2,000 Years of Manchester

2,000 Years of Manchester

First published in Great Britain in 2018
and reprinted in 2021
by Pen and Sword History
An imprint of
Pen & Sword Books Ltd
Yorkshire - Philadelphia

Copyright © Kathryn Coase 2018, 2021

ISBN 9781526715098

The right of Kathryn Coase to be identified as Author of this work has been asserted by him/her in accordance with the Copyright, Designs and Patents Act 1988.

A CIP catalogue record for this book is available from the British Library

All rights reserved. No part of this book may be reproduced or transmitted in any form or by any means, electronic or mechanical including photocopying, recording or by any information storage and retrieval system, without permission from the Publisher in writing.

Typeset in India by Geniies IT & Services Private Limited

Printed and bound in the UK by CPI Group (UK) Ltd, Croydon, CR0 4YY

Pen & Sword Books Limited incorporates the imprints of Archaeology, Atlas, Aviation, Battleground, Digital, Discovery, Family History, Fiction, History, Local, Local History, Maritime, Military, Military Classics, Politics, Select, Transport, True Crime, Air World, Claymore Press, Frontline Publishing, Leo Cooper, Remember When, Seaforth Publishing, The Praetorian Press, Wharncliffe Books, Wharncliffe Local History, Wharncliffe Transport, Wharncliffe True Crime and White Owl.

For a complete list of Pen & Sword titles please contact
PEN & SWORD BOOKS LTD
47 Church Street, Barnsley, South Yorkshire, S70 2AS, England
E-mail: enquiries@pen-and-sword.co.uk
Website: www.pen-and-sword.co.uk
or
PEN & SWORD BOOKS
1950 Lawrence Rd, Havertown, PA 19083, USA
E-mail: uspen-and-sword@casematepublishers.com

For Mum, who loved Manchester

Contents

Introduction		ix
Chapter 1	Early History	1
Chapter 2	From Town to City	9
Chapter 3	'Conditions of the Working Class'	15
Chapter 4	Politics	28
Chapter 5	To Battle!	43
Chapter 6	Religion	49
Chapter 7	Crime & Punishment	67
Chapter 8	Health	94
Chapter 9	Education	103
Chapter 10	Science & Technology	115
Chapter 11	Transport	129
Chapter 12	The Press	138
Chapter 13	Entertainment	142
Chapter 14	Creative Manchester	174
Chapter 15	'Incomers'	199
Chapter 16	Disaster!	207
Chapter 17	Manchester Characters	214

Chapter 18	What's in a name?	230
Chapter 19	Shopping	243
Chapter 20	Iconic Buildings (past and present)	288
Chapter 21	Sport	300
Bibliography		305
Index		307

Introduction

2,000 Years of Manchester takes a (mostly) light-hearted look at the city's past. It is not a chronological history with lists of facts and figures, but rather a series of 'snapshots' which give an insight into the social history of the city and the lives, times, struggles and beliefs of its ever-expanding population. Manchester is, and always has been a centre for ideas, innovation and individualism and I have tried to capture not only the often hard and, in many cases, tragic lives but also the humour, resilience and spirit of its inhabitants.

The book is an eclectic mixture of fact, fiction, legend and myth which illustrate the comic, serious, bizarre and sometimes heart-breaking history of the city's people, events and places. I hope it goes some way in explaining how an insignificant hamlet in the North-West of England became a city at the heart of the Industrial Revolution and a centre for social justice and reform.

I have tried to make the book both educational and entertaining. I certainly learned a lot along the way – I hope you do too.

Chapter 1

Early History

What the Romans Did For Us

One quite important thing the Romans did was to give us the name of our city: 'Manchester'.

Almost two thousand years ago, in 79 AD, the North-West of England was occupied by the Roman army. It was led by General Julius Agricola in his campaign against the Brigantes, the ruling Celtic tribe in the north of England at that time, which was led by Queen Cartimandua. The Romans established major fortresses at Deva (Chester) and Eboracum (York); in the Castlefield area of Manchester lie the reconstructed remains of a Roman fort which was one of a chain of fortifications guarding the Roman road linking the two towns. The fort was strategically placed on a sandstone outcrop at the confluence of the Rivers Medlock and Irwell, which not only provided natural defences, but also gave access to the sea via the River Mersey. The fort was a square wooden building with turf and timber ramparts and was surrounded by a ditch. The site was occupied for over three hundred years, during which time the fort was rebuilt several times. The final structure was built of stone and housed around 500 people on a site of five acres.

A civilian settlement (a *vicus*) grew up alongside the fort providing services and equipment for the Roman army. Excavations of the site have revealed ironworks, potteries and glassworks plus evidence of bronze casting. Many artefacts from this period have been found in and around the Castlefield area, including votive altars, coins, brooches and a gold bulla which was discovered close to the Irwell during the construction of the Bridgewater Canal. A bulla was an amulet worn around the neck to ward off evil spirits; in ancient Rome a bulla was given to a male child nine days after birth. Amphorae (clay pots) of all sizes have also been excavated. Large pots would have been left in the streets; some to collect rainwater and others for urine, which was used for cleaning textiles and softening leather. Smaller pots would have been used to hold, amongst other things, olive oil and wine. One particular treasure is a Samian bowl (brick-red Roman pottery) from c.150 AD decorated with pictures of men hunting for boar with dogs and spears. Another interesting find is a 2,000-year-old paw print of a Roman dog which was preserved when it walked across a newly-made clay tile. Many of these objects are on display in Manchester Museum.

Evidence of an inn at the fort is provided by finds of pieces of glass and gaming counters; the Romans seem to have been fond of a glass of wine and a gamble after a long day's soldiering.

At the beginning of the fourth century, Roman rule came to an end and fort and civilian settlement were gradually abandoned.

Tarquin's Castle   Legend has it ...

It is probable that the fort remained uninhabited after the Romans left, except in legend. The story goes that the fort had fallen, by trickery, into the hands of a cruel and treacherous Saxon knight by the name of Sir Tarquin who for many years had defended it against his enemies, King Arthur and the Knights of the Round Table. The story is told in 'The Ancient Ballad of Tarquin' which begins,

> Within this ancient British land,
> In Lancashire, I understand,
> Near Manchester there liv'd a Knight of fame,
> Of a prodigious strength and might
> Who vanquish'd many a worthy Knight,
> A giant great, and Tarquin was his name.

Sir Lancelot (of the Lake) had heard tales of this wicked knight Tarquin (who apparently ate a child for breakfast every morning) and made his way to 'Tarquin's Castle' which was situated in a barren wilderness. (Apparently all his neighbours had moved elsewhere, especially those with children.) The castle was described as being 'carried to a great height, erected in a good taste, secured at the entrances with gates, and flanked at the sides with high and stately towers'. As he approached, Sir Lancelot met Viviana, a beautiful damsel, who escorted him to the castle gates outside of which stood a tree. On the tree were displayed the shields of the 'threescore knights and four', including two of Lancelot's own brothers, all of whom Sir Tarquin had captured and imprisoned in the castle's dungeon, bound in chains and fetters. Also hanging on the tree was a copper basin on which was written,

> Who values not his life a whit,
> Let him adventure to strike on't if he dare.

With one strike, Lancelot smashed the basin into pieces. Having heard the commotion, Tarquin at once rode out to meet him, accompanied by one of his prisoners who obviously presented a sorry sight.

> 'Villain', said Lancelot, 'Worst of men,
> Hast thou brought this object from thy den?'

Sir Lancelot and Sir Tarquin both took their swords and began to fight. Unknown to his opponent, Lancelot had acquired Tarquin's magical sword of sharpness.

> They wounded were and bled full sore,
> Each wrestling in their princely gore;
> Till Tarquin then for want of breath,
> And loss of blood yielded to death.

(from 'The Ancient Ballad of Tarquin' by J. Aston, 1808)

Sir Lancelot of the Lake slays his opponent, Sir Tarquin. The battle is said to have lasted all of four hours.

Sir Lancelot then proceeded to rescue the sixty-four knights from their captivity.

 On a ceiling in one of the ancient rooms of Chetham's School is a polished oak carving of Sir Tarquin's head. He is evidently mid-breakfast as the limb of a child is sticking out of each side of his mouth.

At Tamworth Castle in Staffordshire walks the ghost of The White Lady who, it is said, was imprisoned there by the same Sir Tarquin. However (à la what centuries later became known as the Stockholm Syndrome) the lady fell in love with her captor and on hearing of his death at the hands of Sir Lancelot, she threw herself off the battlements to her death and forever roams the castle searching for her lost love. **Legend has it ...**

The Romans were not the only people who made their presence felt in Manchester. They were followed by the Saxons, the Danes and the Normans.

Saxons

The Anglo-Saxon settlement of Manchester developed around the confluence of the Rivers Irwell and Irk, near to where Manchester Cathedral now stands. The Romans had given their settlement the name 'Mamucium' (meaning a breast-shaped hill). The Saxon word indicating the site of a Roman fort was 'chester'.

Manchester was born!

More evidence of Anglo-Saxon influence in the town is found in the name 'Aldport', an area which was once at the far end of Deansgate, on or near the site of the Roman vicus. This name is derived from the Anglo-Saxon, meaning 'old town' or 'fortress'.

In a survey of 1322, Aldport covered an area of around 100 acres through which the 'glittering Medlock' flowed. The estate, which belonged to the Lords of the Manor, was described as being a haven for flora and fauna and it was also home to a 'Lodge' which in 1601 passed to the Mosley family. During the Siege of Manchester in 1642 the Lodge was used as the headquarters of the Royalists, led by Lord Strange. It was burnt down by the victorious Parliamentarians and never rebuilt. Aldport became a densely-populated slum area which was later cleared to make room for railway warehouses.

Danes

In addition to the reputed widespread devastation, the Danes also left a lasting legacy in street and place names. 'Gate', the Norse word for street or thoroughfare, can be seen in 'Deansgate', 'Millgate' and 'St. Mary's Gate'.

Normans

After the Battle of Hastings in 1066, William the Conqueror divided up his newly-acquired land and awarded it to his most loyal supporters. The area around Manchester was given to Roger de Poitou who gave the Manor of Manchester to Nigellus, a Norman knight; it then passed on to his son-in-law, Albert de Gresley (sometimes written Grelley).

The Lords of the Manor of Manchester

The Gresley family held the manorial rights for two centuries; in the 1200s Robert de Gresley built a fortified manor house on the site formerly occupied by a rudimentary castle and it was around this manor that the medieval town grew. The Lord of the Manor leased pieces of land to his tenants; the land would have a house, a workshop and maybe a small garden. The lord also owned the only corn mills in the town, on the River Irk by Long Millgate, where tenants would have to pay to grind their corn. (It wasn't until 1759 that the 'right of soke' compelling all inhabitants of a town to grind corn at the lord's mills was repealed.) In addition, there was a 'common oven' which the inhabitants of the town used, again for a fee.

The medieval town had a strong defensive position, bordered as it was by the Rivers Irwell and Irk and Hanging Ditch. Hanging Ditch carried a stream linking the two rivers. By the early 1600s the ditch had become an open sewer; the stream was culverted and the ditch was filled and built on. In the 1800s, as building work was being carried out in the area, the old bridge which had once spanned Hanging Ditch was discovered. It went on show for three months, but was then again lost under a maze of Victorian buildings. It was over a hundred years later that the bridge was rediscovered and restored; it is now on permanent display.

The Manor of Manchester passed into the hands of the De La Warre family; Thomas de la Warre founded the Collegiate Church (later to become the Cathedral).

> A member of the de la Warre family, another Thomas, went to America where, in 1610, he became Governor of and gave his name to Delaware, the 'First State' of the USA.

The last family to own the Manor were the Mosleys. The Mosley (originally Moseley) family was associated with the town and then the City of Manchester for centuries. They were Lords of the Manor of Manchester from 1596, when it was bought by Nicholas Mosley for £3,500, to 1846 when it was sold to Manchester Corporation for £200,000 by Sir Oswald Mosley. Nicholas Mosley was a wool merchant and a shrewd businessman; he also became Mayor of London and was responsible for raising money and recruiting men to build warships to fight against the Spanish Armada, for which he was knighted by Queen Elizabeth I. He became Sheriff of Lancashire and built Hough End Hall (then in Withington) where he died in 1612. Various branches of the Mosley family died out in the coming centuries but the Manchester connection continued. The Mosley Arms Hotel which once stood on Piccadilly is long gone, but the name lives on in Mosley Street. In 1781 John Mosley was made the 1st Baronet Mosley of Ancoats, and the title eventually passed down to Sir Oswald Ernald Mosley, 6th Baronet Mosley of Ancoats.

> **To Quote:**
> No trace is left of the invading Dane,
>
> Or the armed followers of the Norman knight;
>
> Gone is the dwelling of the Saxon thane,
>
> And lord and baron with their feudal might;
>
> The ancient Irwell holds his course alone,
>
> And washes still Mancunium's base of stone.
>
> J.B. Rogerson (president of the Sun Inn poets)

Oswald Ernald Mosley was born in 1896 into an incredibly privileged family. He married twice; his first wedding, to an American heiress, took place in 1920 in St. James's Palace in London with guests including King George V and Queen Mary. His second wedding, in 1936, to Diana Guinness (née Mitford), took place in quite different circumstances. It was conducted in secret, in Germany, at the home of the infamous Nazi Minister of Propaganda Joseph Goebbels; this time there were only six guests, one of whom was Adolf Hitler.

Mosley entered politics at a young age; he was a great orator, but also a great opportunist and he jumped from one political party to another. Although he was acknowledged to have charm and a certain amount of charisma, the former Prime Minister Stanley Baldwin summed him up as a 'cad and a wrong 'un'. Having become disillusioned with the main parties, Mosley set up his own, the 'New Party', which gradually became more authoritarian, right-wing and anti-Semitic. It was superseded by the British Union of Fascists (BUF). The deputy-leader of the BUF was William Joyce (aka 'Lord Haw-Haw') who later defected to Germany and after the war was hanged as a traitor. Mosley travelled to Italy in 1932 on a 'study tour' where he met with the fascist leader, Benito Mussolini; he returned with the conviction that this 'ideology' was the way forward for Britain and Europe. His views unsurprisingly met with great opposition and at the BUF's meetings and rallies, Mosley employed gangs of black-uniformed thugs (known as 'Blackshirts') to deal with any unwanted attention; this usually involved beating up anyone who voiced an opinion different from their own. The party did have some influential supporters and in January 1934 the *Daily Mail* ran a story called 'Hurrah for the Blackshirts!' and even printed the address of the BUF headquarters for any 'young men' who wanted to join them. Six months later the newspaper ceased all connection with the BUF. At its height, the party claimed to have around 40,000 active members. The BUF had its northern headquarters in Salford and there were many meetings and rallies in the area, including one in 1933 at the Free Trade Hall which ended in a riot when they clashed with anti-fascists.

In 1936 Oswald Mosley went to Belle Vue with 500 of his Blackshirts. He stepped onto the balcony to address the crowd, unaware that a protest had been organised; 3,000 people had gathered there and proceeded to sing and chant anti-fascist songs and slogans. Even those sitting closest to Mosley were unable to hear his voice. Defeated and humiliated, Mosley and his thugs had no choice but to leave.

In 1940 Oswald and Diana Mosley were interned in a house in the grounds of Holloway Prison; they had their own garden and were even allowed to employ some of the 'common' criminals as servants. Three years later they were released to live out the rest of the war under house-arrest. After the war Mosley's attempts to rekindle his political career, perhaps unsurprisingly, failed miserably and he and his wife settled in Paris where they lived near to their friends - the Duke of Windsor and Wallis Simpson. Oswald Mosley died in 1980.

In 2006 in the *BBC History Magazine* Sir Oswald Ernald Mosley came top of the 'Worst Briton in the twentieth century' poll.

The Ancoats baronetcy remains in the hands of the Mosley family.

The Mosley Hotel (on the right) in Piccadilly, photographed in 1904

Oswald Mosley and Benito Mussolini, taken during Mosley's visit to Italy in 1932

Chapter 2

From Town to City

Market Town

There was already a weekly Saturday market in the medieval town and in 1222 at the request of Robert de Gresley, Henry III granted the Manor of Manchester a two-day annual fair (extended to three days in 1227) which was initially a market for the sale of sheep, pigs, cows and horses. Gresley, in return, had to pay an annual fee of five marks and a palfrey (a horse ridden by a knight). For hundreds of years Acres Field (previously a graveyard and now St. Ann's Square) was the site of the fair which was held on St. Matthew the Apostle's Day (21 September) plus the day before and the day after. The field was originally surrounded by hedges and ditches and was land on which the people of Manchester had grazing rights. It was also used for growing corn and potatoes, all of which had to be cleared away before the fair. Throughout history, the good people of Manchester have never turned their backs on an opportunity to protest. Even then, Mancunians made their feelings clear on losing their grazing rights for the duration of the fair; the protesters would greet the first animal driven into the field by pelting it with acorns and striking it with whips.

The fair continued to be held there even after St. Ann's Church was built and the grand houses surrounding the Square had been turned into shops. It became one of the most exclusive shopping areas in the town and the shopkeepers, and presumably the customers, were none too pleased at having pigs and cows wandering about, not to mention the noise, smells and crowds of the 'hoi polloi'. The livestock market was moved elsewhere but the fair continued to be held in the Square, selling woollen goods, cotton and haberdashery. In 1821 the fair was moved, first to Shudehill and then to Campfield where it continued until 1876 when, after more than 650 years, the annual fair was abandoned.

In earlier times the fair began with a proclamation: 'Oyez, Oyez, Oyez! The Mayor, on behalf of the Corporation of Manchester, strictly charges and commands all manner of persons not to wear any swords, staves [a piece of wood], falchions [a kind of sword] or any other weapon during the time in which this fair hath its continuance.' This was followed by a solemn procession led by local dignitaries, clergy and the 'gentry' in what was known as 'Acre's Fair Walking'.

The market town (Manchester officially became a market town in 1359.) developed in the area around Hanging Ditch, Fennel Street, Deansgate and Market Stead Lane. The streets would have been lined with rows of timber-framed buildings, occupied by various crafts and trades people, the buildings serving as both homes and workshops. By the sixteenth century, Manchester was a flourishing town and so it remained for over two hundred years until the beginning of the Industrial Revolution in the latter half of the eighteenth century.

> **To Quote:**
>
> John Leland, poet and antiquary, on a visit to Manchester in 1538, described it as
>
> **'the best builded, quickest and most populous tounne in all Lancashire'.**

Textiles

Manchester's association with the textile industry began long before 'Cottonopolis' was born. Encouraged by King Edward III, Flemish weavers began to arrive in the town as early as the 1300s, bringing their expertise in the production of wool and linen. Many documents exist to show that there was at least one fulling mill beside the River Irk as far back as 1282. It was referred to as 'Walke-Milne' (Walkers' Mill). Adjoining the mill was a field where the cloth would be left to dry and bleach in the sun. This gave rise to the name 'Walkers Croft', part of which can still be found near Victoria Station. People were discouraged from stealing the cloth as it lay in the field; the penalty for doing so was death. In 1798 an Irish teenager by the name of George Russell was found guilty of 'robbing a bleaching ground'; he had stolen a piece of fustian cloth from a Mr. Sharrock of Long Millgate. The unfortunate lad was paraded through a tearful crowd, tied in a cart which also held a coffin, a ladder and a rope. He was then hanged on Newton Heath. A children's rhyme marked the event:

> To rob the croft
> I did intend,
> Of Master Sharrock's
> At Mill-gate end.

> James Chetham (1640-92), a celebrated angler of his day, wrote that eels from the River Irk were the most delicious of any river. He ascribed this to the presence of fulling mills on the banks of the Irk which spewed oil, fat and grease into the water.

Two processes were involved in 'fulling' cloth: scouring and thickening. In medieval times fuller's earth was used in the scouring process, hence the term 'fulling'. Fuller's earth is a kind of clay which, when mixed with water (or stale urine) can be used to remove impurities from woollen cloth. Following these processes the cloth would be stretched out on a large frame known as a 'tenter' to which it was attached with 'tenterhooks'.

Manchester became noted for the spinning and weaving of wool, linen and flax and by the late fifteenth century 'Manchester Cottons' (in fact, a variety of woollen cloth) were famous. In the 1600s the textile industry was further boosted by the introduction of cotton, followed by the production of fustian, a strong woven fabric made of linen and cotton.

'Cottonopolis'

By the 1660s Manchester was the largest town in Lancashire and by the end of the century it was already considered a textile 'boom town'. During the next one hundred years the population soared and the town was filled with houses, workshops, warehouses, market squares, inns and mansions for the increasingly wealthy merchant class. In 1701, the profit from cotton export from Manchester was just over £23,000. By 1768 this had increased to £200,000 and only twenty years later the figure stood at £7,000,000. Inventions such as the steam engine, the 'spinning jenny' and the flying shuttle meant that the spinning and weaving of cotton was taken out of the home and into mills. Previously spinners had used the one-thread wheel and weavers the handloom; very often the loom would be in the top floor of a house. Some original weavers' 'cottages' can still be found in the centre of Manchester, for example on Tib Street and the neighbouring Thomas Street.

Until the 1780s mills were water-powered and so needed to be situated on the banks of rivers. In 1781 one of the first steam-powered cotton spinning mills was built on Miller Street, Shudehill, by Richard Arkwright and in the following thirty years a further 85 were built. With the arrival of steam

A weaver's cottage can be identified by the long row of windows on the top floor; this was to maximise the light needed to operate a hand loom. At the side is the opening through which the raw materials and the finished products were lifted and lowered by a pulley. This one is at the corner of Tib Street and Silver Jubilee Walk.

engines, 750 people could do the same amount of work as 200,000 manual workers. The town expanded at an incredible rate, not only in terms of population but also in commerce and construction. In the nineteenth century, Manchester was the fastest-growing city in the world: the number of people living and working in Manchester rose from just over 70,000 to around 544,000. Large mills and factories employing thousands of men, women and children were built on the banks of the canals and rivers and later beside the railways. Other industries developed in Manchester either directly (bleaching, dyeing and printing) or indirectly (iron, glass and chemical works) as a result of the boom in textiles. Manchester also played an important part in the engineering revolution with men such as Whitworth, Fairbairn and

Nasmyth leading the way. Advances in science grew alongside; in the middle of the eighteenth century the bleaching process took at least eight months but with the introduction of chlorine, the process could be achieved in days.

As cotton mills opened in surrounding towns, Manchester became the commercial and financial centre of the world's cotton industry. Grand warehouses were built around the town; not only used for storage, they were also showcases where goods were displayed and sold. They became symbols of the wealth and prestige of the merchants and mill owners.

Manchester was finally given city status in 1853. It had become one of the greatest and most affluent cities in the world, but at what cost? Little wonder that Manchester became the focus for social and political reform.

To Quote:

'Manchester is as great a human exploit as Athens.'

Benjamin Disraeli, British Prime Minister (1849)

Disraeli is also credited with saying, **'What Manchester does today, the rest of the world does tomorrow.'**

Trafford Park

Perhaps unsurprisingly, the first industrial city in the world became the site of the first industrial park in the world. The de Trafford family, one of the oldest recorded families in Manchester, reputedly settled in the area in 1030. One of the de Traffords apparently accompanied King Canute on his journey through neighbouring Cheshire. The family remained in Manchester until selling their five square miles of deer park, meadow, woodland and ancestral home in 1896 to London-based financier Ernest Terah Hooley for £360,000. He then founded and became chairman of Trafford Park Estates Ltd. By this time, the estate, once a haven of tranquillity, was an island surrounded by industry, canals and railways. As it lay on the banks of the Manchester Ship Canal it was ideally located for importing and exporting goods. (Hooley soon gave up his role of chairman and spent the rest of his life between bankruptcy and spells in prison.)

Initially it proved difficult to attract business to the Park which became the site of various leisure activities; Trafford Hall was turned into a hotel, the lake was used for pleasure boats and a polo ground and golf course were established. Gradually the Park was taken over by industry, including local firms such as Brooke Bond and the CWS. By 1915 the Park was home to hundreds of businesses of which over one hundred were American-owned (such as the Ford Motor Company). During the First World War, the Park was mainly used in manufacturing munitions and in the Second World War it was given over to the production of aeroplanes (the AVRO Manchester and AVRO Lancaster bombers) and the Rolls-Royce engines needed to power them. The Park suffered extensive bomb damage in 1940/41; many aircraft were destroyed and Trafford Hall received a direct hit. (It was later demolished.) By 1945 the site employed around 75,000 people but after the war industry in the area declined and by the 1980s was virtually non-existent. However, a regeneration plan was initiated to attract investment; once again Trafford Park is thriving and is the largest industrial park in Europe.

Chapter 3

'Conditions of the Working Class'

In a relatively short space of time the market town of Manchester became the world's first industrial city. The changes which this transformation brought were immense, both on the infrastructure of the town and, more drastically, on the majority of people working and living there. In his book *Manchester Streets and Manchester Men* (1908) the author Thomas Swindells wrote (tongue-in-cheek) that, 'The population of the town a century ago was divided into two classes, the somebodies and the nobodies.' This chapter deals with the latter.

It would be wrong to think that poverty and social inequality arrived in Manchester on the back of the Industrial Revolution. That was certainly not the case. In the records of the Court Leet (the town's governing body until 1846) there are many instances of wealthy citizens making bequests to benefit 'the poor'. One bequest enabled almshouses for twenty-four families to be built on Miller Lane in 1680. (In 1794 the land was sold, the almshouses were demolished and warehouses were built on the site.) Provision for the poor in the eighteenth century included a paupers' workhouse which opened in 1754 on Cumberland Street, soup kitchens and a Relief Committee.

In the first half of the nineteenth century the rise in the population of Manchester was almost without parallel as people flocked to the town looking for a better life. In 1771 the population of Manchester was 20,000; by 1821 it had increased to 180,000. Many immigrants were Irish, both before, after and during the time of the Great Potato Famine (1846-51). By 1851, fifteen per cent of Manchester's population was Irish-born. They had little choice but to settle in the poorest and most squalid areas of the town. One such came to be known as 'Little Ireland'. Another was the equally infamous 'Angel Meadow'.

'Little Ireland'

Although only occupied for just over twenty years, this was one of the most notorious slums in Manchester. Situated on present-day Oxford Road

Station, the area which became known as 'Little Ireland' was a community of mainly Irish immigrants; at least 4,000 people were packed into around 200 (mainly) back-to-back houses (many of them in cellar dwellings) beside the River Medlock. Whenever there was a rise in the river level, the filthy polluted water would pour into their 'homes'. It was not unusual for a hundred families to share one outside 'privy'. The streets were described by Friedrich Engels as being 'without drains or pavement; masses of refuse, offal and sickening filth lie among standing pools in all directions'. Another German social commentator of the time, Jakob Venedey, described the area as a 'hideous hole of misery' and wrote, 'Cholera chose these dwellings of misery and came as a compassionate visitor to put an end to them.' Not quite! Once the epidemic was over, the initial outrage over the living conditions of the poorest abated and plans for improvements were again swept under the carpet. It was only when the land was needed by the railway companies that these slums were finally demolished. The area became so infamous that 'Little Ireland' became a generic term for any ghetto of Irish immigrants.

Angel Meadow

According to local legend this area was named when, in the 1600s, the land was used as a graveyard for thousands of victims of the Plague. The spirits of the dead children buried there were said to play in the fields above, hence the name: Angel Meadow. The land was later used for grazing cattle.

By the middle of the nineteenth century, Angel Meadow was anything but angelic. It was now one of the most densely-packed slums in the industrial miracle that was Manchester. The *Morning Chronicle* journalist Angus Roach described Angel Meadow in 1849 as 'the lowest, most filthy, most unhealthy and most wicked locality in Manchester'. In fact, it has since been described as being the worst slum in the whole of Britain at that time.

These appalling living conditions were not restricted to the areas inhabited by immigrants. One end of Deansgate was another notorious slum. At that time, this long thoroughfare was a street of almost unbelievable contrasts; at one end the opulent and exclusive shopping street, and just a short distance away the 'evil slum of Deansgate' where many families were living in squalor and the utmost poverty without the means to feed and clothe themselves.

'Conditions of the Working Class' 17

A courtyard in Angel Meadow

To Quote:

'What a place! The entrance to hell realised!'

General Napier

As the population of Manchester exploded, the problems of poverty in the town rose exponentially. Commentators on industrialisation and its ensuing problems abounded. Swindells wrote that the conditions 'brought "slumming" in vogue and daintily-dressed ladies were to be seen on fine afternoons paying calls'. As Manchester became increasingly industrialised, those who could afford to do so moved away from the town centre. Initially, they moved to the leafy suburbs of Ardwick Green and Victoria Park. The gap between rich and poor could hardly have been wider. Commentators at the time reported on the segregation of the classes. One such, Cooke Taylor, wrote, 'Rich Ardwick knew less about poor Ancoats or Little Ireland [a mile away] than they knew about China.' Later, with the coming of the railway and improved road conditions, the very wealthiest went even further afield, building grand houses in the Cheshire countryside. In 1841, the canon of Manchester, the Reverend Parkinson, commented, 'There is no town in the world where the distance between the rich and the poor is so great.' Many of those left behind were crammed into poor, densely-packed housing breeding squalor, ill-health and discontent.

Attitudes among the ruling elite were divided; some had 'the poor are always with us' mentality, but there were some who were not satisfied with just visiting and commentating. One of the most famous treatises on the working class in nineteenth century Manchester was written by Friedrich Engels.

> **To Quote:**
> 'An ounce of action is worth a ton of theory.'
>
> Friedrich Engels

Friedrich Engels (1820-95)

Friedrich Engels, the eldest son of a wealthy cotton manufacturer, was born in Barman, Prussia (now Wuppertal, Germany). At a young age he became involved in radical politics and by the time he was 22 he had already written, albeit anonymously, many articles on the ills of industrialisation and the poor living and employment conditions of the workers. It was in order to try and curb his rebellious activities that he was sent to Manchester to work in a branch of his father's business, Ermen & Engels, in Weaste, Salford.

In Manchester Engels met the working-class Irish girl Mary Burns, with whom he was to have a twenty-year relationship until her death in 1862. She guided his visits around the poorest areas of both Manchester and Salford. What he saw there only confirmed his beliefs. How was it possible for anyone with a social and moral conscience to witness such abject poverty and misery and not think that there must be a better way of structuring society? He wrote articles about his experiences of this 'Hell on Earth' and 'these evil slums' which were published in Germany and France. These collected articles became his most famous work – *The Condition of the Working Class in England* – which was published in German in 1845, but not in English until more than thirty years later.

Engels met Karl Marx in Paris in 1844 where they formed a close friendship which would endure until Marx's death. Marx often visited Manchester and it was in the reading room of Chetham's Library that the *Communist Manifesto* was born, a tract outlining the ideology and principles of Communism. It ends with, 'The proletariat have nothing to lose but their chains. They have a world to win ... Working Men of All Countries, Unite!' – more commonly quoted as 'Workers of the world, unite!' Together, they wrote some of the most influential works in history which have impacted on world politics for well over a century. The table where the two founders of Communism collaborated can still be seen in the library.

After time spent in Paris and Brussels, Engels returned to work at his father's office in Manchester so that he could financially support his friend Marx who was now working on another influential tome, *Das Kapital*. Engels almost led a double life: a merchant during office hours and a revolutionary in his free time. Following the death of Mary Burns, Engels began a relationship with her sister Lizzie and married her just a few hours before her death in 1878.

A Matter of Life & Death

In the early 1840s half the population of Manchester was under the age of 22¾ years. In 1841 one half of the total number of recorded deaths (6,774) was of children under 3 years and 11 months. (In Cumberland the figure was under 27½ years.) Though there were more recorded births of boys at this time, the mortality rate in boys was such that after a period of one year, more girls than boys survived. (Only 1 person in 350,000 lived to be 100!)

> **To Quote:**
>
> 'I would like to live in Manchester, England. The transition between Manchester and death would be unnoticeable.'
>
> Mark Twain

In the nineteenth century diarrhoea was the major cause of death among young children while TB was the main killer of adults. Records from 22 August to 24 December 1853 reveal some shocking statistics. In Manchester alone around sixty-eight children under the age of 12 died from being scalded or from their clothes catching fire. Dozens of children under 2 years of age died of suffocation 'caused by accidental pressure whilst in bed with mother'. Many more infant deaths came in the 'accidental death' or 'cause unknown' categories and some inquest records point to death from narcotic substances:

> Mary Wall, died, aged 1 month, from overdose of narcotic.
> Thomas Haley, aged 1 month, died from the effects of narcotic cordial.
> Sarah Cooper died 16th October, aged 5 weeks, from the effect of laudanum.

Mothers were exhausted after working long shifts (very long – up to fourteen hours) in the cotton mills and related industries; they needed their sleep in order to face another day of the same. Parents resorted to drugging their children. Most used opiates, but not the many Irish immigrants who were opposed to these opium-based preparations; they used alcohol to sedate their children!

There was certainly no shortage of morphine-based products to choose from. These tinctures, also known as 'Mothers' friends', were cheap and readily available to anyone, adult and child, either from the local druggist's shop or from the 'crocus men' who sold door-to-door. One such product was 'Godfrey's Cordial' patented as a remedy for colic and other childhood ailments. It was in fact a lethal concoction made up of just morphine and treacle. The treacle and morphine would gradually separate and the morphine would sink to the bottom. The nearer the end of the bottle, the deadlier the dose. In addition to being a poison, the opium was also an appetite suppressor. Many hundreds of children died, either from an overdose of opium or from malnutrition.

Another such product was 'Atkinson & Barker's Infants Preservative'.

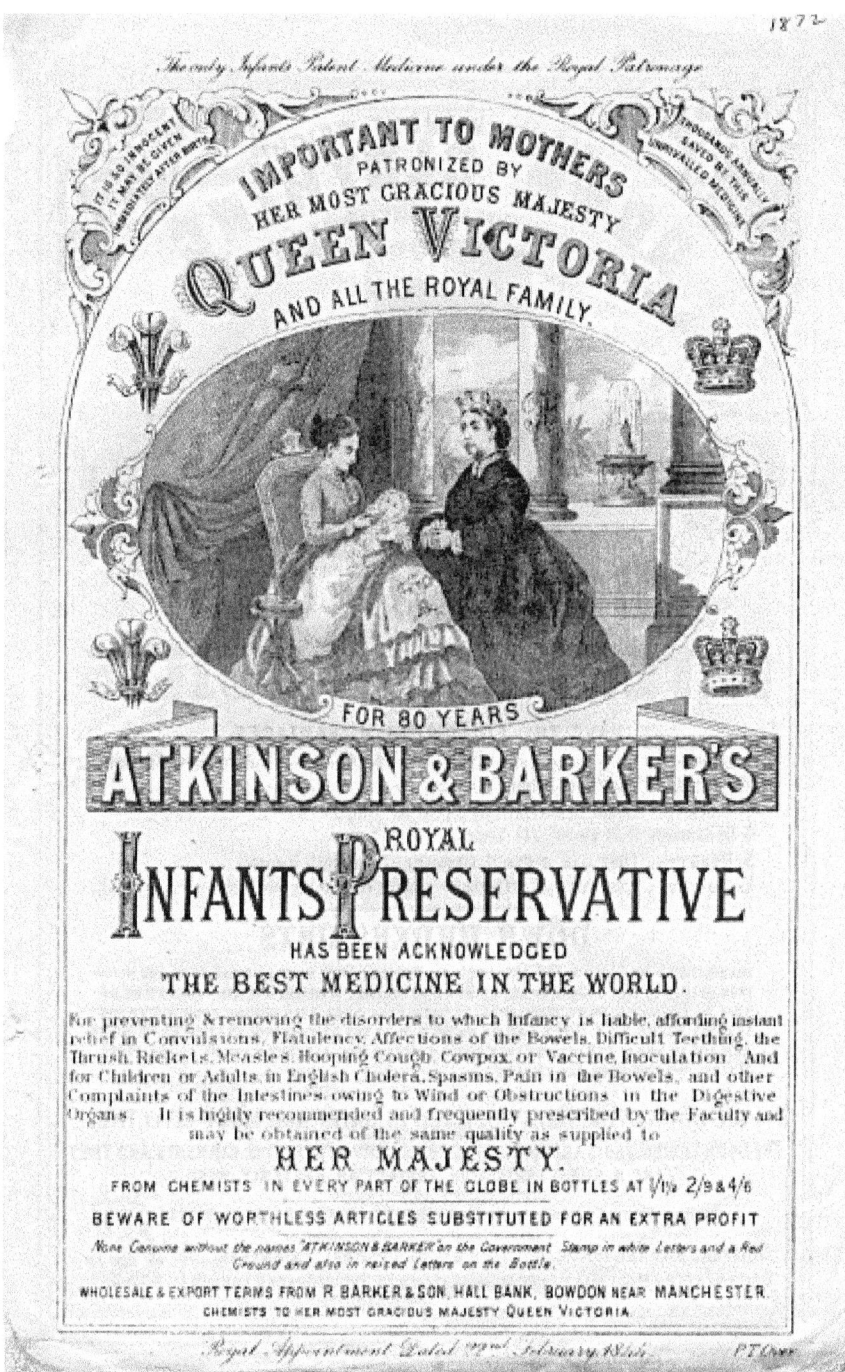

Advert in a London newspaper

> **Atkinson and Barker**
>
> John Atkinson and Robert Barker started their business in the 1790s as 'Druggists and Apothecaries'. Their shop was located at 1, Market Place, Manchester where they began making and selling their 'Infant Preservative'. As can be seen from the advert, they made great claims for their product which seemed to cure every disease known to infants. Quite why it was patronized by Queen Victoria is a bit of a mystery. Although their partnership was dissolved in 1820, Barker continued to run the business and kept the original name.
>
> The mixture was listed as being made up of:
>
> Carbonate of magnesia 6 drs
> White sugar 2oz
> Oil of aniseed 20 drops
> Spirit of sal volatile 2 drs
> Laudanum (a tincture of opium and alcohol) 1dr
> Syrup of saffron 1oz
> Caraway water to make 1 pint
>
> dr – drachm (a unit of weight, once favoured by apothecaries)
>
> In 1886 there was an inquest into the death of a 6-week-old baby at which it was suggested that the cause of death was six drops of the infant remedy.
>
> Not until the early twentieth century was the opium removed from the remedy and amazingly the product was still around in the 1960s (with rather different ingredients). It is still possible to buy Atkinson and Barker's Gripe Mixture made up of caraway oil, dill oil and sodium bicarbonate.

On the very rare occasions when a parent was charged with causing a child's death from opium-poisoning, juries almost never returned a guilty verdict.

****

The Industrial Revolution brought wealth and power to Great Britain, but it brought exactly the opposite to those who created the wealth. As the population rocketed, the supply of labour far outweighed the demand. Workers had a simple choice: accept the conditions imposed by the mill and factory bosses or find employment elsewhere. They had no rights, no vote and no choice. A fourteen-hour day was the norm for many and some were forced to work even longer days; this was six days a week, often in dangerous and insanitary conditions and with no paid holidays. In 1799 and 1800 Parliament passed the 'Combination Acts' making unions illegal.

> **To Quote:**
>
> **'From this filthy sewer flows pure gold.'**
>
> Alexis de Tocqueville, a visitor to Manchester in 1835

Children as young as 6 and 7 were employed in the factories and cotton mills; child labour was the cheapest labour of all as they earned only one tenth of what a man would earn. Young children often worked as 'scavengers' in the cotton mills, a job which involved crawling under the still-operating machinery to collect loose bits of cotton. Many children were maimed and killed after becoming caught in the machines. Mill owners were never held to account.

> **To Quote:**
>
> **'... almost universally ill-looking, small, sickly, barefoot and ill-clad'**
>
> Dr. Turner Thackrah, describing children leaving the cotton mills

Long working hours, terrible housing, poor diet, meagre health provision, little sanitation and the spread of disease all contributed to the miserable lives of many working people. Average life-expectancy in Manchester in the mid-1800s was twenty-five years and in some of the poorest, most-deprived slum areas, the figure dropped to seventeen years. During the nineteenth century hundreds of charities were set up around the town to help alleviate the suffering of the old, the needy and the 'deserving' poor.

These are just a few examples:

The Night Asylum

In the freezing winter of 1838 several homeless people froze to death on the streets of Manchester. In response, a 'Night Asylum' for men, women and children was opened on Henry Street. It had stringent rules, for example, no-one was allowed to sleep there for more than two consecutive nights and it was forbidden to speak in tones louder than a whisper. However, on arrival, each person would receive coffee and a piece of bread. The asylum accommodation consisted of one large sleeping room in the centre of which was a fire. A German commentator, J.G. Kohl, after a visit to the asylum wrote, 'Most of them were smoking because tobacco-smoke is considered a good remedy against infectious disorders.' In 1841, more than 24,000 people slept there. Although the majority of the 'inmates' were Irish, Kohl wrote, 'Africans, Asiatics and Europeans often creep together for shelter from the chilling blasts of an English winter's night.'

> **To Quote:**
>
> 'I would rather be hanged in London than die a natural death in Manchester.'
>
> Julian Harney, Chartist and political activist

The Wood Street Mission

This was founded by Methodist minister Alfred Alsop in 1869. Initially it was on Lombard Street but when that was demolished to make way for Central Station it moved in 1873 to its present location on Wood Street, Deansgate. The Mission's aim was to provide spiritual and practical help to children and their families in the slums of Manchester and Salford; they operated soup kitchens, a night shelter for the homeless, a home for boys and they also donated clothing and bedding. In addition, they ran Sunday Schools and held church services.

How is it possible that in the twenty-first century, in one of the richest countries in the world, the Mission is still in operation, still providing food, clothing and Christmas toys?

This photograph (c.1900) shows children queuing at the Wood Street Mission; they are waiting for the soup kitchen to open.

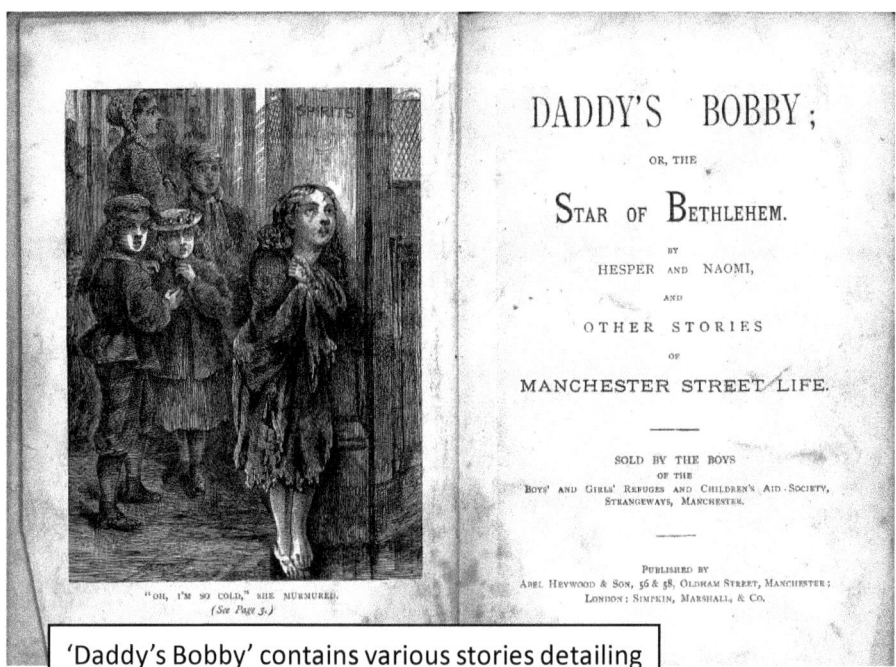

'Daddy's Bobby' contains various stories detailing the lives of children living on the streets in Victorian Manchester. It was sold by Boys' and Girls' Refuges and told the stories of the children in their care. It was hoped that those who read the book would be moved to donate funds to the establishments. It was published by Abel Heywood & Son.

The Workhouse

A workhouse was opened on New Bridge Street in 1793. There was a set of fifteen rules which was read to the inmates on the first Monday of every month. The penalties for disobedience were also laid out:

> WHOEVER shall offend against the above Rules, will be punished either by confinement in the stocks, or in the dungeon, or elsewhere, or by distinction of dress, by abatement of diet, loss of gratuity, by such corporal or other punishment as may be determined and adjudged by the Weekly Board of Overseers, according to the powers vested in them by the Act of Parliament.

Manchester Workhouse on New Bridge Street, close to modern-day Manchester Arena

Engels referred to this workhouse as the 'The Poor-Law Bastille of Manchester'. By the 1860s the workhouse could accommodate over 1,600 inmates.

> **To Quote:**
>
> **'Our object is to establish a discipline so severe and repulsive as to make them a terror to the poor and prevent them from entering.'**
>
> The opinion of one member of the Board of Overseers

This particular overseer certainly got his wish. Joseph Scot wrote, 'He that hath seen this place will never come here till his Limbs or his Reason fail him.'

Next to the Workhouse was a 'Vagrant Office' where 'suitable' vagrants could receive a night's lodgings.

****

> **To Quote:**
>
> **'Dark and smoky from the coal vapours, it resembles a huge forge or workshop. Work, profit and greed seem to be the only thoughts here.'**
>
> Johanna Schopenhauer (mother of the German philosopher) following a visit to Manchester in 1830

Things did begin to change; sometimes so slowly that the rate of progress was imperceptible. Over a period of many, many decades, working hours were cut and conditions in the home and at work improved. Cleaner air and water did much to improve health and raise life-expectancy.

> The building of the very insanitary back-to-back housing was banned in 1844. Other slum areas were cleared to make way for railway buildings, warehouses, etc. However, attitudes take a long time to change: Victoria Square, built at the end of the nineteenth century on Oldham Road, was an attempt to provide better housing for those living in the slums around Ancoats and Angel Meadow. The architect clearly knew little and cared less about the future residents and instructed, 'No wooden skirtings which might be used for firewood; no fresh-air inlets - the working man would block them up; no baths as there are plenty of public ones. It is no great hardship for members of this class to share a scullery with other families.'

Chapter 4

Politics

For many of those in power, workers were mere 'factory fodder', expendable and exploitable. From the beginning of the nineteenth century there were those who began to fight back and demand fair living and working conditions and the right to be heard. They met with resistance every step of the way; many paid with imprisonment and some paid with their lives.

1812 Riots

Wages were low and food prices were high. People were going hungry and discontent was growing. As the government turned a deaf ear to the plight of the masses, so the demand for change gathered momentum. People began to take matters into their own hands. For several days in April 1812 shops were looted, markets were ransacked and people helped themselves to whatever food they could find. The riots were supressed and eight of the supposed ringleaders were tried, sentenced and executed two months later.

The Blanketeers

The first meeting of the group which came to be known as the 'Manchester Radicals' was held in 1816 in St. Peter's Fields, an area of open land surrounded by Georgian townhouses. This was followed by several more (reasonably) peaceful meetings there, often attended by many thousands of supporters. The purpose of these meetings was to petition Parliament for social and political change. At one meeting held in 1817 it was decided to march en masse to London in order to present a petition to the Prince Regent.

The 'Blanketeers' were a group of mainly textile workers who were intending to march from Manchester to London. As they were carrying blankets and rugs to sleep under en route, they became known as the Blanketeers. On the morning of 10 March around 12,000 people left St. Peter's Fields. They were carrying a petition calling for improvements in the cotton industry and in protest against the suspension of the Habeas Corpus Act of 1679 (concerning unlawful detention of citizens by the authorities – still in force today, with some amendments). The cavalry arrived, broke up the meeting and arrested the supposed leaders. 250 people were sent to New Bailey Prison.

Despite, or more likely because of constant suppression by the authorities, the momentum for political, economic and social change grew. However, it was the Peterloo Massacre of 1819 that marked the shift in the gradual decline of Tory influence in favour of a Liberal Manchester Corporation.

> **To Quote:**
>
> ' ... the word Manchester became a synonym for energy and freedom and the right to do and think without shackles.'
>
> *What the Judge Saw* by Judge Parry (1912)

The Peterloo Massacre

> James Murray ran a confectioner's shop at 2, Withy Grove. He attended meetings of the Reformers prior to the Peterloo Massacre, not as a supporter of the cause, but as a government spy. During one meeting, at which he was 'disguised' as a weaver, he was recognized and beaten up. He subsequently became so unpopular that his confectionery business declined and folded.
>
> Just desserts!
>
> &

On 16 August 1819, the radical orator Henry Hunt was on the platform to address a peaceful crowd of tens of thousands of workers and their families in St. Peter's Fields. There was almost a party atmosphere on the day with banners raised and bands playing. The magistrates, fearful of what they considered to be a revolutionary mob, read the 'Riot Act' and then ordered the Manchester & Salford Yeomanry to disperse the crowd and arrest Hunt and the other radical leaders. Led by Hugh Birley, the cavalry (literally) arrived with clubs and sabres drawn. The protesters were trampled on, beaten and bayoneted! Within a few minutes the panicking crowd had scattered; around 15 people were dead and over 600 were injured in what came to be known as the Peterloo Massacre.

James Wroe was the editor of the radical reform newspaper, the *Manchester Observer: sevenpence ready money*. He was the journalist who coined the name 'Peterloo Massacre' ironically likening the heroes of the Battle of Waterloo (four years earlier) to the soldiers killing innocent (and unarmed) men, women and children. One Peterloo protester who had also been at Waterloo compared the two events, 'At Waterloo there was man to man but here [i.e. Peterloo] it was downright murder.' He subsequently died from injuries sustained at the latter.

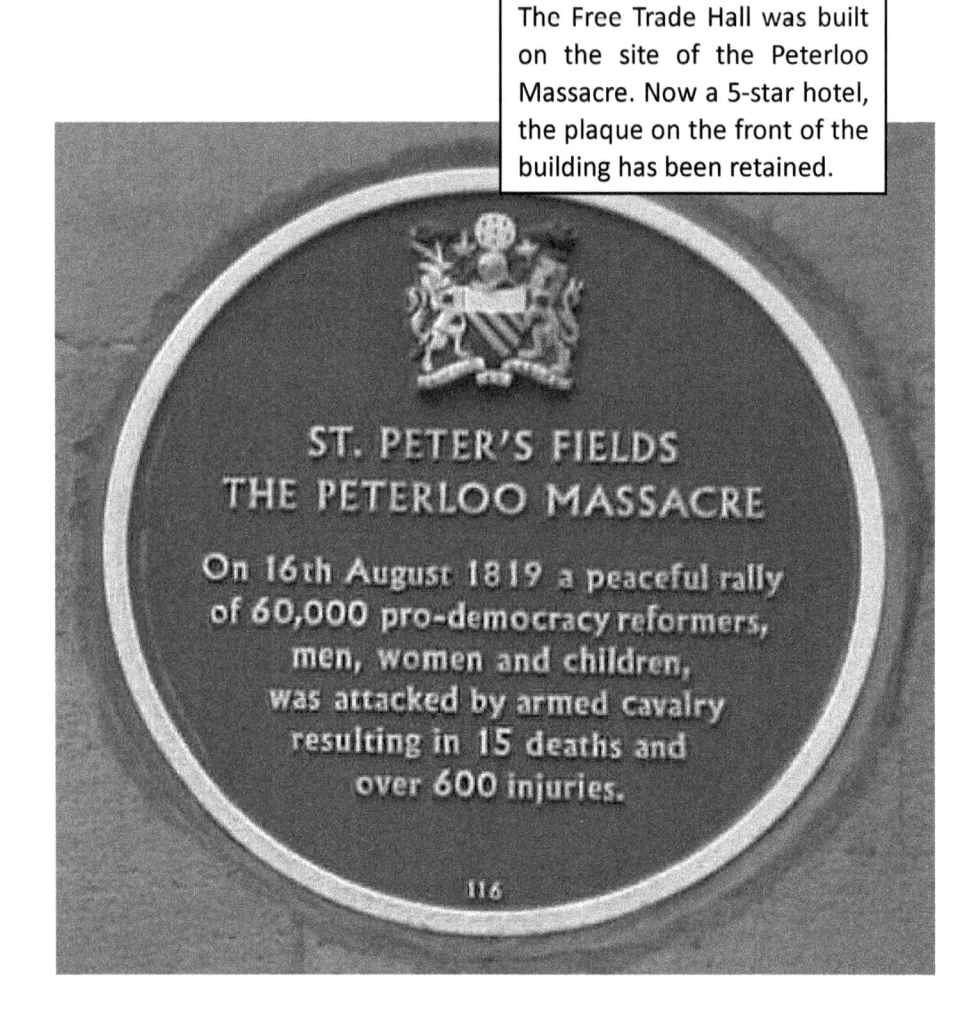

The Free Trade Hall was built on the site of the Peterloo Massacre. Now a 5-star hotel, the plaque on the front of the building has been retained.

ST. PETER'S FIELDS
THE PETERLOO MASSACRE

On 16th August 1819 a peaceful rally of 60,000 pro-democracy reformers, men, women and children, was attacked by armed cavalry resulting in 15 deaths and over 600 injuries.

Much was written about the Massacre, including many satirical observations.

> **How valiantly we met that crew,**
>
> **Of infants, men and women too,**
>
> **Upon the plain of Peterloo.**
>
> A satirical song written shortly after the Massacre

In response to the Massacre, Percy Bysshe Shelley wrote 'The Masque of Anarchy', a protest poem of ninety-one stanzas, advocating non-violent resistance. It is considered by many to be the greatest political poem ever written in the English language. The last verse reads:

> Rise like Lions after slumber
> In unvanquishable number,
> Shake your chains to earth like dew
> Which in sleep had fallen on you –
> Ye are many – they are few.

The authorities banned the poem which did not appear in print until 1832.

In *A Picture of Manchester* (1826) the author Joseph Aston voiced a very different opinion of what happened on that day. He wrote, '…an immense crowd of people, headed by a troublesome fellow of the name of Hunt … several persons lost their lives; being trampled underfoot.'

> Joseph Nadin was one of the most notorious figures involved in the Massacre. Born in 1765, Nadin was first a spinner, then a 'thief-catcher'. For this he was paid by results; in consequence he arrested a great many innocent people. For each person convicted Nadin would receive £2 plus a Tyburn Ticket (a ticket excusing the holder from any public duties) which he could sell for huge sums. In addition, he would extort money from the town's brothels and other dubious establishments. The authorities, in their wisdom, made him Deputy Constable. As such, he was asked to arrest Henry Hunt before he could address the gathering. Nadin replied that he could only do this with the help of the military. The result was the Peterloo Massacre.
>
> Shortly after the Massacre an (unsuccessful) attempt was made on his life. With the proceeds of his ill-gotten gains Nadin was a wealthy man; he retired in 1821 and bought a large estate in Cheshire. Celebrated by the 'ruling class', he was despised by the majority of Manchester's residents.

The government refused to hold a public enquiry into the events of 16 August. Henry Hunt was sentenced to 2½ years imprisonment while the perpetrators of the Massacre escaped scot-free. Not only that, they received a message of congratulation from the Prince Regent!

Parliament then passed the 'Six Acts' in order to curb free expression, ban large public meetings and prevent further disturbances. However, Peterloo had caused outrage and not only amongst the working class; it also acted as a catalyst among Manchester's middle classes. One group helped to establish the *Manchester Guardian*; other groups carried on the fight for the reform of Parliament and the right to vote.

In the 1820s, Manchester, despite its size, growing wealth and importance, still had no MPs. It briefly had two MPs during the Commonwealth era but the town was disenfranchised under Charles II, largely as a result of its former allegiance to Oliver Cromwell. Manchester was still being governed by the medieval institution of the Court Leet. In 1830 a petition was presented asking Parliament to grant two MPs to Manchester; following the Reform Act of 1832 two MPs – the Liberals Mark Philips and Charles Poulett Thomson were elected. However, that same Act became the 'Great Betrayal' for the working class; the government had failed to extend the vote beyond those who owned property. Resentment increased further when the Poor Law Amendment was passed two years later; this meant that those in need, instead of receiving help in the community, were forced into the degradation of the workhouse.

The Chartist Movement for political reform grew as a result of this 'betrayal'. It was a national movement but its strongholds were in the north of England and other industrial areas. The movement took its name from the People's Charter of 1838 which called for the vote for all 'sane' men over 21 years of age; in the following twenty years, petitions with millions of signatures were presented to Parliament. In 1845 Engels wrote, 'Manchester is the seat of the most powerful unions, the central point of Chartism, the place which numbers the most socialists.'

There were many remarkable, often forgotten men and women of Manchester who played such important roles in the struggle for social and political justice and thereby changed the lives of millions of 'ordinary' people. Men and women who fought for the freedoms which today are taken so much for granted. Just a few of those people are mentioned here:

Richard Cobden (1804–65) & The Anti-Corn Law League

Richard Cobden, though not a Mancunian by birth, played a large part in Manchester's political history.

The Corn Law was passed in 1815; this kept the price of bread artificially high by imposing prohibitive taxes on all imported corn. This impacted on wages, food prices and therefore on living standards, especially amongst the poor. Richard Cobden believed in free trade and he, together with John Bright and George Wilson, formed the Anti-Corn Law League in 1838 at the York Hotel on King Street; the League had its headquarters on Market Street. The cause was so popular that a huge wooden pavilion, capable of seating 4,000 people, was built on Peter Street to hold protest meetings and rallies. This was the first of three buildings on the site to be named 'Free Trade Hall'. The Corn Law was repealed in 1846 by Sir Robert Peel, in part owing to food shortages caused by the Potato Famine in Ireland.

Robert Owen (1771–1858)

Robert Owen, often dubbed the 'Father of Socialism' was a Welshman who came to Manchester to work at Satterfield's Drapery in St. Ann's Square. By the time he was 21, he was manager of the Chorlton Twist Mills. In 1793 he became a member of the Manchester Lit. & Phil. Society and he was also a member of the Manchester Board of Health which worked to improve the health of factory and mill workers.

Way ahead of his time, as early as 1817 Owen had mooted the idea of an 8-hour working day, advocating 'Eight hours labour, eight hours recreation and eight hours rest'.

John Doherty (1798–1854)

Doherty was born in Ireland in 1798 and started working in a cotton mill at the age of 10. By the time he moved to Manchester in 1816, he was already an experienced cotton-spinner. Although he could speak little English, he soon became active in campaigning for better working conditions and higher wages.

In 1818 he was one of the leaders of the cotton-spinners' strike. Doherty was involved in preventing 'scabs' (known as knobsticks at that time) from crossing the picket line. There were frequent outbreaks of violence and it was during one of these that a man was shot dead. As a result of this the leaders of the strike were arrested and sent for trial; Doherty was sentenced to two years' hard labour. After his release he remained defiant, becoming leader of the illegal Manchester Spinners' Union in 1828. A year later he led the spinners out on strike again after their wages had been cut. After six months of hardship and near-starvation, the strikers returned to work. Still determined, Doherty founded the General Union of Cotton Spinners; this was also doomed to fail and the Union collapsed in 1831.

A year later, Doherty left the cotton industry and became a printer and bookseller, opening a bookshop, coffee shop and free reading room at 37, Withy Grove. He founded and published a paper, *The Voice of the People*, again championing the cause of factory and mill workers.

Once again Doherty was imprisoned, this time for libel. On his release he worked with Robert Owen to improve working conditions, abolish child labour and to shorten the working day to no more than ten hours – 'The Ten Hours Bill'. Eventually, all their hard work paid off and in the 1847 Factory Act, the bill was ratified and the working day was reduced to 'only' ten hours.

Doherty ceased trading in 1842 and died in 1844, three years before his tireless campaigning bore fruit. He came to be recognized as one of the most influential campaigners and social reformers of his day. John Doherty was a remarkable man, one of the few who dare to stand up and be counted.

> **To Quote:**
>
> 'We are not your slaves, we are your equals. We are one side of the bargain, you are only the other. The idea of those who create all receiving scarcely anything is so monstrous that I can never be persuaded to remain quiet as long as the system remains.'
>
> John Doherty

John Doherty

Factory Acts

The first Factory Act was introduced in 1802 as the 'Health and Morals of Apprentices Act'. In the early 1800s the treatment of many workers was comparable to that of slaves. In 1831 a Factory Act was passed, limiting the working day to a mere twelve hours a day, ten hours a day for those under 16 years of age. However, there was no enforcement of the Act (which only applied to cotton mills) and many employers chose to flout the law. The Factory Act of 1833 prohibited children under the age of 9 from working in any factory and all children from working at night. It also established a small 'Inspectorate of Factories' – very small and completely inadequate, making it almost impossible to enforce the Act.

Ernest Jones (1819–69)

As the son of a royal equerry, Ernest Jones came from an extremely privileged background amongst the nobility of Germany (where he was born and lived until he was 19) and England where he was a frequent visitor at the court of Queen Victoria. He was a gifted writer and by the age of 11 was already a published poet. He married into an aristocratic family and became a barrister. However, his real passions were literature and the rights (or lack of them) of working people. From 1842 he ran the *People's Paper* and three years later became the honorary leader of the Chartists. After giving a lecture at the Hall of Science in Campfield during which he said, 'The green flag of Chartism will soon be flying over Downing Street', Jones was charged with and convicted of sedition; in 1848 he was sentenced to two years' imprisonment. As he refused to pick oakum, he was kept in solitary confinement in a tiny damp cell, often on a diet of bread and water. Given a chance to retract his 'seditious' views and gain his freedom, Jones refused. His uncle threatened to cut him out of his will unless he renounced his radical views. Again Jones refused and the money (£2,000 a year) went to his uncle's gardener. Jones was a member of the Manchester branch of the 'International Workingmen's Association' and was on track to become an MP for Manchester when he died, suddenly, at the age of 50 – his health never having recovered from his time in prison. Around 100,000 people lined the streets of Manchester for his funeral; he was buried in Ardwick Cemetery.

William Marsden

> In St. John's Gardens (the graveyard of the long-since demolished St. John's Church) there is a memorial stone dedicated to Manchester man William Marsden who fought for the Saturday 'half-day holiday'. His campaign was successful despite fierce opposition from mill owners; the Factory Act of 1850 ensured that all women and children finished work by 2pm on Saturdays and this was soon extended to include men. Manchester workers were the first to benefit from a half-day 'holiday' on a Saturday.

Abel Heywood (1810–93)

Abel Heywood's bookshop located at 56, Oldham Street.

Heywood was born into a poor family in 1810, but was lucky in that he gained a basic education before he had to leave school and start work in a warehouse, aged 9, for a weekly wage of 1s 6d (7½p). Highly intelligent and motivated from an early age, he was largely self-taught.

Heywood pioneered the mass distribution of books; the range of books on offer at his shop varied from penny weekly novels, nicknamed "penny dreadfuls", which flew off his shelves at a rate of 6,000 a week, to the novels of Charles Dickens which sold about 250 copies weekly.

At this time, many tobacconists, stationery shops and pubs had small 'libraries' which lent penny fiction and popular periodicals. Heywood also had a 'penny reading room' which was open from 6am to 10pm. In addition to popular fiction, the room stocked political tracts and educational books for those with the time, ability or the energy (after long hours at work) to try and better their lot. In spite of Heywood's (and other booksellers') best efforts, Manchester was still considered to be a town of illiteracy and ignorance.

Abel Heywood never forgot his working-class roots and was a committed social reformer all his life. He took over the Manchester branch of *The Poor Man's Guardian* ('Published in defiance of the law to try the power of Might against Right'). At this time, newspapers (and literature in general) were the privilege of the few. The 'powers that were' were afraid that if newspapers were available to the working classes, they would use them to stir up trouble and promote revolutionary ideas; as a result, the government imposed heavy stamp duties on newspapers. These were known as 'taxes on knowledge'. Heywood was a great believer in cheap newspapers for the masses and refused to pay these duties. As a result, he was imprisoned for four months in New Bailey Prison. The attention given to the case led to the duty on newspapers being reduced from 4d to 1d and in 1855 it was scrapped altogether. Heywood was also heavily involved in Chartism and was responsible for publishing the movement's literature.

In 1862 Heywood was elected Mayor of Manchester for the first time and he was elected again in 1876. When the New Town Hall opened in 1877, it was the world's most expensive building (£1,000,000) and it was expected that Queen Victoria would perform the opening ceremony. She refused. Many believed that this decision was made owing to Heywood's radical past or the fact that a statue of Oliver Cromwell had been erected in the city. In the end, the Town Hall was opened by Abel Heywood himself amidst great celebrations including a procession of around 50,000 people. The procession was over a mile long and took three hours to pass the Town Hall steps where Heywood and his wife were standing. The clock bell in the Town Hall tower is named 'Great Abel' in his honour. It is inscribed with the initials AH and the Tennyson line 'Ring out the false, ring in the true' from his poem 'Ring Out, Wild Bells' which forms part of the beautiful 'In Memoriam'.

Elijah Dixon (1790-1876)

Elijah Dixon moved to Manchester with his family in 1802 and went to work at a mill in Ancoats, first as a scavenger, then as a piecer. He was an intelligent lad and a voracious reader and he soon began to take an interest in the politics of the day. He campaigned and organised petitions for universal male suffrage and in 1817 was present at the Blanketeers' march. A few days later whilst at work, Dixon was arrested, clapped in irons and taken to New Bailey Prison. He was accused of high treason and subsequently taken to a prison in London. Months later he was released without charge and returned to Manchester.

He left the world of textiles and tried many other trades while still remaining a political activist; he was present at the infamous Peterloo Massacre in 1819. Dixon worked (very briefly) as a travelling milk-seller. The milk was carried in cans slung over a donkey's back. Unfortunately on the first day of his milk round, the donkey was stung by a wasp; it (the donkey, not the wasp) went berserk and all the milk was lost. So donkey and cart were sold and Dixon tried to earn a living as a pedlar – again with little success.

In the *Gazetteer* of 1825 he was listed as being a grocer and flour dealer with a shop at 42, Great Ancoats Street. He went on to become a manufacturer and seller of pill-boxes and Lucifer matches. This time luck must have been on his side and the business flourished. He developed the business further, becoming a very wealthy timber merchant.

He remained a reform campaigner all his life, working alongside other prominent figures such as Ernest Jones and Richard Carlile. He continued to champion the cause of the working man, calling for universal 'manhood suffrage', and was a strong supporter of the Co-operative and Temperance Movements and the abolition of slavery. He died in 1876.

A real rags-to-riches story – a true Manchester Man!

The Pankhurst Family

Emmeline (1858–1928)

Regarded by many as one of the most influential women of the twentieth century, Emmeline Goulden was born in Moss Side in 1858, the daughter of a wealthy cotton merchant. When she was 20, she married Dr. Richard Pankhurst, a lawyer more than twice her age, with whom she had five children, three girls and two boys. (Both boys died before reaching adulthood.) In 1903, five years after her husband's death, she founded the 'Women's Social and Political Union' at her home on Nelson Street, Manchester with the help of her three daughters – Christabel, Sylvia and Adela, and fellow-suffragette Annie Kenney; their philosophy was 'Deeds, not words'. The group fought an increasingly militant campaign for women's right to vote, including smashing windows, slashing paintings at Manchester Art Gallery, assaulting police officers and progressing to arson; they, allegedly, set fire to the Rusholme Exhibition Hall which was largely made of wood and consequently burned to the ground. They were also blamed for planting a bomb on the steps of the greenhouse in Alexandra Park which sent a shower of glass over the neighbouring houses; this was just before the Prime Minister Herbert Asquith was due to arrive in the city. Members of the WSPU were imprisoned many times and in 1909 began their campaign of going on hunger strikes. The authorities reacted by force-feeding the women, a practice which continued until the introduction of the 'Cat and Mouse Act'. As Emmeline and Christabel increased their violent tactics, Sylvia and Adela broke away from the group. Hostilities were suspended for the duration of the war and in 1918 women over the age of 30 were given the right to vote. After the war, Emmeline joined the Conservative Party, considered by some as a betrayal. She died in 1928, the year that women over 21 were given the same voting rights as men.

In 2016, after a vote, Emmeline Pankhurst was chosen as the subject for the first female statue to be erected in Manchester since Queen Victoria.

The Daughters:

All the Pankhurst daughters were born in Manchester and were educated at Manchester High School for Girls.

Christabel (1880–1958)

Christabel, named after the heroine of a poem by Coleridge, was always regarded as Emmeline's favourite daughter. She was one of the first female political prisoners when in 1905 she, together with Annie Kenney, was imprisoned for heckling at a political meeting in the Free Trade Hall at which Winston Churchill was speaking and, after being escorted out of the building, spitting in a policeman's eye. Emmeline later wrote, 'This was the beginning of a campaign the like of which was never known in England, or for that matter in any other country.' She was the first woman to gain a Law degree at Manchester University, but, as a woman, found it almost impossible to practise. She became a staunch supporter of the war, calling for all men to be conscripted and all women to work for the war effort. She and her supporters would hand out white feathers (a symbol of cowardice) to all men in civilian clothes. In 1921 she moved to America where she became an evangelist with the Second Adventist group. She returned to Britain in the 1930s when she was appointed a 'Dame' but returned to America at the outbreak of the Second World War where she remained until her death in 1958.

Sylvia (1882–1960)

Less militant than her mother and older sister but just as committed to the cause was Sylvia Pankhurst. She studied at Manchester School of Art and later at the Royal College of Art in London. In 1907 she toured the north of England painting working-class women at work. Sylvia wanted the WSPU to be a socialist party allied to the Independent Labour Party, led by (her good friend) Keir Hardie. A rift followed and widened as Sylvia became a passionate socialist and an anti-war campaigner. She scandalised society (and her mother who refused to have anything more to do with her) by living openly with an Italian anarchist and having his son, whom she named Richard, out of wedlock. In later life, Sylvia became friend and advisor to the Ethiopian Emperor, Haile Selassie, and she and her son moved to Addis Ababa in 1956. She died there four years later.

Adela (1885–1961)

Adela was the youngest of the Pankhurst daughters and, although she too joined her mother and sisters in the fight for the right to vote, she is the least well-known member of the family. When she (together with Sylvia) criticised the tactics of the WSPU, her mother bought Adela a one-way ticket to Australia, gave her £20 and a letter of introduction to an Australian suffragette. They never saw each other again.

Adela became an active campaigner against the war and conscription in Australia. She was also one of the founders of the Communist Party of Australia, but later became disillusioned and founded an anti-communist organisation. In 1941 she was one of the founders of yet another movement – this time, it was the right-wing Australia First Movement. In 1942 she was interned after advocating peace with Japan.

Both Christabel and Sylvia wrote books about their mother and the Suffragette movement. The former paints a picture of her mother as a selfless saint while the latter portrays her as an autocrat and a betrayer of socialist values.

GUTE
Guardian Underground Telephone Exchange

Once called the 'best kept secret in Manchester', the Guardian 'bunker' was built in 1954, as part of 'War Plan UK', to be a communications centre in the event of a nuclear war. It had the potential to withstand a direct hit from an

A-bomb (such as the one which decimated Hiroshima) but ironically, technology advanced at a quicker pace than the building work and by the time it was completed, at a cost of £4 million (funded by NATO), it was already obsolete and would have been worse than useless if hit by an H-bomb. It was constructed by non-English-speaking Poles who believed, as did many others, that it was being built for the GPO (General Post Office); all those 'in the know' were obliged to sign the Official Secrets Act. There was a rumour flying around at the time which suggested that there was, literally, a goldmine being excavated beneath the streets of Manchester.

Had an attack been thought imminent, the bunker would have been sealed with a 35-ton concrete slab. Inside, there was enough food to last for around two months, an artesian well, generators and fuel tanks. The walls of some rooms were painted with artificial windows and countryside scenes. Was this intended to distract them from the fact that they were probably the only people alive within a ten-mile radius? Who knows?

The bunker was built on two levels and is huge, with tunnels stretching from Chapel Street in Salford to Ardwick Green. There were dormitories, a canteen, a bar and even a games room for all for those chosen as 'VIPs' – politicians, civil servants, etc. (Would these people really be VIPs after a nuclear holocaust?) Today, the tunnels have BT cables running through them (or so we are told).

Chapter 5

To Battle!

At one time, in order to be ready for battle, archery was a compulsory activity for the boys and men of Manchester. In the early Court Leet records there are frequent references to archery, including, 'All boys above the age of seven years, and men should possess a bow and at least two shafts or arrows. Archery is to be practised by all on holy days, parents and employers being held responsible for seeing that their children and servants do so at least four times a year.' In earlier times, there were several archery butts situated around the town and men were expected to practise daily.

In 1588 Manchester was required to send '38 barquebusiers, 38 archers and 144 men for bills [lethal-looking swords with a sharp hook at one side] and pikes [long swords] to fight against the Spanish Armada'.

Civil War

The English Civil War (1642-51) was a series of conflicts between the Cavaliers (Royalists) and the Roundheads (Parliamentarians). There were several outcomes of these conflicts: the execution of Charles I, the exile of Charles II (his son) and the establishment of the 'Commonwealth of England' led by Oliver Cromwell. What became known as the Siege of Manchester took place in the early days of the conflict, in 1642. Manchester stood on the side of the Parliamentarians and, under the leadership of the German soldier Colonel Rosworm, had mustered its own fighting force. The Royalist headquarters were in Aldport Lodge, Deansgate, led by Lord Strange (later the Earl of Derby). There were several skirmishes between the two sides. The Royalists tried to besiege the town by firing cannon down Deansgate and when that failed, they made another attack over Salford Bridge. Manchester refused to surrender and the Royalists admitted defeat. Around 200 Royalists and 20 Parliamentarians were killed in a war which would go on to claim the lives of over 200,000 people. As far as Manchester was concerned, the Civil War was over (apart from a later skirmish at Wythenshawe Hall). Strange was executed in 1651 for his part in the Bolton Massacre of 1644.

> **&** The first casualty of the Civil War was Richard Perceval, a Manchester linen weaver who was shot dead on Market Stead Lane during a fracas with Royalist troops.

The monarchy was restored after eleven years when the Protestant Charles II returned from exile and ascended to the throne in 1660.

The Jacobite Rebellions

The first Jacobite Rebellion occurred in 1715 and the second in 1745. The intention of both risings was to replace the Protestant Hanoverian monarchy in favour of the Catholic Stuarts. As always, the good people of Manchester were there to play their part.

The Syddalls

The first act of the 1715 Rebellion was led by peruke-maker (a maker of wigs) Thomas Syddall who led a Jacobite mob which destroyed Cross Street Chapel. Syddall was a staunch Catholic and was fighting to restore the Catholic James Stuart (The Old Pretender) to the throne in place of the reigning monarch, the Protestant King George I. After the rebellion had been suppressed, Syddall was hanged and his head impaled on a spike in the Market Place. As a young boy, Syddall's son, also called Thomas, had witnessed his father's skull which had been left to whiten on the Market Cross and he vowed revenge on the Protestants.

Thirty years later, in the second Jacobite Rebellion when the Rebels came to Manchester, Thomas left his wife, his five children and his business (a barber's shop) to join the officers in the Manchester Regiment. Their aim was to restore the Catholic Charles Edward Stuart, better known as Bonnie Prince Charlie or 'The Young Pretender' to the throne in place of the Protestant King George II. Syddall the younger suffered the same fate as his father; he was charged with high-treason and sentenced to death. He and his fellow conspirators were hanged, drawn and quartered.

Thomas's head was put on display in the same spot where his father's head had once been.

> In 1745 the 'Pretender' resided with Mr. John Dickenson, a merchant who lived on Market Stead Lane. Following the visit, Dickenson's house was referred to as 'The Palace' and years later it became the 'Palace Inn'. After demolition, a warehouse was erected on the site and named 'Palace Buildings'. &

Jemmy Dawson

James 'Jemmy' Dawson, the son of a doctor, was born and educated in Manchester and later went to Cambridge University. Like many young men he enlisted in the Manchester Regiment and, taking the rank of captain, he took part in the Jacobite Rebellion of 1745. After their defeat the soldiers, including Captain James Dawson, were arrested as traitors. (The group became known as the 'Manchester Rebels'.) They were driven through the streets of London, taken to court and charged with high-treason; they were then tried and condemned to death.

On 30 July 1746 Dawson and his fellow conspirators were taken to the gallows where they were hanged and whilst still breathing they were disembowelled, then beheaded before being quartered. Their hearts were also torn out and, together with their entrails, were thrown onto a fire. The executioners cried 'God save King George' and the crowd of spectators cheered. However, there was at least one person who didn't join in the general rejoicing. Jemmy Dawson may have been one of many who met the same fate, but not all achieved fame as the 'hero' of a ballad as he did. The ballad, by William Shenstone, describes Dawson's love of a fair maiden by the name of Katherine Norton and her tragic death after following her lover from the gaol to the gallows and witnessing his barbaric death. As Jemmy died, Katherine said, 'My dear, I follow thee!' and then she too took her last breath. The ballad begins:

> Young Dawson was a gallant youth,
> A brighter never trod the plain:
> And well he loved one charming maid,
> And dearly was he lov'd again.

and ends with:

> The dismal scene was o'er and past,
> The lover's mournful hearse retired:
> The maid drew back her languid head
> And, sighing forth his name, expired.

As was usual in the case of traitors, Jemmy Dawson's head was returned to his home town of Manchester where it was put on public display to act as a deterrent to others contemplating acts of treason.

The Young Pretender was finally defeated at the Battle of Culloden in 1746.

'Ye Hearts of Oak of Manchester'

As Napoleon threatened to invade England in c.1804, the 'call to arms' was again heard in Manchester. Public houses were often the best places in which to find recruits. A popular patriotic song of the time went:

> Ye hearts of oak of Manchester
> Come listen to my song,
> To the marine corps in this town,
> The praise of it belong.

(Chorus)
> This corps, so tight, is the delight
> Of lasses neat and clean,
> No girl that's wise will e'er despise
> A Manchester marine.

> The gentlemen of Manchester
> Five hundred men to raise,
> And more to prove their loyalty,
> Six guineas bounty pays.

> They wear cockades of pink and blue
> For to adorn their head,
> And dress their men in uniform
> Of handsome white and red.

> A band of music sweetly plays,
> Before them in their round,

> While every heart is cheer'd to hear
> Its captivating sound.
>
> The Manchester marines are men
> That's loyal, free, and bold,
> And does declare they'll nobly die,
> Before they'll be controul'd.
>
> To fight the proud insulting French
> They valiantly will go,
> And in defence of Britons' rights,
> Much courage they will show.
>
> When France is taught to know her own,
> If fortune spare our lives,
> To Manchester we will return
> To our sweethearts and wives.
>
> Their bells will ring and music play,
> While Britons drink and sing,
> God bless the Manchester marines
> And save great George our King.

Before they went off to fight, the recruits would congregate in St. Ann's Square and then march through Manchester in a blaze of cockades (coloured rosettes normally pinned on the side of a hat) and red, white and blue ribbons. The sergeants led the parade with loaves of bread impaled on the ends of their swords to indicate that the troops would be well fed. They would have been accompanied by a band playing the song 'Farewell, Manchester'; this was originally a Jacobite song describing Charles Stuart's departure from Manchester in 1745:

> Farewell Manchester! noble town, fare-well!
> Here with loyalty ev'ry breast can swell,
> Wheresoe'er I roam, Here, as in a home,
> Ever, dear Lancashire, my heart shall dwell.
> Farewell Manchester! sadly I depart.
> Tear-drops bodingly from their prison start.
> Though I toil anew, Shadows to pursue,
> Shadows vain, thou'lt remain within my heart.

Sometimes men would be tricked into accepting the King's shilling. One such (name unknown so let's call him Bob) was 'enlisted' by the over-zealous Sergeant Kite. When Bob was presented before the magistrate to be sworn in, the latter decreed that Bob was now a soldier and must go off to fight. Bob replied, 'Well, if I must fight, I must. But first can you tell me if this shilling that the sergeant gave me is a good 'un?' He handed the coin to the magistrate and declared, 'You are enlisted, sir, just as I was!'

The First World War

In Victoria Station, near to its oldest platforms, stands the 'Soldiers' Gate'. It was so named because it was that through which the soldiers passed on the first stage of their journey to the battlefields of France and Belgium during the First World War. This memorial was restored during the station's 2015 redevelopment and is a poignant reminder of the thousands of soldiers who left and never returned.

In 1916 Wilfred Owen, one of the greatest ever war poets, joined the Manchester Regiment as second lieutenant. He was initially not too complimentary about his men, describing them as 'expressionless lumps'.

Blitz!

At the beginning of the Second World War, 172,000 children and 23,000 adults were evacuated from Manchester over a period of three days.

Just three days before Christmas, 1940, the German Luftwaffe carried out a bombing raid over Manchester and Salford which lasted almost twelve hours; more than 1,000 incendiary bombs and almost 300 tons of high explosives were dropped on the two cities and the surrounding areas. The bombers returned the following night to continue their destruction. Altogether, 596 civilians and 64 emergency workers were killed, thousands were injured and tens of thousands of houses were reduced to rubble. The next major air raid took place in June 1941; again there was much loss of life.

> The Grade II* listed Manchester Cenotaph was designed by Sir Edwin Lutyens and was erected in 1924: a memorial to the fallen soldiers of the First World War.
>
> It was relocated in 2014 - from one side of St. Peter's Square to the other.

Chapter 6

Religion

Roman Altars

The Romans believed in many different gods and goddesses who had power over the lives of mere mortals. Altars (known as votive altars) were erected by those who had made a vow to a god or goddess. Three Roman altars have been found in Manchester. One was found near the River Medlock at Knott Mill in 1612 and dates back to the second century AD; it was dedicated to the goddess of 'Fortune the preserver' by Lucius Seniacianius Martius, a centurion. In 2008 an altar was unearthed during excavation work on Chester Road (the old Roman road leading from Castlefield). This one-metre-high column, found in almost perfect condition, was dedicated to two Germanic goddesses by a Roman soldier, Aelius Victor. The Latin inscription on the altar translates, 'To the mother goddesses Hananeftis and Ollototis, Aelius Victor gladly, willingly and deservedly fulfils a vow.' On top of the stone is a hollow which was used for offerings of wine or blood and maybe to burn incense.

Sator Square

In the 1970s when excavation work was being carried out in Castlefield, a fragment of Roman pottery, about 7 inches by 3 inches, was unearthed. It dates back to the second century and is part of a Sator Square; it is believed by many to be one of the earliest pieces of evidence of Christianity in Britain. A Sator Square is a Latin palindromic word square. Like other Sator Squares found in Christendom, the complete square would have read:

```
R O T A S
O P E R A
T E N E T
A R E P O
S A T 0 R
```

This translates to 'Arepo the sower guides the plough with care'. At one time a Sator Square was considered by some to have magical properties: it was thought that the complex four-times palindrome was enough to confuse the devil.

The Sator Square fragment is on display in Manchester Museum.

When the letters are rearranged into the shape of a cross centred around the letter 'N', it reads PATER NOSTER (Latin for 'Our Father') both vertically and horizontally. The two letters left over are A and O which also have a significance in Christianity: 'I am the Alpha and the Omega – the beginning and the end' (from the Book of Revelations). Alpha and Omega are the first and last letters of the Greek alphabet.

The meaning of the Sator Square has been and is still widely debated.

In 1839 a bronze statue of the god Jupiter (some 5½ inches tall) was found by a workman digging the foundations for the Hall of Science in Campfield. Jupiter was the supreme and most powerful deity in the pantheon of Roman gods being the god of sky, thunder and all the heavens.

The Cult of Mithras

In 1821 when drains were being laid in Hulme, three large carved stones dating from the second/third century AD were found. They came from an ancient Mithraeum: a temple for the worship of the eastern god Mithras. The cult of Mithras was an all-male Roman mystery religion which involved a series of seven initiation rites and was popular amongst Roman soldiers. There were many temples of Mithras dotted around the Roman Empire, many of which were in underground caves. Mithras was a god of the sun who always triumphed over darkness; the centrepiece of the temple was a depiction of Mithras killing a bull which symbolised evil.

The Red Bank Urn

In 1850, a sixth century Anglo-Saxon cinerary urn was discovered in the Red Bank area (behind Victoria Station). The urn would have been used to hold the ashes following a cremation.

Angel Stone

In the nineteenth century a stone carving of an angel with a scroll, dating back to c.700 AD was found embedded in the wall of the original south porch of the Cathedral. The 'Angel Stone' points to the presence of an early Saxon church but its location is unknown (although many people have speculated as to where it stood). There is a record of a St. Mary's Church, Manchester in the Domesday Book of 1086 but its location is also somewhat difficult to determine.

The inscription on the stone translates to:

'Into Thy hands, O Lord, I commend my spirit.'

In 1215, however, the then Lord of the Manor, Robert Gresley, decided he would like the parish church of Manchester to be built adjacent to his manor house, on the site of what is now the Cathedral.

Manchester Cathedral

Manchester Cathedral was mainly built in the fifteenth century from sandstone quarried from nearby Collyhurst. As one would expect with such an old building, the Cathedral has had a long and colourful history; over the centuries parts of the original building have been extended, added to, replaced, destroyed and restored.

In 1421, at the instigation of Thomas de la Warre, then Lord of the Manor, the church became a collegiate foundation with eight priests, a warden, four singing clerks and six choristers. He gave the land opposite the church, on which the old Baronial Hall stood, over to the church and funded a 'college' to be used as a residence for the priests. He also began major building work on the church which was dedicated to St. Mary, St. Denys (the patron saint of France) and St. George, reflecting both the English and French heritage of the de la Warre family.

The earliest parish register dates back to 1573; the first entry is the burial of Robert Fisher on 1 August.

Following the consecration of the new St. Ann's, the old Collegiate Church was always referred to as 'th'owd church' (the old church).

> 'Cathedra' is the Latin for 'chair'. When a church becomes the seat of a bishop, it becomes a cathedral. The 'old church' in Manchester achieved cathedral status in 1847.
>
> &

In the 1870s a committee was established to discuss the building of a new cathedral. Plans were drawn up for a huge Gothic building near to the Infirmary in Piccadilly. Instead, a major restoration programme was carried out on the existing cathedral. It is the broadest cathedral in England and the wooden carvings of the sixteenth century misericords are considered to be some of the finest in Europe.

Extensive damage was caused to the Cathedral in December 1940 during the German bombing raids. After Coventry, Manchester Cathedral suffered more bomb damage than any other cathedral in England. There was initially some doubt as to whether it could be saved and almost twenty years were spent in restoring the building, including replacing the stained-glass windows, every one of which had been destroyed in the blast. The cathedral again suffered damage in the 1996 IRA bomb.

> Around the year 1825 a tradesman by the name of Higgins was walking by the Collegiate Church when suddenly, as if from nowhere, there appeared the ghostly apparition of a headless hound. The spectre jumped on his back and, with its paws on Higgins' shoulders, ran him all the way home. On entering his house, the terrified man dashed upstairs and into bed, where with trembling hands he pulled the covers over his head. His wife, however, was not too sympathetic, especially as he had not taken off his filthy work clothes first!   Legend has it ...
>
> The apparition was said to be the spectre of a dog that was buried under the old Salford Bridge spanning the River Irwell. Legend has it that the dog was condemned to walk the earth for 999 years.

Cathedral Characters:

Dr. John Dee

John Dee was born in Wales and always maintained that he was descended from Welsh princes. He was extremely intelligent and had a voracious appetite for learning. At the age of just 15 he went to study mathematics, chemistry and astronomy at Cambridge University where he later claimed that he had studied for eighteen hours each day and slept for four hours, leaving two hours for food and recreation. When he was 19 he was appointed a fellow of the newly-established Trinity College. In the coming decades he became one of the most famous and eminent mathematicians, logicians and astronomers in Europe; at one time he owned the largest personal library in England. His lectures were so popular that many people had to stand outside and listen through the open windows.

Dee believed that the universe was based on principles of 'Magic', but that its rules and laws could be explained by mathematics. Since his teens, Dee had been exploring the power of astrology (the interpretation of the effects of celestial bodies on humans) and he later turned his attentions to alchemy. The 'science' of alchemy had two objectives: to transmute base metals into gold by means of a philosopher's stone and to discover the *Elixir Vitae* – the gift of eternal life, youth and health. A belief in alchemy was not confined to the credulous or the ill-educated; it was practised by doctors, scholars and those high up in the Church, not to mention kings, queens and popes. However, Dee gradually earned the reputation of being a practitioner of the 'dark arts'.

During the reign of Queen 'Bloody' Mary, Dee was accused of 'practising against the queen's life by enchantment'. He was imprisoned for three months, but later released owing to lack of evidence. He had more luck with the next monarch, Queen Elizabeth I, especially after he produced an astrologer's chart to determine a propitious day for her coronation, which proved to be a huge success. This was an age of great superstition, even among the 'upper echelons' of society and the Queen called for Dee's help on many occasions, for example following the appearance of a comet and after a wax effigy of her with a stake in its heart had been found: these 'mysteries' and more were handed to Doctor Dee to explain and alleviate her paranoia. He earned the nickname of 'the Queen's Merlin'.

In 1582 Dee began a friendship with Edward Kelly and this became one of the main reasons why he was damned in so many people's eyes. Kelly had once been a lawyer but had been convicted of forgery and was punished by having his ears cut off (a not uncommon punishment in England during the sixteenth and seventeenth centuries, sometimes known as 'cropping'). To disguise the fact, he always wore a huge black hood to cover his head and neck. Dee claimed to possess a magical mirror given to him by angels which he used to cast horoscopes and a crystal (again brought by angels) which he claimed was the portal to the world of spirits. Kelly claimed that he was a 'seer' (a modern-day medium) and that, unlike Dee, he could use the crystal to conjure up and speak with the spirit world. Kelly related countless conversations he claimed to have had with the spirits, all of which Dee assiduously scribed.

In 1595 Queen Elizabeth appointed Dr. Dee as Warden of Manchester's Collegiate Church. Here he was described as a man who 'took little interest in Papist or Protestant theology', being more devoted to the study of the occult. Dee's reputation of 'dealings with the devil' had obviously followed him to the town. Although he was still respected by some for his scholarship and learning, he was feared by many for being a necromancer and a magician. His interest in alchemy and spiritualism led the Fellows at the Church to equate Dee's activities to witchcraft and devilry. Although Dee always claimed that he dealt only with 'good spirits', there were many people who thought otherwise. Dee was not wanted in Manchester; he petitioned the new monarch, King James I, to be allowed to stay, but his request was denied and Dee left the town in 1603.

During his stay in Manchester, Dr. Dee lived in what is now Chetham's School of Music, then a residence for the clergy of the Collegiate Church.

> Amazingly, the school is still in possession of a table that was used by Dr. Dee. It has a large circular burn mark in one corner which is said to be a hoof mark, made when Dee had conjured up the devil to ask his advice.

Legend has it ...

Photograph: Courtesy of Chetham's Library

Doctor Dee died in 1608 in 'the utmost poverty'; clearly his attempts at alchemy had not been too successful! However, his legacy lives on. Many believe that he was the model for Christopher Marlowe's 'Doctor Faustus', a man who sells his soul to the devil in return for power and knowledge. It is also thought that the character Prospero in Shakespeare's *The Tempest* was based on Dr. Dee. He was certainly the inspiration for *Doctor Dee: an English Opera* by Damon Albarn and Rufus Norris which received rave reviews when premiered in Manchester in 2011.

Joshua Brookes

A local lad, educated at Manchester Grammar School and then Oxford University, the Reverend Joshua Brookes was chaplain of the Collegiate Church from 1790 until his death in 1821. During his tenure, the town's population exploded from 17,000 to 180,000. Before 1847, nearly all baptisms, marriages and funeral services in Manchester were conducted there and Brookes is reputed to have baptised, married and buried more people than any other clergyman in England.

Brookes was renowned for his eccentricities and he would often interrupt services to 'box the ears' of a misbehaving boy or to pop out to the shop on Half-Street for a bag of his favourite sweets: horehound drops. At baptisms, if he didn't like the name the parents had chosen for their baby, he would promptly change it. Weddings were routinely carried out for thirty couples at a time and it was not unknown for Brookes to marry a bride to the wrong (often drunk) groom. The busiest time for weddings was Easter; during Lent, the marriage fee would be double.

One observer of a "mass marriage" painted a dismal picture in his description of the "happy couples" – "… all of them unbrushed, unshaven, unwashed, uncombed and wrinkled with penury and care… They were, in short, the mere rags and tatters of the human race."

Cecil Daniel Wray

Eccentricity seems to have been a trait in Manchester clergymen. Wray (who went on to become canon and sub-dean) spent fifty-six years at the Cathedral. On his 88th birthday he founded 'Canon Wray's Birthday Gift'. Every year, on 21 January, two pairs of 'good, Worsted stockings' were to be given to eight men and eight women in need.

****

Cross Street Chapel

Cross Street Chapel, originally called the 'Dissenters' Meeting House' is a Unitarian Church founded by Henry Newcome in 1694 following the 'Act of Tolerance'. (Dissenters were those who would not conform to the new rules set out by the Church of England.) The first chapel was built on a piece of land which went by the name of 'Plungeon's Meadow'; the congregation still meet on the same site today. The chapel was destroyed in the Jacobite Rising of 1715 and replaced by another which lasted for over two centuries before being obliterated in the Blitz of 1940. Rebuilt in the 1950s, the third chapel lasted a mere forty years and in 1997 was replaced with the present building.

In 1828 William Gaskell, husband of the novelist Elizabeth Gaskell, became a minister at the Chapel, a position he was to hold until 1884. He and other Unitarians played a key role in the fight for social justice and in providing education for the working classes.

The Chapel originally had a graveyard attached to it. In 2014, during the construction of the Second City Crossing tram line, the remains of over one hundred bodies were found; they were re-interred in Southern Cemetery. Also discovered during excavation work for the tram line was the vaulted crypt of St. Peter's Church which was built in what is now St. Peter's Square in 1788.

St. Ann's Church

This Georgian church was built on part of Acres Field on land donated by Lady Ann Bland (daughter of Sir Edward Mosley) and Lady of the Manor who laid the foundation stone in 1709. Built in response to dissatisfaction with the High Church teachings at the Collegiate Church, it was consecrated three years later and dedicated to St. Ann in homage to the founder and also to Queen Anne, the reigning monarch. The name of the area was changed to St. Ann's Square.

The 'Hidden Gem'

St. Mary's RC Church on Mulberry Street is the oldest Catholic church in Manchester; it acquired its nickname when a visiting bishop remarked, 'No matter on what side of the church you look, you behold a hidden gem.' When it was built in 1794, the area, which had so recently been meadows and grazing pastures, was one of the poorest in town, becoming increasingly built up with slum dwellings. Today, the church is lost among a warren of Victorian buildings and twentieth century office blocks; it truly is a 'Hidden Gem'.

L.S. Lowry made a chalk and charcoal sketch of the church in 1962 and on 20 August 2007, Anthony Wilson's funeral service was held here.

Martyrs:

Saint Ambrose Barlow

Edward Barlow was born in 1583 in Barlow Hall, Chorlton-cum-Hardy, the son of well-to-do Catholic parents and one of the first pupils at Manchester Grammar School. This was a time of religious persecution and to be a practising Catholic was to risk imprisonment, torture and even death. His grandfather had died in prison the year before Edward was born, imprisoned owing to his refusal to give up his faith. Edward's father, Sir Alexander Barlow, had also had much of his land confiscated as a result of his Catholicism, following which he and his family had converted to the Church of England. At an early age Edward realised he had a vocation and was sent off to France and then Spain to study. He eventually became a Benedictine monk and two years later he was ordained as a priest, taking the name Father Ambrose. He returned to his home in England where he conducted forbidden Masses in secret chapels in the grand houses of devout Catholics living in Lancashire. These families also provided him with funds to enable him to hold Mass in the homes of the less well-off Catholics in his parish. He continued to do this for many years.

On 7 March 1641 King Charles I gave all Catholic priests one month in which to leave the country or risk being arrested as traitors, for which, if convicted, the penalty was death. Father Ambrose refused to go. On Easter Day of the same year, only days after the 'one month' deadline had elapsed, John Jones, a Protestant minister, heard that Father Ambrose was holding Mass in the nearby Hall of a noted Catholic family. Jones and his bloodthirsty congregation of around 400 left their own church service and, armed with swords and clubs, marched to the Hall to hunt down the priest. Father Ambrose gave himself up immediately on condition that those who had been present at the Mass were free to go. He was taken to Lancaster Castle where he was tried and condemned to death by being 'hanged, dismembered, disembowelled, quartered, beheaded and boiled in tar'. His head was then impaled on a spike and exhibited in Manchester's Market Place. The skull was later stolen, only to turn up many years later.

Wardley Hall, the black and white half-timbered Tudor House in Salford, earned the nickname 'The Skull House' on account of the human skull which for centuries has been on display in an aperture built into the wall between the Great Hall and the staircase. There were many myths and legends told about the provenance of the skull, but it is now acknowledged to be that of Father Ambrose. It was believed to have been stolen by a Catholic sympathiser and hidden at the Hall. In the eighteenth century when an old part of the building was being demolished, a box containing the skull 'with a goodly set of teeth and a good deal of auburn hair' was discovered.

> The skull was found by a servant and thrown into the moat, an action which was immediately followed by deafening claps of thunder. The owner of the Hall drained the moat and retrieved the skull. Ever after it was thought to possess magical powers; whenever it was disturbed, a violent storm would break out - trees were uprooted, roofs were lifted and windows were blown in. According to legend, the skull is indestructible and all attempts to destroy it are doomed to failure; the grinning (some say screaming) skull always reappears in one piece!
>
> **Legend has it ...**

The skull remains in its little cubby-hole to this day!

St. Ambrose Barlow was one of a group known as the 'Forty Martyrs of England and Wales' who were canonised by Pope Paul VI in 1970.

John Bradford

Catholics were not alone in being executed for their beliefs. John Bradford, born in Blackley and also educated at Manchester Grammar School, was a Protestant preacher who fell foul of the Catholic Queen Mary; he was first imprisoned in the Tower of London, then publicly burned at the stake in 1555 after being found guilty of heresy. He was chained to the stake with a young man by the name of John Leaf. As the fire was lit he turned to Leaf and said, 'Be of good comfort brother; for we shall have a merry supper with the Lord this night!'

The Shakers

Ann Lee was born into poverty in Toad Lane, Manchester in 1736 and was christened in the Collegiate Church. Her father was a blacksmith and too poor to provide any education for his children; like so many people at that time, Ann never learned to read and write. When she was old enough (though still very young) Ann was sent to work in a textile mill. She later worked as a fur cutter and then as a cook in the newly-built Manchester Infirmary. From such humble beginnings Ann Lee would seem an unlikely prospect to become the charismatic leader of a religious sect and founder of a unique way of life that would last for over 200 years. But that she did!

Ann's parents were deeply religious and Ann grew up to be a spiritual and serious-minded girl. Disillusioned by the Anglican Church, she joined a Quaker sect known as 'The Shaking Quakers', so called because during worship they would dance, shake and speak in tongues; the sect had been founded by Jane and James Wardley. In 1762, and much against her better judgement, Ann was reluctantly persuaded into marriage and went on to have four children, all of whom died in infancy. After the death of her fourth child, Ann claimed to have had a vision in which God told her that celibacy and confession of one's sins provided the only true path to the Kingdom of Heaven.

Ann Lee began to gather a loyal group of followers who became convinced that she represented the second coming of Christ. The Shaker movement, later also known as 'The United Society of Believers in the First and Second Appearance of Christ' was born, with 'Mother Ann' as its leader. She herself believed that 'just as Adam and Eve were the "natural" parents of humanity, she and Christ were the "spiritual" parents of a new and higher order of humanity'. She espoused many of the ideas of the Wardleys and taught that by dancing and shaking during worship, the body would be purged of sin. In what was a period of religious persecution Ann Lee was imprisoned several times, charged with blasphemy and breaking the Sabbath. Yet in spite of persecution and frequent acts of violence against her and her supporters, she remained undaunted and continued to preach. It was during one stay in prison that she had another vision – of a tree – with the message that God had prepared a place for them in America.

Nine Shakers sailed for America in 1774; the nine included her husband, Abraham Stanley, who, shortly after their arrival, abandoned her and ran off with another woman. (He had obviously decided that a celibate existence was not for him.) The remainder stayed in New York for five years during which time they worked to earn the money to establish their unique colony near Albany. During this time, Ann Lee worked as a laundress and at times had so little money that she was unable to buy food.

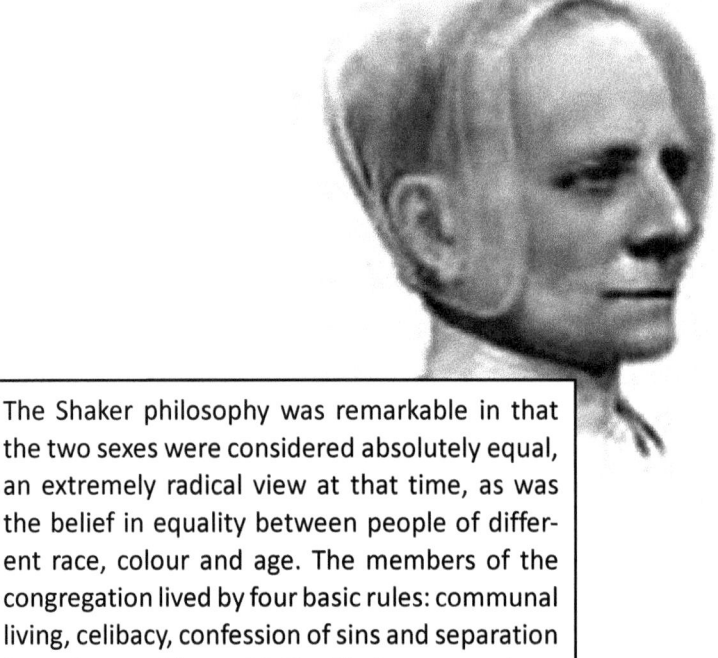

> The Shaker philosophy was remarkable in that the two sexes were considered absolutely equal, an extremely radical view at that time, as was the belief in equality between people of different race, colour and age. The members of the congregation lived by four basic rules: communal living, celibacy, confession of sins and separation from the outside world. The Shakers were also a pacifist sect and in 1780 Ann Lee was again sent to prison, this time for refusing to sign an oath of allegiance.

'Mother' Ann Lee

The Shaker philosophy was 'Put your hands to work and your heart to God'.

Shakers at worship

Mother Ann envisaged a community free from the ills which plagued 'the World' – war, greed, violence and exploitation. She also included lust in the category of 'ills' and believed sex to be the ultimate sin against God. She advocated perfection in every aspect of life; each person in the community was trained to master a specific task or craft, all of which were deemed equal. Simplicity, utility and perfection were their guiding principles and in order to support themselves, they produced beautiful high-quality goods to sell. Original Shaker items now command huge prices and the Shaker name today conjures up images of furniture, oval boxes and folk art rather than any religious connotations.

Ann Lee's proposed colony was to be the first of nineteen thriving Shaker colonies that were established in several states across America. Amazingly, the movement lasted for over 200 years. Despite their vow of celibacy, they were able to recruit enough new members to ensure continuity of their 'Utopian' ideals; at its height in the mid-1800s, membership was around 6,000. Sadly, Ann Lee didn't live to experience the full fruition of her labours. It was only after her death and under the leadership of her chosen successors, Joseph Meacham and Lucy Wright, that all the 'Believers' came together in settled communities. Each community had its Sisters and its Brethren who worshipped together, though the whirling and shaking were toned down to become a simple uniform dance.

Just before her death in 1784 at the age of 48, Ann Lee had another vision which predicted that when membership fell to just five, the movement would be reborn.

In 2017 there were only two Shakers remaining.

Vegetarianism & the Bible Christians

Vegetarians have been around for millennia – in various parts of the world and for various reasons. However, it is fair to say that the modern vegetarian movement has many of its roots in Salford and Manchester.

William Cowherd was born in the Lake District, trained to be a priest and became a preacher in a working-class area of Salford. Cowherd was initially an adherent of the Swedenborgian doctrine which was named after the Swedish scientist and mystic Emanuel Swedenborg. His followers believed that God and nature should be viewed as a whole, meaning that God inhabited every living thing. Therefore, to kill an animal was to kill a part of God. Cowherd later went on to establish his own denomination called the 'Bible Christian Church', which could be classed as the first European vegetarian institution (since the Pythagorean Society almost 1,500 years earlier). He commanded his entire congregation to give up both meat and alcohol which he considered to be the source of almost all the evils of society. Cowherd built the Chapel of Christ Church in King Street, Salford and declared it to be 'Christ's Universal Church on Earth', open to those 'who wished to shun the common evils and errors of the world'. A minister from a nearby church nicknamed Cowherd's church the 'Beefsteak Chapel' and suggested that his followers would die from a lack of meat. The Bible Christians soon had several churches in the area, but they were practically unknown outside Manchester and Salford, though they did later establish some churches in the USA.

Vegetarianism was not only a matter of diet for the Bible Christians, it was a way of life. Cowherd believed that vegetarianism was the way to achieve physical, mental and spiritual health and a way of showing compassion to 'God's sentient creation'. He saw self-denial as a way of focusing on one's own spirituality and one's relationship with God. The philosophy of God being part of every living thing led the Bible Christians to discuss the social issues of the day, such as the equality of the sexes and the social classes (revolutionary ideas at the time) and to fighting for workers' rights and against slavery. They later also established a fund to help the victims of the Peterloo

Massacre. Cowherd preached that eating meat had a brutalising effect on people, making them more aggressive and 'liable to engage in brawls'. Also, a meat-free diet was much cheaper, leaving the extra money to be spent on 'self-improving pursuits'. As idealistic as his teachings were, especially considering the conditions in which most working-class people had to live and work, William Cowherd was a man who practised what he preached: he ran Salford Grammar School and Academy of Sciences, opened up his own library to his parishioners, ran a (vegetable) soup kitchen, gave free medical service and provided free burials. He even wrote his own 'vegetarian hymns' including the classic 'Little lamb, who ate thee?' Needless to say, many people thought he was mad or dangerous (in espousing such socialist views) but he had a loyal following.

When William Cowherd died, Joseph Brotherton, another liberal reformer and Salford's first MP (a position he held for twenty-four years) took over as head of the Bible Christian Church. In 1847 there was a meeting on Manchester's Bridge Street at which the Vegetarian Society was formed. (It was actually Brotherton who coined the term 'vegetarian'.) Another vegetarian group was involved in this process – the Alcott House Concordium led by the American William Alcott. Unlike the Bible Christian Church, this group was based more on socialist rather than religious ideals. William Alcott had been converted to vegetarianism by missionaries from the church in Salford when they had settled in the USA. In 1817 forty-two Bible Christians had left Salford to establish churches in America where the movement soon attracted the attention of, amongst others, John Harvey Kellogg (as in Cornflakes) who became a key figure in the American vegetarian movement. Unlike the English Vegetarian Society, the American Society was on the whole more concerned with the health-giving benefits of not eating meat than with compassion for the animals' suffering. Joseph Brotherton was the author of many of the first tracts on teetotalism and his wife Martha wrote what is regarded as the first vegetarian cookbook in the western world, *A New System of Vegetable Cookery: With an Introduction Recommending Abstinence from Animal Foods and Intoxicating Liquors* of 1812, (though ten years previously, George Nicholson, a printer from Bradford, had written *The Primeval Diet of Man: Arguments in Favour of Vegetable Food with Remarks on Man's Conduct to [other] Animals*). Martha Brotherton's book is included in a list of the forty most important books ever written on Animals and Ethics. In addition to hundreds of tasty recipes such as herb pudding and the somewhat unusual 'omelette without eggs and butter', the book also contained household cleaning tips and herbal remedies.

In 1849 the *Vegetarian Messenger* was launched; it was a monthly magazine costing one penny. Despite several name changes, the magazine, now called *The Vegetarian* is still going strong (though costing rather more than 1d).

Three years later, the Vegetarian Society held its annual meeting (and vegetarian banquet) in Salford Town Hall in a room which had been decorated with the portraits of famous vegetarians, including Pluto, Pythagoras (who was a vegetarian owing to his belief in the transmigration of souls) and Benjamin Franklin. Other early pioneers of vegetarianism include the Irish playwright George Bernard Shaw, the Russian author Leo Tolstoy, and the English poet Percy Bysshe Shelley.

The Bible Christian Church gradually lost its members and faded away, but its legacy remains and the headquarters of the Vegetarian Society are still located in the Manchester area.

Manchester became the home of British vegetarianism. By the end of the nineteenth century there was a large vegetarian restaurant in Piccadilly and various others around the city; in fact, there were more vegetarian eateries in Greater Manchester then than there are in the twenty-first century. There was even a vegetarian Gentleman's Club in the city centre.

At his own request, Cowherd's epitaph was, 'He was understood by few, feared by all and loved by none.' This was misunderstood by some, but referred to Alexander Pope's 'Essay on Man'–

> Truths would you teach, or save a sinking land?
>
> All fear, none aid you and few understand.

****

Many churches have come and gone in Manchester during the past couple of centuries, including some magnificent buildings such as St. Peter's, St. John's and St. Matthew's.

Throughout its history Manchester has always had a diverse and cosmopolitan population. As various groups have settled in the city, new churches and other places of worship have appeared and disappeared over the years. The city has places of worship for many ethnic groups, including Jewish, Armenian, German, Muslim, Hindu, Polish and Buddhist.

Chapter 7

Crime & Punishment

The Court Leet

The Manchester Court Leet was the body that governed the Manor of Manchester from medieval times to the mid-nineteenth century. Originally it met in the 'Booths', a large wooden manorial courthouse situated in the Market Place. Here are just a few examples from the Court Leet records which begin to shed some light on what life must have been like in the early days when Manchester was a mere village.

The Court Leet doth –

1573

'present John Skilliekorne, plumber, to be a common easing-dropper (eavesdropper), a naughty person, such a one as doth abound in all misorders; therefore we desire that he may be avoided the town, and have such punishment as unto such doth appertain.'

1577

'order James Smith, capper, and William Savage, the catchpoll, to attend the Parish Church on Sundays and holidays to note who wore hats contrary to law.'

1578

'order that no man nor women shall stand with any turnips, besoms [brooms] or straw hats, no higher in the street than now the dwelling house of Edward Cunliffe.'

1585

'order that no stranger not Inhabiting within this town shall buy any apples or other fruit before ix of the Clock.'

1589

'order that no person shall cast any more dung over the church wall here-after.'

1595

'order that no person be allowed to use butter or suet in cakes or bread; fine 20 shillings.'

(A year later 12 officers were appointed to oversee and fine 'them that put butter, cream or suet in their cakes'.)

1597

'order that no foreigner nor any other stranger shall sell or measure any corn upon any other day than the Saturday and Monday, and that to be after the bell rings.'

1600

'order that no inhabitant shall suffer any other minstrel to play at his house at wedding dinners, but only the waytes.'

(Waytes or Waits were the town minstrels appointed by the Court Leet. They had to conduct the bride and groom to and from church and then at, and after the wedding dinner, they were obliged to play 'lively music and dances'.)

1676

'doth amerce (fine) John Hardman and John Wallworke two shillings and sixpence apiece for bringing shoes to be sold in the market made of insufficient Leather.'

Giddy-Gaddy

Giddy-gaddy, also known as 'cat's pallet', and later as 'tip cat' was a children's game that seems to have been peculiar to Manchester in the sixteenth century. The game involved laying a 6-inch piece of wood, sharpened at each end, on the ground. One end of the wood was then whacked with a stick, launching it up into the air. It was then hit as hard as possible towards a target, the winner being the one who could hit it the furthest. Quite often the said piece of wood would miss the target and instead cause injury to other children or innocent passers-by. After many complaints, the Court Leet decreed:

1579

'that whereas there is great abuse in a game used in the town called gede gadye or the cat's pallet that no manor person shall play at the same game being above the age of xii years upon pain of every person so playing to be imprisoned in the dungeon for the space of ii hours ... This order is made because diverse of the inhabitants do find them grieved that their children be hurt and in danger to be hurt.'

(Four years later the order was re-issued; this time anyone over the age of 7 years was threatened with a spell in the dungeon.)

Bull-baiting

Bull-baiting was introduced into Britain in the early thirteenth century and continued until 1835 when the practice was made illegal. The bull would be placed in an enclosure, chained to a post and have its nose sprayed with pepper in order to enrage it; then a bulldog would be unleashed. All this would have happened against a backdrop of a cheering and baying crowd. This was a spectator 'sport' enjoyed by people of all classes. However, bulls were not only baited for 'entertainment'; at one time, all bulls had to be baited by dogs before being slaughtered as it was thought that vigorous exercise improved the flavour of the meat and made it more tender. In the early Court Leet records, there are many examples of people being fined for selling 'unbaited' beef.

1676

'amerce Robert Hough for selling half a bull unbaited.'

Although one might imagine that vandalism and hooliganism are comparatively recent phenomena, the Court Leet records indicate otherwise. During just one night in December 1775 a gate belonging to the Collegiate Church was torn down and thrown into the River Irwell, one end of the stocks in the Market Place was removed and damage was caused to the gateposts of St. Ann's churchyard. A reward of twenty guineas was offered for the capture of the perpetrators – an enormous sum of money at that time. In later years there were reports of door knockers being wrenched from doors and thrown through bedroom windows.

Early Prisons

One of Manchester's earliest 'prisons' was known as 'The Dungeon'; it was situated on Salford Bridge in a former chapel which had been built in 1368, during the reign of Edward III. Thomas del Booth, a rich yeoman, had left the tidy sum of £30 to be used for erecting a stone bridge to connect Manchester and Salford (the first bridge to link the two medieval towns) which was also to incorporate a chapel (in the hope that, as the founder, people would pray for his soul). The original chapel had been made of wood but was replaced a century later by one built of stone; the building contained not only the chapel but also a 'cell' for the priest. In the sixteenth century one visitor to the town wrote, 'Manchester has several stone bridges, of which the best is called Salford Bridge; it crosses the Irwell by three arches and has an attractive chapel on it.' Travellers could break their journey there in order to pray and also to ask for food and drink to help them on their way. The chapel was later converted into a prison for Manchester and Salford to hold 'felons, deserters and other military prisoners'. The welfare and comfort of criminals was certainly not considered a priority in those days; the Dungeon was two storeys high and was plagued by rats, especially on the lower floor. One unfortunate man, who had been put in there to sober up, woke to find that the rats had bitten off several of his toes. As the chapel had been built into the base of the stone bridge, it was also liable to flooding from the River Irwell and at least one prisoner drowned there. The dungeon was demolished in the late 1770s in order to widen the bridge.

In 1575 a statute was issued which required every county to have a 'House of Correction'; the one in Manchester was built between 1575 and 1580 on Hunt's Bank (the site of present-day Victoria Station) and was known as 'New Fleet'. Originally it was used to hold 'popish recusants', i.e. Catholics who refused to renounce their faith in favour of the Church of England. The wealthier prisoners were even made to pay for the privilege of being locked up by contributing to the running costs of the prison. It later became a regular prison and remained in use until being demolished in 1790. Until 1774 the House of Correction had cells with windows opening out onto the street and it was a common sight to see the prisoners standing at the barred windows and begging for alms (money, food, tobacco) from the passers-by;

for this purpose ropes with bags attached hung from the upstairs windows. Very often any money collected would be used to buy alcohol from the gaolers. When the old building was replaced there were no windows overlooking the street; instead there was a poor-box in front of the building which bore the legend 'Sick and in prison, and ye visited me not'.

Up to the end of the eighteenth century, prison was not considered as a punishment in itself, but rather as a holding-place until a punishment, usually capital or corporal, could be administered. From Saxon times to the twentieth century, hanging was the most common form of capital punishment in England, though until 1747 beheading was the method reserved for the aristocracy. The worst crime was considered (by the 'powers that were') to be treason, for which the sentence was hanging, drawing and quartering; until 1820 the 'drawing' (cutting open the stomach and removing the entrails) might be done while the person was still breathing. In 1746 a law was passed which allowed the bodies of those hanged to be given to surgeons for the purpose of dissection.

You Are Sentenced To ...

> Although gossiping is now a national pastime, in times past the penalties for being a gossip and a scandalmonger were not pleasant. Up until the early 1800s the brank or scold's (gossip's) bridle was still used in Manchester. It would render the wearer speechless; if s/he (normally she!) tried to speak, her/his tongue would be pierced with spikes! The gossip would often be led through the streets by a chain and then tied to the pillory.

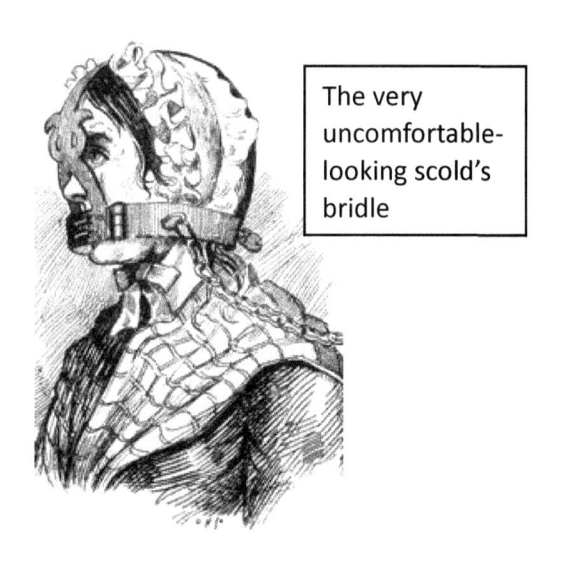

The very uncomfortable-looking scold's bridle

The last recorded wearer of the scold's bridle in Manchester was a 'dwarf' called Charlotte who claimed that she could drink 'twenty-four noggins of gin on end'.

In Manchester, the pillory (sometimes called the neck-stocks), the whipping-post and the stocks were placed side by side close to the Market Cross in the old Market Place. The Cross was erected there for two reasons: one was as a place of prayer and the other was in the (often forlorn) hope that it would inspire honest dealing amongst the market traders. The town beadle or catchpole would open the market by ringing a bell and then he would read out any local 'news items'. Finally, he would announce the names and misdemeanours of those receiving punishments that day.

In 1405 an Act of Parliament was passed decreeing that every town and village in the land must have a pair of stocks. For centuries this was the most common form of punishment for minor offences or for holding prisoners when no prison was available. In the 1600s every person convicted of being drunk had to spend six hours in the stocks. They were also used for tramps, card tricksters and other 'undesirables'.

The stocks

The whipping post was used until the middle of the 1800s; the culprit was tied to the post, whereupon s/he (usually he) would receive a public flogging. In 1774, Rebecca Mee, a 'single lady of Manchester' was convicted of stealing some wool. She was sentenced to fourteen days hard labour at the House of Correction and also received a public whipping in the Market

Place. A man by the name of Edward Ashwood received a whipping for defacing a library book. Punishment by the cat-o'-nine-tails was also handed out; in one instance, two boatmen received fifty (!) lashes each for 'tapping' a barrel of brandy they were transporting along the canal.

The pillory

The pillory in the Market Place was nicknamed 'the tea table'; it was erected c.1627 and remained in use for almost 200 years before being removed in 1816. It was used as a punishment for more serious offenders such as dishonest tradesmen who had been found guilty of 'doctoring' their goods or selling food unfit to be eaten (for example, a landlord watering the ale or a butcher selling bad meat). Once in the pillory, the culprits would be left to the mercy of the market-day crowd who would jeer and pelt unpleasant things (such as bad eggs, rotten fish and fruit) at them.

The intention of many forms of punishment in days gone by was to degrade and humiliate, none more so than the ducking stool. Where Boots is today (at the corner of Cross Street and Market Street) there once stood the half-timbered Radcliffe Hall, also known as Pool Fold Hall, an Elizabethan mansion which was surrounded by a moat (with drawbridge), fields and orchards.

Radcliffe Hall

Cross Street was originally named Pool Fold. The 'pool' in question was situated in the grounds of Radcliffe Hall and was that in which the town's ducking stool was located in the sixteenth century, though this was apparently not much appreciated by the Radcliffe family who seemed to have had no say in the matter. The ducking stool was mostly used as a punishment for 'Lewde women and Scoldes', 'common prostitutes' and women bakers who sold under-weight bread. This ducking stool was in use until 1619 when a new one was installed at Daub Holes (modern-day Piccadilly) where it remained for another 150 years. A 'scold' would often be carried around the town in a tumbrel (cart) on the way to the ducking stool. The duration of a 'ducking' depended on the whim of the person operating the contraption and the severity of the crime; it could range from a few seconds to repeated 'duckings' throughout the day. These punishments were carried out whatever the season; sometimes the shock of the freezing cold water would kill the culprit, especially if she were old or feeble. In the early 1600s, two 'common scolds and disturbers of their neighbours' – Isabel Richardson and Alice Worthington – were sentenced to several duckings in mid-October.

In *Travels in England* written in c.1700, the author (a Frenchman called Misson) describes the ducking stool: 'The way of punishing scolding women is pleasant enough... They place the woman in the chair and so plunge her in the water, as often as the sentence directs, to cool her immoderate heat.' Benjamin West took an equally light-hearted tone in his poem 'The Ducking-Stool' (published in 1780) in which the following lines appear:

> If noisy dames should once begin
> To drive the house with horrid din,
> 'Away, you cry, you'll grace the stool,
> We'll teach you how your tongue to rule.'
> No brawling wives, no furious wenches,
> No fire so hot, but water quenches.

The ducking stool at Pool Fold, Manchester

New Bailey Prison

In 1790 New Bailey Prison, built next to the River Irwell, was opened to serve both Manchester and Salford. Turrets with loop-holes were later added to the building through which muskets could be fired at anyone attempting to storm the prison. In addition to the more serious crimes, there were also some hefty sentences handed out for more trivial (and obscure) misdemeanours, for example, in 1809 a man was sentenced to six months for selling 'obscene songs'. This was in addition to a stint in the pillory in the Market Place.

The conditions inside the prison were better than those outside for many people – at least the prisoners received a bed to sleep in and an ample diet which included 'Butchers' Meat, Potatoes and Pease'. Initially, the prison had a garden in which vegetables would grow in abundance. However, as the Irwell became increasingly polluted, the only thing that would grow was rhubarb! In his book *Manchester as it is*, published in 1839, B. Love wrote, 'One of the female prisoners contrives to get committed at stated periods for the purpose of recruiting her health.' A German commentator of the time, J.G. Kohl, visited the prison in 1841 and wrote, 'The lodgings of the prisoner are always clean, spacious and airy.' He listed the weekly rations for an adult male as:

7 loaves of bread, each weighing 20 ounces,
31 ounces of flour,
5 pounds of potatoes,
1 pint of pease,
3½ ounces of salt,
1 pound of beef
1 quart of beer.

In 1824 the Treadmill was introduced as a punishment for those sentenced to hard labour, and hard labour it certainly was. Walking the treadmill, prisoners would climb the equivalent of Mont Blanc every two days. In a biography of the physicist James Joule, the author, in a footnote about the New Bailey treadmill which was used to grind logwood for the dyestuff industry, included the following: 'Instead of festering idleness, a prey to evil thoughts and designs, the prisoner now had healthful exercise and the moral benefit of knowing he was engaged in economically productive labour.' An eight-hour shift of this gruelling torture sounds enough to give even the most upright and honest citizen some 'evil thoughts and designs'. In 1866 Thomas Connor, a man in his sixties (a ripe old age in those days) was sentenced to six months' hard labour – for stealing a fuchsia. He died after only three months.

Victorian prisons operated the 'separate' and 'silent' systems. Under the former, prisoners were kept in solitary confinement for most or all of their sentence. This was described by one reporter from *The Times* as the 'maniac-making system'. Under the latter system, prisoners were able to mix for work and exercise but had to remain silent at all times. New Bailey Prison adopted the 'silent system' in 1834, but with so few staff it was almost impossible to enforce. By 1850 the prison was criticized for being 'thoroughly bad… with lax discipline, overcrowded cells, little instruction and unproductive labour'.

New Bailey Prison

> In 1841, one hundred and seventy-seven children under the age of 17, from Manchester alone, were sentenced to transportation for periods of up to fifteen years. **&**

'Only' six people were hanged at the New Bailey Prison; this included the three men who became known as 'The Manchester Martyrs'. On 18 September 1867 two leaders of the Irish Republican Brotherhood, Thomas Kelly and Timothy Deasy, both Irish-Americans, were being taken to Belle Vue Gaol in a horse-drawn police van. The van was ambushed by a group of around forty Fenians (those fighting for an independent Ireland) which resulted in the fatal shooting of Police Sergeant Charles Brett (the first policeman in Manchester to be killed on active duty). Brett had been looking through the keyhole of the van to see what was happening outside at the same time as one of the mob was attempting to shoot open the lock. The bullet passed through Brett's eye and into his brain, killing him instantaneously. Kelly and Deasy escaped, never to be seen on British soil again. It was thought that they had returned to America.

There was a general outpouring of anti-Irish feeling following the shooting and dozens of people were taken into custody. Five members of the IRB were tried for the crime and three – William Allen, Michael Larkin and Michael O'Brien – none of whom had fired the fatal shot – were chosen as 'scapegoats' and sentenced to death. As the sentence was passed, they shouted, 'God save Ireland!' They became the last people to be publicly hanged in Manchester.

On the day of the execution, 23 November, thousands of bloodthirsty spectators gathered around the site; some had even queued up all night to get the best view! Great preparations had been made to prevent a rescue attempt; all traffic in and out of the city was stopped and hundreds of policemen and soldiers were positioned in and around the prison. William Calcraft was chosen as the executioner. Already nervous after receiving death threats, he was more incompetent than usual; Allen died almost immediately but Calcraft had to climb into the pit to pull on Larkin's legs to hasten his death. The priest in attendance, Father Gadd, refused to let the same thing happen to O'Brien. Half-dead, he was taken down from the gallows and Gadd held his hand and recited prayers for the three-quarters of an hour it took O'Brien to die.

All appeals for clemency had been rejected. Queen Victoria described the Irish as 'really shocking, abominable people – not like any other civilised nation'.

The bodies of the three men were buried in quicklime in the prison grounds. Friedrich Engels wrote that the hangings had 'accomplished the final act of separation between England and Ireland'. It may not have been the final act, but it certainly took the cause of the Fenians a step further.

The 'Manchester Martyrs'

Crime & Punishment

The New Bailey Prison closed in 1868, the same year that public hanging was abolished.

Assize Courts

The Manchester Assize Courts (Law Courts) was a huge Gothic building located on Great Ducie Street, Strangeways, on the site of the former Strangeways Hall. Following a competition with over one hundred entries, it was designed by the renowned architect Alfred Waterhouse and finished in 1864. The entrance was topped by a statue of Moses, the law-giver. The new Strangeways prison, also designed by Waterhouse, was connected to the Assize Courts by an underground tunnel.

Badly damaged in the 1940 Christmas Blitz and again in the June Blitz of 1941, the building was finally demolished in 1957. It is regarded by many as one of Britain's great 'lost buildings'.

At 279 feet tall, this was the tallest building in Manchester. The record lasted until another Waterhouse building, the Town Hall, was built.

Strangeways

Strangeways Prison, now called (but never referred to as) HM Manchester Prison, was built in 1868 (at a cost of £170,000) on the site of Strangeways Hall and Park, once the ancestral home of the Strangeways family, which had stood there since medieval times when the land was acquired by John de Strangeways.

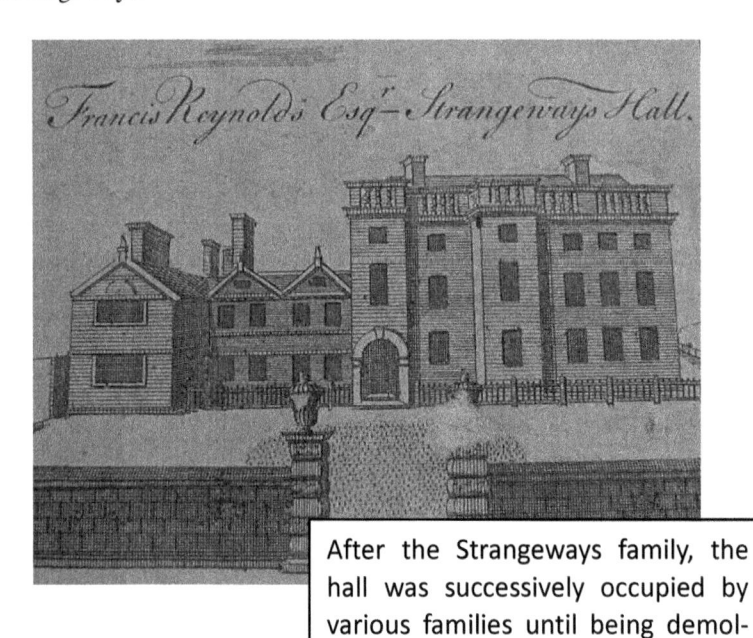

After the Strangeways family, the hall was successively occupied by various families until being demolished in 1863.

HM Manchester Prison is a beautiful building; the gatehouse and the ventilation and watch tower both received Grade II listed building status in 1974.

Strangeways was one of the few prisons to have a permanent gallows. The first person to be hanged on them was Michael Johnson, aged 20, who was convicted of murder in 1869. The executioner was Calcraft who, despite his alleged incompetence, was the longest-serving hangman of the nineteenth century; he carried out hundreds of hangings, most of them in public.

During the next 100 years the gallows were used a further one hundred times. In 1951 James Inglis was convicted of murdering a prostitute. Before being sentenced, he asked to be 'hanged as quickly as possible'. He got his wish. The record for the 'world's fastest hanging' was set by Albert Pierrepoint at Strangeways Prison on 8 May; it took just seven seconds for Inglis to die.

Strangeways held both male and female prisoners until 1963. 'Only' four women were ever hanged at Strangeways; the first was Mary Ann Britland in 1886. She was convicted of poisoning her daughter and her husband (to get the insurance money) and the wife of her lover (to get the husband, presumably).

In 1909 Emily Davison, the militant suffragette and member of the Women's Social and Political Union, was sentenced to a month's hard labour in Strangeways Prison for throwing stones at (the future Prime Minister) David Lloyd George's carriage. She went on hunger strike and was force-fed. To avoid any further force-feeding she barricaded herself in her cell. The prison guards used a hose and began to fill the cell with water; as she still refused to come out, the door was eventually broken down. On her release, Davison sued the prison and was awarded forty shillings. In 1913 Emily Davison ran out into the path of the king's horse during the Epsom Derby; she died four days later as a result of her injuries. During the early years of the century there were horrendous images in newspapers and magazines of suffragettes being force-fed. The practice was finally abandoned following the introduction of the Cat & Mouse Act of 1913 which allowed the release of prisoners who were at risk of death as a result of being on hunger strike. Once their health had improved however, they were returned to prison.

Pierrepoint

Alfred Pierrepoint was perhaps the most well-known hangman of the twentieth century. He was also the most prolific and during his 'career' he carried out over 430 executions, including those of many Nazi war criminals in Germany. Being Chief Executioner was not a full-time job and Pierrepoint also ran a pub in Hollinwood, Oldham, which was called, somewhat macabrely, 'Help the Poor Struggler'. However, when it came to helping one of his regular customers, it was business as usual for the hangman. James Henry Corbitt was a frequent visitor to Pierrepoint's hostelry and although they were not great friends, the two of them were wont to have a bit of a sing-song around the piano together. They even had the nicknames Tish and Tosh for each other. One Saturday evening the two of them, as on many previous occasions, had performed a duet of 'Danny Boy'. Later that night Corbitt went to the Prince of Wales Hotel on Stamford Street in Ashton-under-Lyne with his girlfriend Eliza Wood where, during an argument and in a fit of jealous rage, he strangled her with a shoelace and, with an eyebrow-pencil, scribed 'whore' on her forehead. Corbitt stood trial and received the death penalty. On the morning of his execution he greeted his former singing partner with 'Good morning, Tosh' to which Pierrepoint replied, 'Hello, Tish. Come on, old chap'. This story forms the plot of the film *Pierrepoint*, released in 2005. After his retirement Pierrepoint expressed doubts as to whether capital punishment was an effective deterrent or an 'antiquated relic of a primitive desire for revenge'.

One of the last two hangings in Britain was carried out at Strangeways in August 1964. Gwynne Owen Evans (an alias of John Robson Walby) was hanged at exactly the same time as his partner in crime, Peter Anthony Allen, for the murder of John West. As early as 1863 there had been a meeting in the Free Trade Hall to form an association for the abolition of capital punishment; it was just over one hundred years later that the death penalty in England was finally abolished.

What was the condemned block of the prison is said to be haunted by a hangman – his ghostly figure, dressed in a dark suit and carrying a small briefcase, can be seen walking from the condemned cells (where the prisoners awaited their execution) and if followed, the phantom disappears. It is believed to be the ghost of hangman John Ellis who, having executed several criminals there in the 1920s, committed suicide in 1932.

Garrotted!

During the mid-1860s gangs of garrotters were terrorising the streets of Manchester and other Lancashire towns and cities. They usually worked in threes, one woman and two men, who would frequent dark and lonely streets and lanes at night. One of the men would creep up behind his victim and tighten a rope around his neck, the second man would rob him of all his possessions and the woman would keep watch for the police. Although the intention was not to kill, many people received horrendous injuries and never recovered. Initially, sentences handed out to the culprits were terms of imprisonment – not much of a deterrent for hardened criminals. The attacks were so sudden and so quick that anyone was a potential victim, and as they became more prevalent and more daring, something had to be done. In 1865 at the Manchester Assizes it was decided to hand out the severest punishments possible to twenty-three of those convicted of the crime; the judge sentenced them all to terms of penal servitude, the length of the sentence depending on the level of brutality they had inflicted on their victims. They were also sentenced to be flogged – once, twice or three times, again dependent on the severity of their crimes. Some of those being flogged began almost immediately to cry and beg for mercy. Others tried to brave it out and taunted those carrying out the floggings with comments such as 'Lay it on, my mother could do better than that.' and 'You would not do for a schoolmaster.' However, their bravado was short-lived and they all ended up pleading for mercy. Not surprisingly, these punishments soon put a stop to the widespread practice of garrotting and the streets and lanes were (comparatively) safer to walk.

Suggestion for an 'anti-garrotting' device?

A Victorian Inspector

Jerome Caminada was born and brought up in the slums of Manchester, the son of two immigrants – an Italian father and an Irish mother. During his time in the police force, he rose through the ranks from constable to Detective Superintendent; his career reads like a collection of Victorian detective stories, full of dangerous escapades, cunning disguises and dastardly ne'er-do-wells. He used to meet his informers in the back pews of St. Mary's Catholic Church (the 'Hidden Gem').

The Manchester Cab Murder

One of Caminada's most famous cases became known as the 'Manchester Cab Murder'. John Fletcher was a wealthy businessman and also a bit of a boozer. One evening, in February 1889, he embarked on a pub crawl in the company of a much younger man. The two had later hailed a cab near the Cathedral, asking the driver to take them to Hulme. They were nearing their destination when the younger man jumped out of the cab and ran off. The cabbie, Henry Goulding, jumped down from his seat and looked into the carriage to find the older man slumped forward, dead. It was later discovered that his gold watch, a purse containing gold sovereigns and his gold-rimmed glasses had all been stolen. Using his remarkable powers of deduction, Caminada quickly built up a picture of the evening's events which led him to 18-year-old Charles Parton. Purely by coincidence, Caminada had come across a police report about a theft of chloral from a chemist's shop in Liverpool; he put two and two together and, amazingly, came up with the correct solution. Parton was identified by both the cabbie and the chemist and, on examination, traces of the poison were found in Fletcher's body. Parton was tried and sentenced to death. In the condemned cell, when asked what his last request would be, he opted for a cup of tea. However, just a few days before he was due to hang, his sentence was commuted. His mother had mounted a campaign and with the help of medical experts, it was concluded that John Fletcher had had a heart condition and the dose of chloral had not been lethal in itself. Parton did eleven years hard labour which he spent breaking rocks. On his release he travelled around the world, working (?) to pay his way.

Super-sleuth Jerome Caminada

Photograph: Courtesy of Greater Manchester Police Museum

Fancy Dress Ball

Another famous case involving Caminada occurred in late September 1880. A group calling themselves the 'Manchester Pawnbrokers' Association' hired a temperance hall a short distance away from the city centre. But there was something sinister afoot; all but two of the windows had been covered and the only music was provided by Mark Letcher, a blind accordionist. Not only that, the local constabulary had received a tip-off about a 'dance of immoral character'. Detective Sergeant Jerome Caminada organised a band of police officers and some local volunteers to be at the ready. Caminada managed to climb onto the roof of an adjacent building from which, hiding behind a chimney stack, he was able to peer through a small window into the party. There he saw a group of forty-seven men, half of whom were dressed as historical figures and the other half as women. Some were dancing the can-can and others drifted off to another smaller room. He seems to have watched the proceedings for around three hours (!) before deciding to take action. Having ascertained that the password was 'sister', Caminada did a fair impersonation of a woman and gained admittance to the building. The police stormed in and arrested all those present.

Headline news!

EXTRAORDINARY OCCURRENCE.
MIDNIGHT RAID BY THE MANCHESTER POLICE.

One of the strangest spectacles ever witnessed in a court of justice was presented at the Manchester City Police Court on Saturday morning, when 47 men, some of them dressed in the most fantastic fashion, and eight of them in the garb of women, were brought up in custody on a charge of having assembled in a room in Hulme Place, York-street, Chester Road, for an improper purpose. The names and addresses of the defendants were as follow:—

> Article in the *Manchester Guardian* on 27 September 1880

Images: Courtesy of Greater Manchester Police Museum

All the party-goers were handcuffed and taken to various police stations and then on to the cells in the Town Hall. The prisoners seemed to be a mixed bunch of men, coming from different social classes and different parts of the country. When they appeared in court, they were still wearing their 'party clothes' and seemed to be 'much embarrassed' by all the attention. In his evidence Caminada indicated that the events of the evening of 24 September were 'too coarse to describe' and then went on to state that in society, 'There existed a class of men, almost unknown to many gentlemen, who prowl about the streets almost to the same extent as unfortunate women and some of the prisoners belonged to that class.' He described how they were engaged in 'grotesque dances such as are familiar at low-class music-halls'. The prisoners were remanded in custody and when they next appeared before the judge, the court was packed with hundreds more people waiting outside to enjoy the spectacle, which they found highly amusing. The prisoners were charged with 'meeting together for the purpose of inciting one another to commit abominable, unnameable offences'. Although at that time the penalty for homosexual acts carried a sentence of ten years penal servitude, on this occasion the magistrates were desperate to avoid a scandal and so the forty-seven men were bound over to keep the peace for a year, fined and then acquitted.

Bob Horridge

What Professor Moriarty was to Sherlock Holmes, so Robert (Bob) Horridge was to Manchester's No.1 detective Jerome Caminada. Horridge began his life of crime at the age of 13. He followed in his father's footsteps and became a talented blacksmith (in between his spells in prison), but, unlike his father, he was not content with making an honest living. Horridge was involved in many escapades with the police but finally met his nemesis in Caminada. Horridge was on the run after having shot two policemen when they caught him breaking into a shop on Rochdale Road. Disguised as a labourer, Caminada followed Horridge's wife 'Little Ada' who led him to Liverpool Docks. The detective spied his quarry outside a pub, approached him and pressed the muzzle of his gun into his face. Despite a struggle and with the help of other police officers, Caminada arrested his 'Moriarty' and brought him back to Manchester where he was sentenced to life. After twenty years of trying, Caminada had at last put the notorious criminal behind bars for good.

Not someone you'd like to meet on a dark night (or even a bright day) - Bob Horridge

Photograph: Courtesy of Greater Manchester Police Museum

'Purring'

Clogs were worn by most working-class people who toiled in the factories, mines and mills of the industrial north; they were warm, hard-wearing and easy to repair. They were also cheap. Children who would otherwise have gone barefoot also wore clogs.

> **Pop goes the weasel**
>
> A weasel was a shoemaker's tool and pop was slang for pawn. A pawnshop was also known as a 'popshop'.
>
> &
>
> To 'pop one's clogs' meaning 'to die' uses the word in the same context. However poor people were, their clogs would only be popped (pawned) after they had died.

Mill workers would tap their feet to the rhythm of the clacking machines and would later recreate the steps outside, giving rise to clog-dancing. It became a popular entertainment, both for those participating and also for the spectators. (Charlie Chaplin began his show business career as a clog-dancer.)

Clogs were also put to other uses. One particularly brutal way of settling a dispute in nineteenth century Manchester was clog fighting or, as it was more commonly known, 'purring'. This involved two men with their metal-tipped wooden clogs, climbing into and then sitting on the rim of a barrel. They would then proceed to kick each other's shins to a pulp. Although this practice was illegal, by some it was considered to be a sport. It had its own venues and rules and was a good opportunity to place a bet. (Children would be used as lookouts for any passing policemen.) An opponent was allowed to lift his legs out of the barrel a maximum of three times before losing the fight. Sometimes the clog-fighters would dispense with the barrel and sit on chairs facing each other. Occasionally opponents didn't bother with either barrel or chair and would just use their clogs to kick each other senseless. It seems that the men would sometimes fight naked (except for the clogs, of course). Both clog-fighters would receive horrendous, sometimes fatal injuries. One reporter of the time wrote, 'The common tendency to substitute the clog for the fist in Lancashire is without parallel in any other county in the kingdom.'

Scuttlers

Look on any website about Manchester in the nineteenth century and the chances are that you will see this young man staring back at you.

> His name was William Henry Brooks and he was the Irish-born leader of the Greengate gang in Salford in the 1890s. He thoroughly enjoyed his notoriety when alive and would no doubt have been delighted to know that his face would still be on public view well over a century later. He was described as a formidable opponent and was one of the most feared gang members.

Photograph: Courtesy of Greater Manchester Police Museum

The cult of gang warfare is certainly not a recent phenomenon, especially in Manchester. In the latter part of the nineteenth century gangs of youths (mainly male, but with girlfriends not far behind) ranging from about 13 to 19 years of age terrorised the streets of the inner city areas of Manchester and Salford. Conflicts between these territorial gangs began in the early 1870s in Ancoats and Angel Meadow, but soon spread to Salford and areas further afield such as Openshaw and Harpurhey. They became known as 'scuttlers', a term they had coined themselves and they are widely regarded as Britain's first youth cult. They came from some of the most deprived neighbourhoods in the country; growing up in the slums, violence would have been an everyday fact of life, not only on the streets but in many homes where domestic violence was commonplace.

The scuttlers were distinctive in their appearance. Their hair was cropped except for a long fringe which became known as a 'donkey fringe'. They wore a 'uniform' which consisted of bell-bottom trousers, a cap tilted on the back of the head and clogs fitted with brass tips. They would have made an ominous, deafening sound on the cobbles as they marched en masse, announcing both their arrival and their intention to fight. They also made an impact when kicking a rival gang member! A neckerchief was part of a scuttler's outfit, the colour or pattern of which denoted membership of a particular gang. They would arm themselves with various weapons but two things were essential for all gang members: a knife and – a 'scuttler's' most prized possession – a belt with a heavy metal buckle which could also be used as a weapon and frequently was!

Fights between rival gangs often involved several hundred scuttlers; their intention was to hurt and disfigure the opponent, rather than to kill. Deaths were rare, but they did occur. In 1887 Owen Callaghan, aged 19, and a member of the 'Meadow Lads' (from Angel Meadow) was convicted of the manslaughter of Joe Brady, aged 18, a member of the 'Bengal Tigers', perhaps the most notorious gang, which came from the nearby Bengal Street area of Ancoats. Callaghan was jailed for twenty years. In his summing up of the case, the judge said, 'Life in parts of Manchester is as unsafe as it is amongst a race of savages.' (However, when a journalist from the *Manchester Guardian* interviewed four members of an Ancoats gang in the 1890s, he described them as 'articulate, amusing and refreshingly respectful'.)

Many gang members received horrendous injuries and it was not uncommon for a scuttler to be sentenced to five, ten or even twenty years imprisonment. However, prison and punishment seemed to be no deterrent and did nothing to curb the violence which continued unabated until the end of the century. The gang members, then as now, were those on the margins of society: many were poorly educated and saw no way of escaping their monotonous, impoverished lives. Only when the authorities realised that prison was not the answer (combined with the fact that when recruits were needed to fight in the Boer War it was discovered just how unhealthy most working-class males were) did the situation begin to improve. Moves were made to involve teenagers in activities other than scuttling. Working lads' clubs were set up as were football and other sports' clubs. City and United were in their infancy and rivalries began to be played out on football pitches rather than on the streets. Another major factor in the decline of the scuttlers was the much-needed and long-awaited programme of slum clearance in the worst areas of Manchester and Salford which finally began towards the end of the nineteenth century.

Suicide

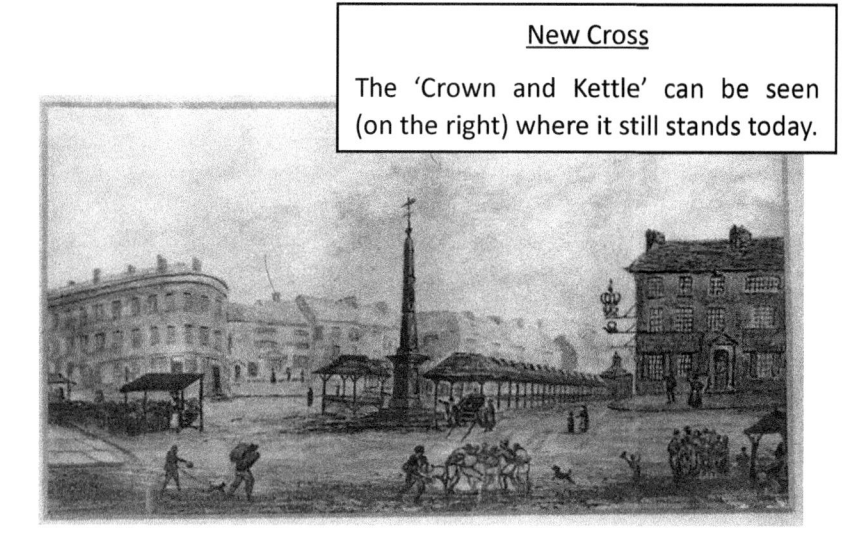

New Cross

The 'Crown and Kettle' can be seen (on the right) where it still stands today.

The Crown and Kettle was the second pub on this site; the previous building was a two-storeyed double-fronted cottage which, as early as 1734, became the wonderfully-named 'Iron Dish and Cob of Coal'. This was when Newton Lane (later Oldham Road) was described as 'a broad country lane fringed on either side by hedgerows'. The name of the area 'New Cross' is no longer in common usage.

&

To Quote:

'To the greater proportion of the people who do their shopping in Oldham Street, New Cross is nothing more than the boundary that denotes the division between respectability and slumdom.'

from *Manchester Streets and Manchester Men* (1906) by T. Swindells

In 1846 two coffins were unearthed at New Cross. They were found to contain the remains of two victims of suicide. One was a boot closer (someone who stitched the uppers to the soles) called Smith who had ended it all in a fit of unrequited love and the other was a young woman who had poisoned herself in 1808; both had been buried at the crossroads.

Although suicide had always been considered a mortal sin by the Church, it was the middle of the thirteenth century when it became a crime by law, as indicated in the word 'commit' suicide. It was also referred to as 'self-murder' and the treatment of suicides reflected this inherent criminality. In 1753 an ostler at the Swan and Saracen's Head on Market Stead Lane (now Market Street) hanged himself in the stable. He was convicted of self-murder and sentenced to be 'drawn upon a sledge, and buried at four lane-ends [a crossroads] with all his clothes on, and to have a stake driven through his body'. This sentence was carried out before a crowd of curious (not to mention ghoulish) spectators.

If it was proven that a victim of suicide was 'sane', then s/he would be denied a Christian burial in consecrated ground. Instead, s/he would be taken to a crossroads (thought to confuse the spirit of the dead person) in the middle of the night and dropped into a pit. A stake would then be hammered through the body and into the ground to help prevent the spirit from escaping. All this with no clergy, no prayers and no mourners. Until 1822 the deceased's family could be stripped of all their worldly goods which would then be given to the Crown. So in addition to losing a loved one, the family would also be thrown into poverty.

Amazingly, suicide was only decriminalised in 1961 in the UK (one of the last countries in Europe to do so). Before this date, even as late as the 1950s, there are numerous stories of people being imprisoned following failed attempts at suicide.

Pig Tales

In 1845 William Chambers, aged 20, was transported to the penal colonies of Australia for a period of fifteen years for 'pig stealing'.

*****

On 6 March 1866 a 21-year-old labourer called John Alty was sentenced to fifteen months of hard labour. His crime? He 'feloniously, wickedly and against the law of nature did casually know a certain pig and then did feloniously perpetrate an unnatural act at Manchester'.

*****

In 1883 a sentence of five years of hard labour was handed out to Dorcas Mary Snell for stealing one rasher of bacon. She was released after serving just two years!

> **To Quote:**
>
> **'If you say in any other part of England that you are from Manchester, you are at once supposed to be a thief.'**
>
> Taken from the statement of a thief and quoted in *Juvenile delinquency in Manchester: its consequences and some suggestions concerning its cure.*
>
> William Beaver Neale (1840)

Chapter 8

Health

The Infirmary

Garden Street, off Shudehill, was the site of Manchester's first infirmary, albeit a very small one having only twelve beds. It was founded in 1752 for the 'benefit of the poor' by Charles White, an eminent surgeon, and Joseph Bancroft, a local industrialist.

The first known outpatient was a young man called John Boardman who was suffering from a skin disease with the unpleasant-sounding name 'scrofula'. It was more commonly referred to as 'King's Cure' or 'King's Evil', as at that time it was believed the only cure was to be touched by a king. (The last English monarch to carry out this practice was in fact not a king but Queen Anne at the beginning of the eighteenth century.) Luckily for Mr. Boardman, he was cured without the need for any royal intervention. In 1764 a James Leech advertised his services in the *Mercury* (an early Manchester newspaper). As the seventh son of respectable parents, he claimed to be able to cure the King's Evil – for a reasonable fee, of course!

The first inpatient of the infirmary was a 12-year-old boy by the name of Benjamin Dooley who was admitted with 'sordid ulcers of the leg'.

In 1757 the wounded rioters from the 'Shudehill Fight' were treated here; four people were killed and fifteen wounded when soldiers opened fire on those who were protesting about food shortages.

It soon became apparent that a much bigger hospital was needed. On land (modern-day Piccadilly Gardens) donated by Sir Oswald Mosley, then Lord of the Manor of Manchester, a new fifty-bed infirmary was built, opening in 1755 at a cost of over £4,000. In 1766 a Lunatic Hospital was added; it had facilities for 22 patients and twenty years later another 40 beds were added.

In the foreground of this print is the Infirmary pond, formerly part of Daub Holes, which had been quarried in earlier days when many of the houses in Manchester had been made of wattle and daub. The pond was also, at one time, the location of the town's ducking stool.

Health   95

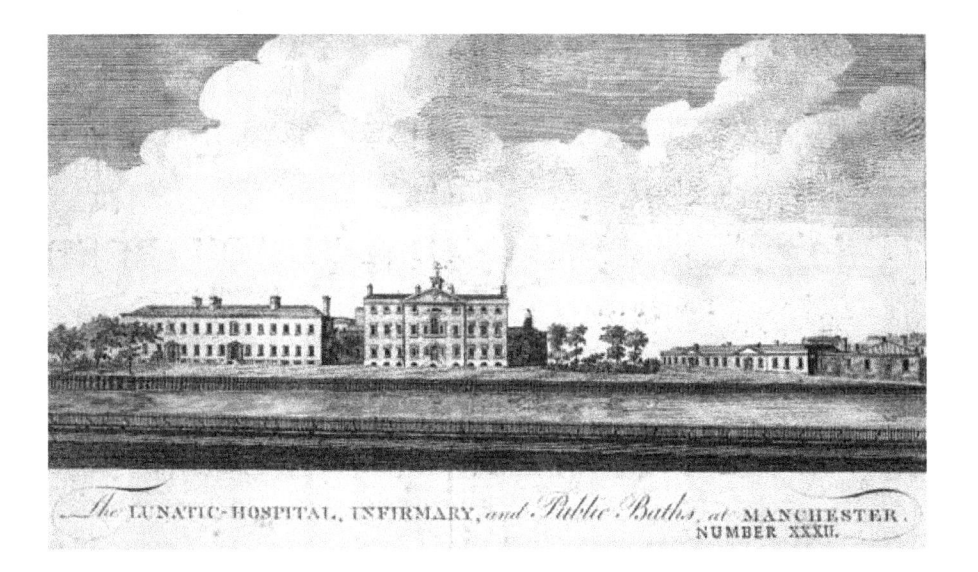

The LUNATIC-HOSPITAL, INFIRMARY, *and Public Baths, at* MANCHESTER.
NUMBER XXXII.

The Lunatic Hospital

Until the Vagrancy Act of 1714, the mentally ill were treated as vagrants or criminals; this act allowed the 'furiously mad' to be legally detained. The Madhouse Act of 1774 gave some of the first guidelines on the care of 'lunatics'.

One early patient of the Lunatic Hospital was Daniel Newton, an apprentice grocer, who in 1772 made a vow to eat and drink nothing but bread and water from March to October. In September, having failed to persuade Newton to abandon this extreme diet, a clergyman sent him to the Lunatic Asylum. On returning home, he (Newton) fell into a 'six-week trance' in which he had visions of another world. These visions were written about in *Extraordinary Warnings from the Invisible World*, a book written in 1813.

The purpose of the Lunatic Hospital was to offer the patients 'an alternative to exploitation or abuse by private madhouse proprietors'. It wasn't long before the patients were segregated into paupers and non-paupers. 'Poor Lunaticks' were charged five shillings a week (paid out of charitable funds) and the rates rose to one guinea for the most affluent patients. When the hospital was extended in 1783, there was separate accommodation for 'poor Persons' and for those of 'superior Fortunes'. The latter would be entitled to receive 'the greatest Privacy, the best Advice, the most tender Treatment and every comfort and Assistance that can be afforded to them… as befitted their unhappy Condition in Life'. It is nowhere mentioned what the 'poor Persons' were entitled to in their "unhappy Condition".

The hospital complex was continually expanding and in 1791 was renamed 'The Infirmary, Dispensary, Lunatic Hospital and Asylum in Manchester'. The Asylum housed the wealthier mentally-ill patients while the paupers continued to stay in the Lunatic Hospital.

The threat of violence was a constant concern and various methods of restraint were used, with varying degrees of success. One keeper of the Manchester Lunatic Hospital was stabbed to death by a patient in 1774. Suicide was also a problem and in that same year a man 'found the means to destroy himself' just a few hours after being admitted. In 1801 Matthew Jepson 'a reputable tradesman from Sheffield' tried to kill himself by sitting on the fire. Although engulfed in flames, he was bravely rescued by a fellow patient, Hugh Williams.

In the mid-1800s a new wing was added to the Infirmary, built with donations; one donor was Jenny Lind, the opera singer from Stockholm known as the 'Swedish Nightingale', who gave the hospital the proceeds from two concerts in Manchester, one at the Free Trade Hall, the other at the Concert Hall. Frederic Chopin, the Polish pianist and composer, was also a benefactor.

An unusual exhibition was held at the Infirmary in 1826: the body of Alexander M'Keand was put on public display before being dissected. Alexander and his brother Michael (dealers in tea and linen) had both been convicted of the wilful murder of Elizabeth Bates, a servant at the Jolly Carter pub in Salford. The landlady, Martha Blears, had also been attacked, but miraculously survived despite being stabbed in the neck. A (not very good) song was written shortly after the incident:

> Oh Betsy Bates we murdered thee,
> For which we're on the fatal tree.
> We stabbed the mistress in the bar,
> And gave her many a cruel scar:
> And in her head we left the knife,
> But William Higgins saved her life.

Both were hanged at Lancaster; Michael's body was sent to the hospital in that city and Alexander's was returned to Manchester. Quite why the corpse was put on display for the ghoulish public to ogle remains unclear. Even to this day, the ghost of the servant is said to haunt the scene of her murder on the anniversary of her fatal stabbing.

In 1832 King William IV became patron of the hospital which thereafter became Manchester Royal Infirmary.

In 1849 the Manchester Lunatic Asylum was moved to Cheadle. It became the Cheadle Royal Mental Hospital, now the Cheadle Royal. The Manchester Royal Infirmary moved to its present site on Oxford Road in 1908.

The Lying-in Hospital

Charles White, one of the founders of Manchester Infirmary, also helped to set up the first lying-in (maternity) hospital in the town. This developed into St. Mary's Hospital.

The Lock Hospital

Joseph Jordan was born in Manchester in 1787; he studied medicine and became a practising surgeon. In 1812 he started a School of Anatomy and Surgery in a house on Bridge Street.

Until the Murder Act of 1752 was passed, it was illegal to obtain dead bodies for the purpose of dissection (apart from several old universities which were allowed a quota of bodies – but only those of executed criminals and, at one time, suicides). Following the Act, the bodies of executed criminals became available to all medical establishments. However, by the nineteenth century, the demand for dead bodies far outweighed the supply. This led to a 'black market' in cadavers and body parts. Jordan used the Burke and Hare method of procuring bodies for his students to dissect (stealing them from graveyards that is, not committing murder!). Jordan was taken to court where the judge was reluctant to punish him as he recognized the need for students to learn. Jordan was fined £20, but the resurrectionist (i.e. the man who actually dug up the bodies for which he charged £10 each) was sent to prison for a year.

In 1819, in two small houses on Cumberland Street, Joseph Jordan, together with William Brigham and Michael Stewart, founded a Lock Hospital 'for the relief of females whom poverty and the diseases consequent upon a certain course of vice, have rendered outcasts' or, as one social commentator of the time described them 'a certain class of deplorable objects rendered miserable by imprudence and destitute by long sickness and sufferings'. There were several Lock Hospitals around the country at that time which were used to treat those suffering from venereal diseases, such as syphilis. These 'unfortunate women' were often left to die on the streets but Jordan offered them a refuge where they could be treated away from the public's disapproving gaze. Other institutions, such as the Manchester Infirmary, refused to treat such patients, raising 'moral, economic and medical objections'. Only occasionally, and with great reluctance, did they relax this rule if a woman had contracted the disease 'innocently'.

Unlike other charitable institutions, the Lock Hospital faced an endless struggle to collect funds. Many people refused to donate money to those they considered to be 'undeserving' and some were strongly opposed to the very existence of such a place in their town, believing that by treating such diseases, the medical establishment was 'encouraging vice'.

In 1822 a connected 'Lock Asylum' was established and named 'Manchester and Salford Asylum for Female Penitents'; this became the main charity for 'rescuing and reforming prostitutes'. This was where the 'penitents' were trained as servants, laundrywomen, etc. and instilled with 'habits of industry and forethought' in order to find employment on leaving the institution.

Despite being plagued by financial difficulties and having to change locations several times, the Lock Hospital proved successful. It was reported in the 1860s that it treated 20 inpatients and 56 outpatients daily. In 1873 the hospital moved to its last home – Duke Street, off Deansgate - behind the Oxnoble pub and a male ward was established in some cottages in the nearby Stone Street. In 1920 the hospital changed its name to St. Luke's, a name it retained until closing in 1974.

In *A Picture of Manchester* (1816) by Joseph Aston, the author dismisses the Lock Hospital in a few curt sentences describing it as being 'for the cure of a disease arising from a course of guilt'.

****

> **&**
>
> **Plague**
>
> The bubonic plague arrived in Britain in 1348 and over 2½ years it claimed the lives of more than a third of the population of Manchester as it did across the entire country.
>
> In 1603 another plague hit the town killing 1,078 Mancunians in just one summer.

Following outbreaks of typhus and other contagious diseases, moves were made to tackle the problem. A "Fever Hospital" or "House of Recovery for Infectious Diseases" with beds for 100 patients opened on Portland Street opposite the Infirmary and moved to the corner of Aytoun Street in 1804.

This was the first institution in the country to be used to try and stem the spread of an epidemic. The wealthy citizens of the town gave generously to the cause, some in the spirit of philanthropy and others out of fear for their own well-being. Cholera was a frequent visitor to the town in the 19th century with outbreaks in '32, '49, '54, and '66.

Cholera!

In the early 1830s there was an outbreak of cholera in England. In Manchester over 1,300 people caught the disease, half of whom died. Symptoms were sickness, diarrhoea and sweating and were so severe that after the first signs of the illness, a victim could die within hours. The disease swept through the town and was especially virulent in the poorest areas such as Angel Meadow and 'Little Ireland'.

One Irish victim was a 4-year-old boy called John Brogan; his grandfather wanted to see his grandson's body, but when the coffin was opened, it was to discover that the child's head was missing. At that time the Irish, who were considered by many to be the 'lowest of the low', believed their cholera victims were being murdered for medical science. Thinking that the child had fallen victim to 'burkers' (so-called after the infamous body-snatcher, one half of Burke & Hare) there was a huge outcry amongst the Irish community; a crowd formed at New Cross and proceeded to storm the old factory-building on Swan Street which had been set up as a cholera hospital and where the boy had died. The coffin with the headless corpse was held aloft as the street rang with the cries of 'Burkers! Burn the hospital!' Once there, they smashed windows, wrecked furniture, attacked staff and attempted to remove the patients. Order was only restored by the intervention of a priest (and a group of special constables). It was discovered that John Brogan's head had actually been sawn off by a medical student to sell for research, all without the knowledge of the Medical Board. The boy's body was taken to the Town Hall where the head was sewn back on by a surgeon and he was buried the following day.

In fact, the first 300 victims of this outbreak of cholera were dissected to try to discover how the disease was transmitted. In the early nineteenth century it was believed that cholera was caused by 'bad air'; it was only decades later that infected water, contaminated food and excrement were identified as the causes of the disease. Bearing in mind the atrocious conditions in which so many people lived, it seems amazing that the epidemic didn't wipe out half the population of Manchester.

Many of the cholera victims were placed in a vast open pit in Walker's Croft cemetery. This area (which now lies under part of Victoria Station) was a mass paupers' graveyard which had been established in 1815. Previously, paupers had been buried in the New Burying Ground which was situated next to St. Michael's Churchyard (in which the wealthy were buried). By 1815, the New Burying Ground was full (with some 40,000 bodies) and a new space was needed. Walker's Croft was a large piece of land which had been walled and consecrated with a tiny chapel on it. During the cholera epidemic a huge pit was dug and the coffins piled in, side by side and on top of each other.

> O, where are the mourners? Alas! there are none,
> He has left not a gap in the world, now he's gone,-
> Not a tear in the eye of child, woman, or man;
> To the grave with his carcass as fast as you can:
> Rattle his bones over the stones!
> He's only a pauper whom nobody owns!

(from 'The Pauper's Drive' by Thomas Noel)

> Nationally, the cholera epidemic of 1832 claimed 32,000 lives.

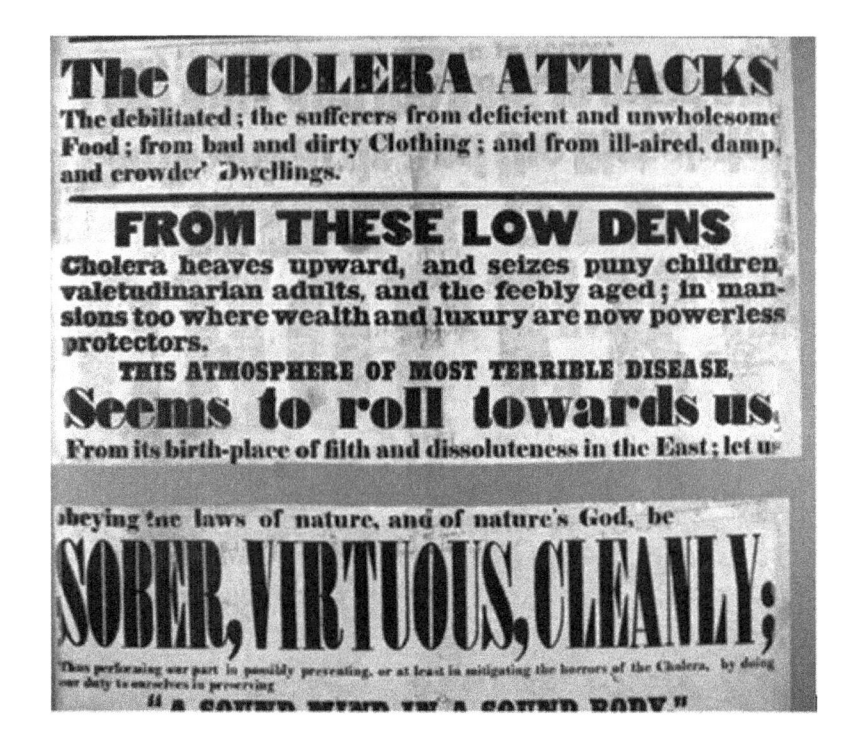

The CHOLERA ATTACKS
The debilitated; the sufferers from deficient and unwholesome Food; from bad and dirty Clothing; and from ill-aired, damp, and crowded Dwellings.

FROM THESE LOW DENS
Cholera heaves upward, and seizes puny children, valetudinarian adults, and the feebly aged; in mansions too where wealth and luxury are now powerless protectors.
THIS ATMOSPHERE OF MOST TERRIBLE DISEASE,
Seems to roll towards us,
From its birth-place of filth and dissoluteness in the East; let us

obeying the laws of nature, and of nature's God, be
SOBER, VIRTUOUS, CLEANLY;
Thus performing our part in possibly preventing, or at least in mitigating the horrors of the Cholera, by doing our duty to ourselves in preserving

"A SOUND MIND IN A SOUND BODY."

Some skeletons which were found during alterations and construction work at Victoria Station have been reinterred in Southern Cemetery.

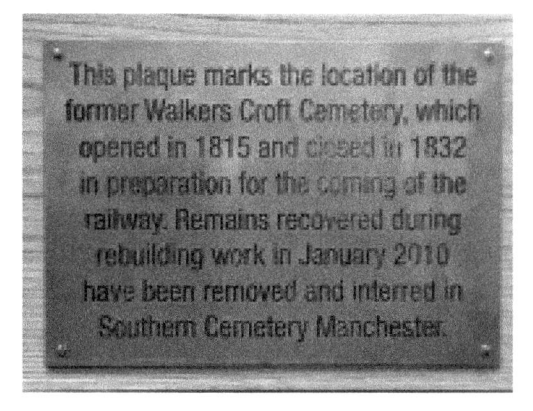

> This plaque marks the location of the former Walkers Croft Cemetery, which opened in 1815 and closed in 1832 in preparation for the coming of the railway. Remains recovered during rebuilding work in January 2010 have been removed and interred in Southern Cemetery Manchester.

Plaque in Victoria Station

The space where the old Paupers' Graveyard had been was later used for cockfighting, bare-knuckle fights and other nefarious activities. It was later paved over with flagstones after it was discovered that the desperate residents of Angel Meadow had resorted to selling the soil to farmers to use as fertilizer.

> This 'font' or 'plague stone' on Aspin Street was used during the cholera epidemic when it would have been filled with vinegar; provisions were left near the stone and coins would be placed in the vinegar which was thought to prevent the disease from spreading.

Not only did the residents of these squalid areas have to contend with diseases caused by their sewage-contaminated water and filthy living conditions, the very air was so filled with smoke and pollution billowing out of the factories that the town was often covered in a thick layer of smog (smoke and fog) giving rise to asthma, pneumonia and other bronchial problems. In the nineteenth century pulmonary tuberculosis, caused by poor diet and horrendous living and working conditions, accounted for ten per cent of all Manchester deaths.

> In 1918 1,500 Mancunians died in a period of three months during the flu epidemic. Soldiers were recruited to become coffin-makers and grave-diggers. &

Water

Isabella Beck may be an obscure name in the annals of Manchester's history but she it was who funded the construction of the first 'waterworks' in the town. In the mid-1500s, in what is now the Spring Gardens and Fountain Street area, there were a few scattered houses with gardens attached. In one of these gardens was a spring from which clean, fresh water was conducted, via Market Stead Lane, through pipes made of hollowed-out elm trunks, to a conduit in the Market Place. This became the town's main supply of water for the next two centuries. The first Theatre Royal was later built over the site of the spring.

In 1808, as the population of the town soared, Holt Town Reservoir was built and stone pipes were constructed to carry the water, not an ideal choice in that they frequently cracked and burst. This was followed in 1826 by the Gorton reservoirs and this time iron pipes were used to carry the water. In 1851 Manchester began to receive water from Longdendale Reservoir.

Chapter 9

Education

Manchester Grammar School

> School motto:
>
> 'Sapere Aude' - 'Dare to be wise'

Courtesy of 'The Victorian Web'

Manchester Free Grammar School was founded in 1515 by Crumpsall-born Hugh Oldham, who in 1505 had been made Bishop of Exeter. He paid £5 to buy a piece of land from George Trafford (who, in return for having prayers offered up for his soul, accepted less money than the land was worth) and a further £208.13s 5d (exactly!) to build the school which was located in the Long Millgate area (now Cathedral Gardens), close to the River Irk. He endowed the school with an income from the profits of the water-driven corn mills on the banks of the river and from land in Ancoats. Originally, the school was intended for '40 healthy boys, born in wedlock who, having pregnant wit, have been for the most part brought up rudely and idly' and was open to boys from all over the country, provided they were not suffering from any disease, such as 'pox, leprosy and pestilence'. Each new boy had to pay one penny for the benefit of two 'poor scholars' who in return had to keep the registers and clean the school once a week. Until 1881 new pupils also had to give one shilling to the head boy.

At one time the boys boarded with a master; one of the most well-known masters was Charles Lawson, also known as 'Millgate's Flogging Turk'. The boys faced a harsh regime; lessons began at 6 am in summer and 7 am in winter. The rules stipulated that the boys were not allowed to carry knives or staves, nor participate in cockfighting or jousting. In 1690 there was a 'mutiny' when the boys locked themselves inside the school and the masters out. Some local residents supplied the pupils with food and, bizarrely, weapons and ammunition, which the boys would use to fire near the legs of anyone trying to enter the building.

The school had an annual Shrove Tuesday tradition which involved the boys shooting at a target with a bow and arrow in order to win a prize. In the early days, the target was a live cock which was buried in a hole in the ground with just the head and neck showing. The boys would shoot, in turn, from a distance of around thirty yards and the first boy to draw blood would gain the cockerel as his prize. After the contest, boys and masters would form a procession and walk to the 'Bull's Head' in the Market Place where the masters and older boys would feast on roast beef and plum pudding while the younger boys had to make do with fermenty (an ancient dish made from boiled, cracked wheat and milk).

More buildings were acquired to cope with the ever-increasing number of pupils. Gradually the area around Long Millgate deteriorated. The Irk itself was described (by Engels) as a 'narrow, coal black, foul-smelling stream full of debris and refuse'. The school was surrounded by poor, insalubrious houses, taverns and shops; in addition, an apple market was held on Long Millgate three times a week, thronging the street with people and traffic. Nevertheless, an impressive new extension, designed by Alfred Waterhouse, was added in the 1870s. (It is now part of Chetham's Music School.)

Despite its unpromising location, the school had a reputation for academic excellence and by 1880 it had 750 pupils. The school, despite several extensions, eventually became too small for purpose. In 1931, after more than 400 years, the school moved to its present location in Fallowfield at a cost of £240,000.

Chetham's

Dating back to 1421, Chetham's is a collection of medieval sandstone buildings which stand on the site of the fortified manor house belonging to the Lords of the Manor of Manchester (formerly the site of Manchester Castle). When the nearby Parish Church of St. Mary's (later to become the Cathedral) was made collegiate the Lord of the Manor at that time, Thomas de la Warre, endowed a college (a residence) for the priests. In 1654 the buildings were bought by the trustees of Humphrey Chetham in order to establish a 'hospital school' and a free library.

Humphrey Chetham (once fined for refusing a knighthood) was a wealthy banker and fustian merchant; he was born in 1580 at Crumpsall Hall and educated at Manchester Free Grammar School. He believed ignorance to be the cause of poverty and education to be the only escape from it. He planned to buy the empty Collegiate Church 'college' buildings and convert them into a free public library and a residential school. The College House had been neglected; during the Civil War it had been used as a prison and an arsenal and later became a pigsty. Chetham gave detailed instructions that the school was to house and educate forty boys, between the ages of 6 and 14, of 'honest, industrious and pains taking parents and not of wandering, or idle beggars or rogues ... the boys shall not be bastards, nor such as are lame, infirm or diseased'. He even stipulated where the boys should come from – 14 from Manchester, 6 from Salford, 3 from Droylsden, 2 from Crumpsall, 10 from Bolton-le-Moors and 5 from Turton. The boys wore a distinctive uniform – a long blue tunic, blue stockings and yellow underclothes. On leaving school, the boys were apprenticed into a 'useful trade' and given two suits of 'cloaths'. Today the same buildings are home to the largest speciality music school in the UK, the world-renowned Chetham's School of Music, founded in 1969.

Although Humphrey Chetham didn't live long enough to see his dream realised, his wishes were carried out by the executors of his will and the school known as 'Chetham's Hospital' and the library (which is now the oldest surviving public library in the English-speaking world) were opened in 1653. Chetham had left instructions that the books in the library should be of good quality and also should be chained to the bookcases. Karl Marx and Friedrich Engels were frequent users of the library when they were collaborating on the *Communist Manifesto*. The library now holds more than 100,000 volumes, including one of the largest collections of works on the history of Manchester.

Literary & Philosophical Society

> The Manchester Literary and Philosophical Society was established in 1781; it was the first and remains the oldest society of its kind in the world. It has counted some of Britain's greatest academics amongst its members; John Dalton and James Joule were two prominent members in the nineteenth century, while Ernest Rutherford, Niels Bohr and Alan Turing were notable members in the twentieth.

The Society originally met in the Cross Street Chapel and had twenty-five members. In 1799 it moved to George Street where it remained until 1940 when the building had to be demolished to provide a firebreak during the Blitz. A concrete structure was built in its stead and the Society remained there until that too was demolished in 1980. The Society now has around 400 members and its headquarters are within Manchester University. Women were only allowed to become members of the Society in the early twentieth century.

Despite its title, the Society's aim was to promote and advance all areas of education (apart from religion and politics which were regarded as potentially divisive topics). Many of its early members played an important role in the Industrial Revolution and included not only scientists, but engineers, mathematicians, cotton merchants and manufacturers.

Portico Library

The Portico Library opened in 1806 as library and newsroom; 400 members each contributed 13 guineas to fund the construction of the building on Mosley Street which was at that time, according to John Dalton, 'the most elegant and refined street in Manchester'. The first secretary was Dr. Peter Mark Roget, who began writing his 'Thesaurus' here. The library was a private one, open only to subscribers. It also housed an eatery offering such delicacies as oysters, pies and ice cream. Famous past members include John Dalton, the Gaskells, Thomas de Quincey, Sir Robert Peel and, more recently, Eric Cantona.

The library 'celebrates both the historic and contemporary culture of Manchester'. The building became Grade II* listed in 1952.

> A guinea was 21 shillings (equivalent to £1.05) and was named after Guinea in Africa where the gold was mined to make the first coins. **&**

Manchester University

In nineteenth century England, students had to take religious tests before entering higher education, thereby excluding non-conformists, such as Quakers, Unitarians, etc. Manchester merchant John Owens believed that education should be accessible to everyone and left a £97,000 bequest for the foundation of a college open to all, irrespective of religious beliefs. Owens College opened in March 1851 at 21, Quay Street; it had 7 staff and 25 students (all male). It formed the first college of what was to become Manchester University. When it moved to new premises on Oxford Road in 1873, the College had 334 day and 557 evening students. Three years later it changed its name to the Victoria University of Manchester. From such small beginnings, it is now, following its amalgamation with UMIST in 2004, the largest single-site university in the UK.

One of the first professors at Owens College was Richard Copley Christie. His name is commemorated in the world-renowned Christie Hospital which was founded in 1893 with money left by Sir Joseph Whitworth; Christie was the hospital's first president.

21, Quay Street, which first housed Owens College, has had an interesting history. Prior to becoming a college, it was the home of Richard Cobden, one of the founders of the Anti-Corn Law League. The house later (in 1878) became the Manchester County Court. In July 1898, Judge Parry was pronouncing sentence against William Taylor. Taylor, not too happy with the verdict, took out a gun and shot Parry three times in the head and neck. Luckily, a doctor from the Infirmary happened to be in court and the Judge survived. Taylor was convicted of attempted murder and sentenced to twenty years' hard labour. The building, now with blue plaque, is still standing.

Deaf and Dumb Institute

Born around 1839, Mary Bradley was the first deaf-blind person in Britain to learn how to communicate by touch. At the age of three Mary contracted a serious illness; her mother (described as a 'loose woman who had taken to evil courses') abandoned her in a damp cellar where she was found and taken to the infant department of the nearest workhouse. When she recovered from the illness, she had lost her sight, hearing and speech. Being deaf, blind and dumb, Mary became an obvious target for the other children who tormented her relentlessly. Thankfully she was rescued from this misery when she was moved to the Deaf and Dumb Institute in Old Trafford. The first impression of her there was that she was 'one of the most uncouth and wild-looking objects it is well possible to conceive'. Her head had been shaven as a consequence of a skin disease and she looked more like a wild, cowering animal than a 'human being with a rational soul'. She used no signs at all to communicate her wants; she would merely scream and shout. The headmaster, Andrew Patterson, must have been a man of infinite kindness and patience. He had heard of a meeting that Charles Dickens had had with Laura Bridgman (the first ever deaf-blind person to be educated) during his travels in America in the early 1840s and how she had been taught to communicate by having letters and words signed in her hand. Until then most people had believed that it was impossible for deaf-blind people to communicate. Indeed, many readers of Dickens' *American Notes* of 1843 were sceptical of the story of Laura Bridgman, thinking it a highly exaggerated account of her life.

Patterson spent many weeks trying to make Mary understand the connection between the sign in her hand and the related object 'when all at once, like a sudden burst of sunshine, her countenance brightened up one day with a full intelligence beaming in it'. After that, her thirst for knowledge was unquenchable; with the help of cardboard letters and then using typeset letters Mary learned to read and write. She even went on to exchange letters with Laura Bridgman. In addition, she helped her fellow pupil Joseph Hague, also deaf-blind, to learn how to sign by touch. He then became the second deaf-blind person in Britain to learn how to communicate in this way. Mary and Joseph both made amazing progress and it was said that they seemed to possess an 'extra sense' to compensate for those they had lost.

Mary became a devout Christian and although she was plagued by illness in the last years of her life, she firmly believed in a future afterlife of happiness. She died in the institute at the age of 26.

Joseph Hague was the son of a deaf and dumb mother who had also been educated at the Deaf and Dumb Institute. He had been born deaf and lost his sight before he was 2. He was able to return to living with his parents and ended his days, not unhappily, in the Sheffield Workhouse, where he continued his education.

> Joseph Hague Departed this life on 26th February 1879.
>
> Wall'd in by Deafness, Dumbness, Blindness all!
> Could life exist beneath that dreadful pall?
> It did! Life, Love were there: The living Soul
>   Beat hot against the bars that held it in,
> Striving among the best, to reach the goal,
> And, through Christ's Death, immortal life to win. …
>   Kind Death hath bid the captive soul go free,
>   Where the Deaf hear, Dumb sing and Sightless see.

(This epitaph is taken from *The deaf and dumb and blind-deaf mutes* published in Canada in 1886).

Asylum for the Indigent Blind

Also in Old Trafford was the 'Asylum for the Indigent Blind' endowed by Thomas Henshaw, the successful owner of a hatting business. It opened in 1837 to educate the blind and enable them to earn a living and also 'to afford asylum to the impotent and aged blind'.

Manchester High School for Girls

The MHSG, now in Rusholme, was founded in 1874 by a group of forward-thinking Mancunians who believed that education was an end in itself and that the daughters of Manchester should be given 'what has been provided without stint for Manchester's sons'. In addition to housewifery and secretarial skills, maths and science also formed a large part of the curriculum, a progressive and uncommon practice at the time.

Institutions designed to promote education amongst the working classes began to appear in the early nineteenth century:

Manchester Mechanics' Institute

The Manchester Mechanics' Institute was founded in 1824 to offer education in basic science to working men plus literacy and numeracy classes for both men and women. It initially occupied a building on Cooper Street but moved into the (now Grade II* listed) building on Princess Street in 1855. The Institute is notable for being the birthplace of the Trades Union Congress in 1868 and the Co-operative Insurance Society in 1867. In 1883 a Technical School, which was the beginning of UMIST, was established here.

Ragged Schools

In 1847 the 'Juvenile Refuge and School for Industry' opened on Dantzic Street. In 1861 the building was taken over by 'Angel Meadow Ragged School' which shared the premises with a 'low-class dancing saloon, frequented by thieves and prostitutes'. This was the first industrial ragged school in Manchester and in order to rid themselves of the dancing saloon and its clientele, they bought the building for £200. In 1867 the name was changed to 'Charter Street Ragged School'. The aim of these charitable organisations (the name taken from the ragged clothes of the pupils) was to equip destitute children, aged from 5 to 13, with the skills necessary to become respectable citizens able to contribute to society. They were fed and clothed; in addition, they were taught the '3 Rs' and had to attend Bible study and Sunday School. The school also provided adults with literacy lessons and free meals. Good behaviour was rewarded by an annual trip to the seaside; sometimes as many as 1,000 children would descend on Victoria Station to take the train to Lytham.

It was renamed 'Charter Street Ragged School & Working Girls' Home' in 1892. The Working Girls' Home provided safe accommodation for servants and other girls with low-paid jobs; each girl had an individual cubicle for sleeping and the use of a bathroom, kitchen and laundry. The existing building, which dates back to 1866, was extended several times, but still retains features of its original use.

'Sharp Street Ragged School', also in Angel Meadow, was established in 1853 by an evangelical Christian called Christopher Sharp, though the existing building dates back to 1869. Ragged Schools were not universally popular and some felt that education and knowledge were wasted on working people. One such group tried to oust the school by offering a higher rent for the building. In 1970 Violet Carson, who played Ena Sharples in Coronation Street, became president of the school. In 2012 the building was converted into private offices.

Schooling for all

Before schooling for all became a reality, education of the poor was mainly in the hands of religious organisations, with the Bible being the focus of the teaching. The first Sunday School in Manchester began in 1784 in a building on Gun Street, Ancoats. For many children, Sunday Schools provided the only education they ever received. By 1834, forty thousand children were attending Sunday Schools in this town alone. The first Infant School in Manchester was established by the Society of Friends (Quakers) on London Road and had a playground attached. Many charity schools opened in the nineteenth century to educate the poor and in 1833, for the first time, the state became involved in universal education and allocated a yearly fund for the building of schools. Four years later, a meeting in Manchester established the 'Lancashire Public Schools' Association' which advocated that the cost of education should be funded from public taxes. Compulsory education up to the age of 10 was only introduced in 1880. It was increased to 13 years in 1899.

Hall of Science

The Hall of Science in Campfield (near present-day MOSI) was opened in 1840 by the 'Father of Socialism' Robert Owen as a home for the Owenite Co-operative Movement which had previously had its headquarters in Salford. The aim of the group was to provide education for working-class adults and children; the teachers were all volunteers and the tuition was free. The building cost £7,000 and contained the largest lecture hall in Manchester, capable of holding 3,000 people. In addition to lessons and lectures, the group also organised concerts, parties and excursions. The institution soon earned the reputation of promoting radical ideas and at least one attempt was made to burn it down 'by person or persons unknown'. The building was sold in 1850 and became home to the new library. It was demolished in 1877 after being declared unsafe.

Hall of Science

Manchester Free Public Library

Under the Public Libraries Act of 1850 Manchester became the first place to establish a public lending and reference library; it was supported by a local tax of one penny. The Mayor of Manchester, Sir John Potter, led the campaign to raise money for a building and books. Donations arrived in abundance from many quarters, including from Prince Albert. The building chosen was the Hall of Science at Campfield which had been built in 1839 and in 1852 the library opened. Both William Makepeace Thackeray and Charles Dickens supported the cause and spoke at the opening ceremony. In accepting an invitation to the event, Dickens wrote, 'My engagements are very numerous, but the occasion is too important and the example too noble to admit of hesitation.' In the week following the opening, a police officer had to be on duty to control the crowds. Ten years later the first children's library opened there. When the building was demolished, the library collection moved into the old Town Hall on King Street before finding a permanent home in Central Library.

Central Library

Central Library, which has recently undergone a major refurbishment, was erected between 1930 and 1934; its design was influenced by the Pantheon in Rome. It was built on the site of St. Peter's Hotel and the Waldorf Restaurant. The foundation stone was laid by the Prime Minister, Ramsay Macdonald, and the library was opened four years later by King George V and Queen Mary on a day so hot that many people in the cheering crowd fainted. (The King laid the foundation stone for the Town Hall extension on the same day.) When completed, it was the largest public library in the country. Amidst the surrounding black-sootened buildings, the new library sparkled and was dubbed the 'Corporation Wedding Cake'. Over one million books, magazines, etc. were carried, mostly by hand, from the old library to the new.

John Rylands Library

John Rylands was a cotton merchant and one of the most successful businessmen in Victorian England. He was also Manchester's first multi-millionaire. A religious man and a great philanthropist, he established orphanages and homes for 'gentlewomen' and 'poor ministers' (presumably not together) and also printed and gave away Bibles. He was married three times and had seven children; however, he outlived all his children and on his death in 1888, his widow inherited more than £2½ million.

Considered as one of the great libraries of the world, the John Rylands Library, a neo-Gothic building on Deansgate, was designed by Basil

Champneys and took ten years (and £250,000) to build; it opened to the public on 1 January 1900. It was founded by Mrs. Enriquetta Rylands as a lasting memorial to her husband and also as a gift to the people of Manchester. In 1899 Mrs. Rylands became the first woman to be awarded the Freedom of the City. She bequeathed a further £200,000 to the library which was used to build an extension and to add to the collection. In 1979 the library became part of Manchester University library.

The library is home to around 1½ million items: books, maps, photographs, manuscripts and many rare, priceless treasures which span an incredible five millennia. These include 5,000-year-old clay tablets (examples of the earliest known forms of writing), a 1476 William Caxton edition of Chaucer's *Canterbury Tales*, and the earliest known piece of New Testament writing: a papyrus fragment of St. John's Gospel from the second century AD. There is also a copy of the extremely rare *Wicked Bible*, known as such because it omits the word 'not' from 'Thou shalt not commit adultery'.

Chapter 10

Science & Technology

William Crabtree (1610–44)

The Great Hall in Manchester Town Hall is home to a series of twelve large murals painted by Ford Madox Brown depicting significant events in the city's history. One of the panels shows the amateur astronomer William Crabtree observing the transit of Venus (when that planet passes between Earth and the Sun). Crabtree was born in Broughton and educated at Manchester Grammar School. In later life he was a wealthy cloth merchant and had both the time and money to pursue his hobby. He and a fellow astronomer, Jeremiah Horrocks, were the first people ever to predict and observe the transit of Venus – on 24 November 1639, an event considered by many to mark the beginning of serious research by British astronomers. They also predicted, correctly, that there would be a transit of Venus on 8 June 2004. The transit will next occur in the year 2117.

Driven by the Industrial Revolution, Manchester became a place of many 'firsts', especially in the fields of science and technology.

John Dalton (1766–1844)

John Dalton was born in Cumberland in 1766 into a modest family; his father was a handloom weaver and both his parents were Quakers. He attended the local village school, as a pupil until he was 11 and then as a teacher. At 15 he helped to run a Quaker school in Kendal with his brother and at the age of 19 became the principal, a position he held for six years. As a Quaker, a university education wasn't an option so Dalton was largely self-taught. In 1793 he moved to Manchester where he would spend the rest of his life. A workaholic, Dalton had little time for relaxation; he made just one annual visit to the Lake District and one weekly visit to the bowling green at the 'Dog & Partridge' in Old Trafford.

Dalton investigated many aspects of science. He took a great interest in meteorology and kept a daily 'weather diary' for 57 years, recording over 200,000 observations on rainfall, air temperature and humidity, etc. In doing so, he helped to turn the study of weather into a recognized science. He was also the first person to investigate and put forward a theory on the causes and the hereditary nature of colour blindness, a condition from which both he and his brother suffered. He revealed his discovery in 1794 at a meeting of the Lit. and Phil. Society (of which he would later become president). Daltonism became a recognized name for colour blindness though the term is no longer in common usage. The French word for colour blind is 'daltonien'.

> In 1995 John Dalton's preserved eyeball was examined; it was discovered that his was a rare form of colour blindness and that he was missing the photoreceptor for perceiving the colour green.

It was in 1803, again at a Lit. & Phil. Society meeting, that John Dalton propounded his atomic theory and the first table of atomic weights and elements. In doing so, he earned a place in history as one of the founders of modern chemistry.

In later life, Dalton was tutor to several pupils, one of whom was the Salfordian James Joule, the physicist who gave his name to the international unit of energy. Much of Dalton's written work was destroyed in the Christmas bombings of 1940, prompting the American author (and Professor of Biochemistry) Isaac Asimov to say, 'It is not only the living who are killed in war.' What remains of his papers are kept in John Rylands Library.

Following his death, Dalton's body was laid in state in Manchester Town Hall. The day of his funeral was declared an official day of mourning and 40,000 people turned out to watch the funeral procession.

John Benjamin Dancer (1812–87)

John Benjamin Dancer was a Victorian optician, maker of scientific instruments, inventor, and a pioneer of photography. He opened his shop on Cross Street in 1845 where two of his most eminent customers were John Dalton and James Joule. Dancer invented microphotography; he reduced photographs of famous paintings down to one millimetre in diameter which he then mounted on slides for viewing through a microscope. In 1859 he exhibited his microphotographs in Paris. He is also credited with taking the first photograph of a flea.

In addition, Dancer was commissioned by Queen Victoria. He took five photographs of her family, each one had a diameter of only $\frac{1}{8}$ of an inch. He then set them into a signet ring with a magnifying jewelled lens.

> Microphotography is involved in the production of the microdot, usually a circle of 1 mm diameter, famously used in espionage! It was first used in the Franco-Prussian War of 1870 to send secret messages, by carrier pigeon, into the besieged city of Paris.

> Dancer is credited with taking the first photographs of Manchester, the earliest known of which features 1, Market Street - a cutler's shop.
>
> This amazing photograph was taken by Dancer from the top of the Royal Exchange building in 1842.

The Henrys

Thomas Henry, one of the founding members and later president of the Manchester Lit. & Phil. Society, was a Manchester surgeon-apothecary with premises on King Street. In addition to his medical work, he was also an experimental scientist. He developed an antacid from magnesium carbonate; patented as 'Henry's Magnesia', it was a popular medicine for over 100 years. He also investigated gases, especially 'fixed air' (an early name for carbon dioxide) to find methods of preserving food and water. Buying bottled water, especially bottled sparkling water, might be seen as a fairly recent fashion, but the practice actually began way back in the late eighteenth century when Thomas Henry became one of the first people in the country to successfully manufacture and sell mineral and soda waters, initially for medicinal purposes. In an 1808 directory of the town, a 'mineral water-works' is listed at 19, Cupid's Alley (now Atkinson Street) off Deansgate, being run by Thomas and his son, William Henry.

William Henry, in addition to continuing with his father's lucrative business, became one of the leading British scientists of the early nineteenth century. He shared his father's passion for chemistry and carried out investigations into the solubility of gases in water, the result of which became known as 'Henry's Law'. He was also one of the founders of the Mechanics' Institute, the forerunner of UMIST, now part of Manchester University.

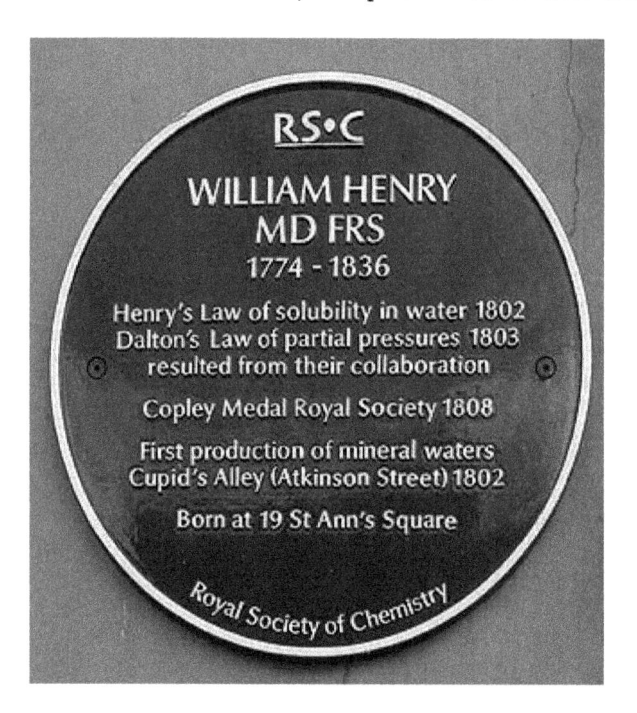

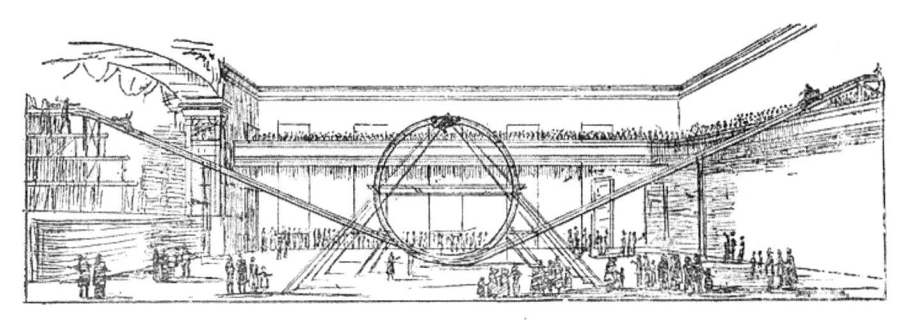

Grand Centrifugal Railway

CENTRIFUGAL RAILWAY
Constructed by C Esplen & J Higginbottom and others from a Model by Mr Roberts the Firm of Sharp Roberts & Co Manchester. The first constructed upon a scale large enough to convey a living Traveller. Railway 200 Feet long Vertical Circle upwards of 40 feet in Circumference

The forerunner of the roller coaster was not intended as a pleasure ride but as a spectacle to attract 'the curious and scientific'. The machine was first demonstrated at the Mechanics' Institute in Manchester in 1840 (without human cargo). The first full-scale (Grand) Centrifugal Railway was introduced in Manchester in 1842 as a 'scientific theatrical exhibition'. It had been constructed by Tarr & Riley of Manchester, 'on a scale never before exhibited in the World'. The entrance fee was 6d during the day (with reserved seats for ladies) and 3d in the evening.

At over 200 feet long, the contraption was huge; the advertisement claimed that a carriage would safely carry 'living men', heavy weights and a bucket of water (without a drop being spilt) around the 40 feet vertical circle at a speed of almost 100 mph. Before carrying people the machine had been rigorously tested with sandbags and a monkey, but it must have been a brave person who first volunteered to be strapped into the carriage. One journalist wrote, 'Females have had the fortitude, in Manchester, to travel by this extraordinary conveyance.' The model was then taken to Liverpool, Belfast and other cities around the country; in Bristol, it was described as 'one of the greatest wonders of the age'.

James Braid (1795–1860)

Regarded as the 'Father of Modern Hypnotism' and the 'first genuine hypnotherapist', James Braid was the man who coined the terms 'hypnosis' and 'hypnotism'. He was born in Scotland in 1796 and studied medicine at Edinburgh University. By 1828 he was a practising surgeon in Manchester and it was at a public performance at the Manchester Athenæum in 1841 that he observed the travelling Swiss 'animal magnetiser' Charles Lafontaine who was in town to demonstrate his ability to induce trances in animals and humans. Braid expected to be able to prove that Lafontaine was a charlatan, but after several visits to the demonstrations, during which he was invited onto the platform to witness the 'magnetiser's' abilities at close quarters, Braid realised that the subjects were indeed in an altered physical state and so he decided to perform some experiments of his own. Hypnotism was at that time known as Mesmerism after the Viennese physician Franz Anton Mesmer who used hypnotic suggestion to cure his patients of various ailments, including 'hysterical' disorders. Mesmer propounded the theory of 'Animal Magnetism'; he believed that some illnesses were caused by depleted levels of magnetism in the body and that a physician could transmit his own magnetic force to the patient by touch (known as the 'Mesmeric pass') when the patient was in an induced trance. Braid disputed this and began experimenting first on himself and then on his wife, friends and servants; in so doing he was able to prove that physical contact between 'operator' and subject was unnecessary. He believed that his subjects were in a kind of sleep and so he named the phenomenon after Hypnos, the Greek god of sleep. He later realised his mistake in thinking that the phenomena pertaining to hypnotic trances were sleep-induced and came to the conclusion that a trance could be induced by concentrating the patient's attention on a single object or idea. He tried to rename the practice 'monoideism' (the focusing of attention on a single idea), but without success: the terms 'hypnosis' and 'hypnotism' had taken hold and were here to stay!

Braid remained in Manchester until his death in 1860.

Sir Joseph Whitworth (1803–87)

Joseph Whitworth was one of the giants of the Industrial Revolution. He was born in 1803 in Stockport and from an early age showed an interest in engineering and machinery. He worked at various factories around the country before returning to Manchester to set up his own engineering business on Chorlton Street in 1833. Initially it was run from a small room in a mill but as he prospered he moved to larger premises and employed more people; by 1880 he owned a huge factory in Openshaw, employing over a thousand workers. Whitworth's key to success was in making accuracy and precision a priority in all his endeavours, whether perfecting existing ideas or devising methods and machinery of his own; it was this that won him international acclaim and secured his place as one of the foremost mechanical engineers of his age. He is considered by many to be the 'father of precision engineering'. In the first half of the nineteenth century a measurement with an accuracy to within a sixteenth of an inch was generally acceptable; Whitworth devised an instrument which could measure to a millionth of an inch. He invented and patented many pieces of machinery, but it is perhaps the Whitworth screw-thread for which he is most remembered. He first introduced his standardised screw in his own factory but by 1858 it was in universal use. He also earned a place in military history as an inventor of rifles; the War Office paid to have a shooting gallery built in the grounds of Whitworth's home so he could work on the accuracy of the rifles. In addition, he designed a field gun which was the most accurate and the most rapid-firing in the world. Not only that, he invented the first mechanical street-cleaner. He was knighted in 1869.

Whitworth made a fortune. He had a house, The Firs, built in Fallowfield, later moving to a Hall in Derbyshire. As his health began to decline, he spent his winters in the south of France and died in Monte Carlo in 1887. He left almost £1,250,000 to his trustees to be used for educational purposes and to benefit the people of Manchester. The money was used to set up scholarships for young engineers and to found the Whitworth Art Gallery and Park.

Resurgam

Q: What is the connection between Manchester and submarines?
A: The Reverend George William Garrett!

Unlikely as it seems, the Reverend Garrett was a pioneer in the design of submarines. Born in Moss Side in 1852, he attended Manchester Grammar School followed by Owens College (forerunner of Manchester University) and Trinity College, Dublin. In 1873 he became a curate in his father's parish.

In 1877 Garrett invented a diving suit which he demonstrated to the French government in the River Seine. On his return to Manchester he raised £10,000 from local businessmen and set up his own company (on Deansgate) looking into the military possibilities of submarines. In 1879 he designed and made a 45-foot-long steam-powered submarine which could reach a depth of 150 feet; it was built in Birkenhead at a cost of £1,500. He called it *Resurgam*, Latin for 'I shall rise again'. The trials of this machine were apparently successful, but unfortunately *Resurgam* didn't live up to its name and sank off the coast of Wales when being towed in a storm. Despite this, it impressed a wealthy Swedish arms dealer enough to finance him. Together, they made submarines for Greece and Turkey. Garrett was even commissioned as a commander in the Imperial Ottoman Navy (mainly because he was the only person who knew how to operate the machines)!

Although Garrett's submarine still had many design faults – the inside of the submarine was like a furnace, the only light was provided by candles and there were some major stability problems – the *Resurgam* is classed as the first engine-powered submarine and Garrett is regarded by many as the 'Father of the Submarine'.

Deciding to give up on his invention and being rejected by the church, Garrett and his family emigrated to America where he joined the US Army as an engineer. He died in New York, penniless, at the age of 50.

A man by the name of William Scanlon-Murphy, a radio producer, spent a lot of time, not to mention a lot of money looking for the wreck of the *Resurgam*.

Some years earlier, Uri (famous for bending spoons) Geller had predicted the exact location of the submarine, but Mr. Scanlon-Murphy was sceptical of Geller's psychic powers and ignored the advice. *Resurgam* was discovered in 1995, about five miles off the coast of Rhyl, exactly where Geller had predicted it would be. The wreck is now a protected site and some would like to raise it, but for now, the world's oldest submarine remains at the bottom of the sea.

Garrett, his daughter and two crew members on the *Resurgam*.

Robert Angus Smith (1817–84)

Born in Scotland, Smith came to Manchester in the early 1840s after studying chemistry in Germany. Working from his laboratory in Grosvenor Square, off Oxford Road, he investigated air pollution (What better place than Manchester?) and the link between industrial pollution and the acidity of rain; he discovered what came to be known as 'acid rain'. In 1844 he sent a letter to the *Manchester Guardian* in which he stated, 'Coming in from the country last week on a beautiful morning when the air was unusually clean and fresh, I was surprised to find Manchester was enjoying the atmosphere of a dark December day.'

In 1863 Queen Victoria appointed him to the role of Inspector-General of the Alkali Inspectorate, the first national pollution-control agency in the world. A far-sighted campaigner, Smith encouraged mill and factory owners to take responsibility for their industrial waste (with varying degrees of success) and was the first to advocate the use of smokeless fuels.

Manchester and Salford became the first cities in Britain to have 'smokeless zones'.

Sir Henry Enfield Roscoe (1833–1915)

Roscoe (who was the uncle of Beatrix Potter) moved to Manchester in 1857 when he became Professor of Chemistry at Owens College. By the time he left in 1886 that small college had become Victoria (later Manchester) University. Amongst many other accomplishments in his field, in 1858 he, together with Robert Bunsen, took the world's first flash-light photograph using magnesium as a source of light. He is also credited with establishing the first purpose-built chemistry laboratory in Britain.

Ernest Rutherford (1871–1937)

In the early 1900s three of the greatest scientists of the twentieth century came together at the Victoria University of Manchester: the Danish Niels Bohr (pioneer of Quantum Physics), the German Hans Geiger (inventor of the Geiger Counter) and Ernest Rutherford.

Born in New Zealand to an English mother and a Scottish father, Rutherford arrived in Manchester in 1907 to take up the position of Professor of Physics and a year later he was awarded the Nobel Prize in Chemistry for his previous work on radioactivity at Montreal University. However, it was in Manchester, working from his laboratory on Bridgeford Street, that he discovered the atomic nucleus and became the first person to 'split the atom'; in doing so, he laid the foundations of nuclear physics. He also discovered and named the 'proton'. Albert Einstein called him 'a second Newton'.

Marie Stopes (1880–1958)

Marie Stopes was the first female lecturer at Manchester University where she taught fossil botany in the Faculty of Science. In 1905 she went on to become Britain's youngest Doctor of Science. However, she is most well-known for her pioneering work on sex and family planning. In 1918 she scandalised society when her book *Married Love* was published (which soon became a best-seller). She returned to London where, in 1921, she founded the 'Mothers' Clinic for Birth Control', a free service mainly aimed at working-class women and which was branded as 'criminal' by many, especially the Catholic clergy.

Her first marriage was unconsummated and so annulled. She later married Humphrey Verdon-Roe.

A.V. Roe (1877–1958)

(Edwin) Alliot Verdon-Roe, brother of Humphrey, was born in Patricroft in 1877. He is famous for designing, building and flying the first British-made plane in 1908. Two years later he and his brother founded the Avro Company in Manchester. He went on to design a plane with an enclosed cabin which established a British flying record of 7½ hours. In 1913 he built the Avro 504 biplane – the most used military plane in the First World War and a design which became a prototype for future military aircraft. He sold the company in 1928.

Two of his sons inherited his love of flying; both became fighter pilots and, ironically, both were killed in the Second World War.

Alcock and Brown

In April 1913, the *Daily Mail* offered a prize of £10,000 to the first aviator to fly, non-stop, across the Atlantic Ocean. When war broke out, the offer was suspended but was reinstated following the Armistice.

John Alcock was born in Old Trafford in 1892; he was a military pilot in the war and on one of his missions the engine of his plane failed and he was taken prisoner in Turkey. Arthur Brown's family came to live in Manchester soon after his birth; he too was taken prisoner after his plane was shot down in Germany.

Once the war was over, Alcock accepted the *Daily Mail*'s challenge; he was to be the pilot and Brown the navigator. They wanted to prove, in the face of all the doubters, that it was possible to fly 'non-stop from the New World to the Old'. The plane was a Vickers Vimy and was powered by two Rolls-Royce engines. On 14 June 1919 they left Newfoundland and arrived in Galway, Ireland, 16 hours and 12 minutes and almost 2,000 miles later. Thinking they had found a lovely green field in which to land, it must have been a bit of a surprise to find that they had actually touched down in a bog! The plane was damaged, but they were unhurt. After they had been helped out of the plane, they communicated their success using Marconi's first transatlantic wireless station which was situated nearby.

> Ooops!
>
> Alcock and Brown, if not their plane, landed in Ireland in one piece.

Their adventures during the flight read like a tale from an old *Boys' Own* annual. It was extremely windy and turbulent, they flew through thick, dense fog, an exhaust pipe split and began shooting out flames and the batteries of the heating inside their flying suits ran out – all in the first five hours of their flight! The radio transmitter had also died, leaving those in the newsroom of the *Daily Mail* to fear the worst. The pair went on to fly through rain, hail and a snowstorm. In the freezing, blinding snow Brown had to climb out of the cockpit and onto the wings to remove all the ice – a feat he performed four times! On their return to England they were hailed as heroes and just a few days later they were both knighted by King George V at Buckingham Palace. They later flew to Manchester where they were given a civic reception.

Alcock was tragically killed just a few months later when his plane came down in France. His body was returned to Manchester, he was buried at Southern Cemetery and a memorial service was held in the Cathedral. It is amazing to think that all that happened around only a hundred years ago. Looking at their plane, it would have been hard to imagine that fifty years later, man would have travelled to the moon and back.

Alan Turing (1912–54)

Born in 1911, Alan Mathison Turing is perhaps most famous for leading the team which cracked German military codes at Bletchley Park during the Second World War. The Germans used a machine, 'Enigma', for encrypting all military and naval communications. Turing developed a new machine named the 'Bombe' which could crack the Enigma codes. It is widely believed that this shortened the war by two to four years, saving many thousands of lives. Three years after the war he came to Manchester University.

In 1936 his *The Turing Machine: On Computable Numbers* was published, establishing the basic principles of how a computer functions. This is widely recognized as the foundation of modern computer science and in Manchester he continued to work on computer programming and the possibility of artificial intelligence. In 1950 he developed the idea of an 'imitation game' for comparing the output of humans and machines in what came to be known as the 'Turing Test'.

In 1954 Turing committed suicide at his home in Wilmslow by swallowing cyanide; the previous year he had been prosecuted for his homosexuality and had then had to undergo 'treatment' with hormones (i.e. chemical castration) as the only alternative to being sent to prison. He was also automatically considered a security risk and his contract with the government code-breaking department was revoked; he also came under police surveillance. In 2009 a campaign, backed by thousands, including Stephen Hawking, was launched and in 2013 Turing was granted a (much too little, much too late) posthumous royal pardon and received an apology from the Prime Minister.

Computer

Given the nick-name 'Baby', the world's first electronic stored-programme computer was developed at Manchester University by Tom Kilburn and Frederic C. Williams in 1948. It was 5.2 metres long and 2.2 metres tall, weighed one tonne and could take half an hour to perform an operation which would nowadays be performed in millionths of a second. The successor of 'Baby' was the Manchester Mark 1 and in 1952 the local electronics firm Ferranti worked with the university to produce the Ferranti Mark 1 computer (also known as the Manchester Electronic Computer) which became the first commercially available computer in the world.

Sir Alfred Charles Bernard Lovell (1913–2012)

Bernard Lovell came to Manchester in 1936 to join the Department of Physics at Manchester University where he carried out research into cosmic rays. However, in his laboratory which was close to Oxford Road, he found that there was too much background interference from passing electric trams. He moved to a quieter, rural location near Goostrey in Cheshire and this was where he established and became the first director of the Jodrell Bank Observatory.

> The land on which the observatory was built was once owned by William Jaudrell, a Cheshire landowner, who had fought with the Black Prince at the Battle of Poitiers in 1356.

From 1951 to 1980 Lovell was Professor of Radio Astronomy at Manchester University. He was leader of the team which built the largest (at the time) steerable radio telescope in the world, now named the 'Lovell Telescope'. In 1948 Lovell had estimated the cost of building the telescope at £60,000 but the final figure was actually £670,000 – a massive overspend by any standards. The project was mired in controversy from beginning to end: questions were asked in Parliament, many condemned the telescope as a 'white elephant' and Lovell was faced with ruin and even possible imprisonment over his debts. The telescope, which stood at 249 feet tall, was finished in 1957.

Although it wasn't part of Lovell's vision for the telescope to be used as a political tool in the Cold War, the critics were well and truly silenced when, just weeks after it was put into operation, it detected the first ever artificial satellite – the Russians' Sputnik 1 and their first intercontinental ballistic missile.

The radio telescope has since led to many discoveries about the origins of the universe.

Graphene

At only one atom thick, graphene is the thinnest material possible but, amazingly, in certain conditions, it can be seen with the naked eye. It is 200 times stronger than steel but is extremely light and flexible. It can also carry a thousand times more electricity than copper. It was known many decades ago that graphite (used in pencils) is made up of millions of layers of graphene; the problem was to isolate them. This was achieved in 2004 by two Manchester University physicists, Professors Andre Geim and Kostya Novoselov; they were awarded the Nobel Prize for Physics in 2010 and later received knighthoods. The potential of graphene is immense and is predicted to revolutionise technology in the future.

Chapter 11

Transport

Stagecoach

In 1753 a stagecoach named *The Diligence* left Manchester at 6am, stopped in Irlam for breakfast, in Warrington for lunch and in Prescot for tea, finally arriving in Liverpool around twelve hours later. In 1754 another new service was advertised: 'However incredible it may appear, this coach will actually (barring accidents) arrive in London in four days and a half after leaving Manchester.' It was named the *Flying Coach* and was a four-wheeled, horse-drawn vehicle which 'flew' at a steady rate of around 5 mph. By 1773, with improvements to both roads and coaches, the journey-time had been reduced to just two days.

Canals

The Bridgewater Canal

At the behest of the Duke of Bridgewater, engineers James Brindley and John Gilbert built the Bridgewater Canal to carry coal the seven miles from the Duke's mines in Worsley to the mills and factories of Manchester and Salford. It opened in 1761 and was the first modern artificial waterway, marking the beginning of the 'Canal Age'. The price of coal coming into Manchester and Salford was almost immediately reduced by half. The Barton Aqueduct became one of the first 'tourist attractions' of the Industrial Revolution.

The world's first steamboat began operating on the Bridgewater Canal in 1773.

The Manchester Ship Canal

20,000 men, 6 years, around £17,000,000 and the removal of 82,000,000 tons of earth all went into the construction of the 35 miles long and 28 feet deep waterway, locks, docks and quays of the Manchester Ship Canal, finally providing the city with a direct passage to the sea. (The original estimated cost of the canal was just £1 million.) Daniel Adamson was the originator and first chairman of the Manchester Ship Canal but he died before the canal was officially opened on 21 May 1894 by Queen Victoria.

Railway

First Railway – First Fatality

> This is the tragic story of the Right Honourable William Huskisson, Member of Parliament, former Cabinet Minister and the first person ever to be killed in a railway accident.

The fifteenth of September 1830 saw the grand opening of the first passenger railway in the world: the Liverpool and Manchester Railway (L&M), which was 31 miles long and had been built at a cost of £820,000. Arthur Wellesley, aka the Duke of Wellington (then Prime Minister and 'guest of honour') and William Huskisson, MP for Liverpool, were both passengers on the ceremonial train procession from Liverpool to Manchester. Crowds of spectators lined the track and were entertained by bands as they waited. Halfway along the line the train made a scheduled stop to take on water. The passengers were advised to stay on board, but around fifty people, Huskisson being one of them, chose to ignore the advice.

Huskisson had played an influential role in the creation of the British Empire, but his calls for parliamentary reform had led to a rift with Wellington. Huskisson saw an opportunity to be reconciled with the Prime Minister and walked along the track to Wellington's private carriage. Having shaken hands, the pair were deep in conversation and Huskisson failed to see, or hear, the arrival of George Stephenson's *Rocket*. When he did become aware of the approaching machine, he understandably panicked and tried to get into the Duke's compartment. Unfortunately the carriage door swung open and Huskisson was knocked onto the track and under the wheels of the oncoming *Rocket*. Still alive, though with horrendous injuries to one leg which was described as 'almost entirely severed', Huskisson was taken by train to Eccles. The train was driven by George Stephenson (who was L&M's chief engineer) and on that journey he actually set the world record for speed, travelling at a dizzying thirty-six miles an hour! The weather seemed to echo the tragedy and they arrived in the middle of a violent thunder and hail storm. Huskisson was taken to the vicarage where he was given wine, brandy and laudanum while waiting for the surgeons to arrive from Manchester. On being told that he was unlikely to survive, he made a codicil to his will which he had drawn up only the day before. On his death bed he said, 'I hope I have no enemies in the world. I have no enmity to any human being.' He died in agony just a few hours later. Ironically, in his pocket, was his unread speech praising modern technology and including a toast to the 'organized power of steam'.

A graphic illustration of the unfortunate Mr. Huskisson as the *Rocket* hurtles inexorably towards him.

The Duke of Wellington was reluctant to carry on the day's celebrations but was persuaded to continue to Manchester. On arriving at Liverpool Street (the first passenger railway station in the world) the Duke was booed and pelted with rotten fruit and stones. He refused to leave the train and demanded an immediate return to Liverpool.

The L&M Railway Company had intended the opening of this railway to attract as much publicity as possible, but they could never have envisaged just how much coverage the event would receive; Huskisson's death was widely reported around the world and heralded the arrival of the age of the railway. The inquest returned a verdict of 'accidental death' and Huskisson was buried with great ceremony at St. James's Church in Liverpool.

Within five years of its inauguration, the Liverpool and Manchester Railway had carried over five million passengers. In the early days, passengers had to book their ticket in advance, giving details of their reason for travelling and next of kin (in case of accidents). The first train tickets were introduced in 1837 and in addition to the printed name of the destination, there was also a pictorial symbol to help those ticket collectors who were unable to read. Timetables were still in their infancy; although the departure time was given, the arrival time was not. Basically, at whatever time the train arrived was its arrival time. This was further complicated by the fact that there was no standardised time in those days: it was only in 1847 that Manchester changed its clocks to Greenwich Mean Time.

Until 1833 the second class carriages of the L&M Railway were completely open to the elements and when they did eventually get a roof there were no windows. When, in 1840, second class passengers were promoted to having carriages with windows, the new third class passengers had to be content with window-less (and sometimes seat-less!) journeys. There were many unforeseen hazards associated with this new form of travel: some people tried travelling on the roof of a railway carriage instead of inside it and, unsurprisingly, several people were knocked off the roof by bridges, causing a bye-law to be passed which made the practice illegal. After several deaths, and to prevent more passengers jumping out of the wrong side of the carriage and into the path of an oncoming train, all the doors not opening onto a platform were locked. In 1842 five people were killed when they decided to take a nap on the railway line.

The advent of the railway was received in various ways: one of George Eliot's characters in the novel *Felix Holt* regarded Huskisson's death as a 'proof of God's anger against Stephenson', though why He vented His rage on Huskisson and not Stephenson is unclear. The novelist H.G. Wells cited 'a steam engine running on a railway' as the defining symbol of the nineteenth century.

Central Station

After eighty-nine years the last train left Manchester Central Station in 1969 after falling victim to Dr. Beeching. Despite receiving Grade II* listed status in 1983 the massive iron and glass building was left to the elements and vandals and it fell into disrepair. Luckily, before it was completely destroyed, the building was bought and converted into conference/exhibition space. When the old station clock was being dismantled during restoration, a Victorian time-capsule was found inside.

The building reopened in 1986.

> **&**
>
> The area around Castlefield where the first canals and the first passenger railway meet has been designated as Britain's first Urban Heritage Park.

Exchange Station

With Exchange Station in the background, the statue in the foreground is Oliver Cromwell and was erected in 1875 amidst much controversy; the Irish community was especially outraged owing to Cromwell's brutal suppression of Irish uprisings. Queen Victoria was not amused either and allegedly refused to open the new Town Hall unless the statue was removed. It wasn't, so she didn't. Seen here in a prominent position between the Cathedral and the Station, Cromwell was later downgraded and now occupies a spot in Wythenshawe Park.

Cromwell's Statue and Exchange Station, Manchester

Manchester Underground

The idea of an underground rail system in Manchester goes back as far as the 1800s. However, in the mid-twentieth century the idea looked set to become a reality. Over a period of twenty years plans, maps and drawings for an underground, starting with the Picc-Vic line linking the two main railway stations, were completed. Work was due to start in 1973 with a completion date of 1978. Nine metres below Top Shop in the Arndale Centre is a huge void where building work began and which would have been a station. The project was abandoned for political and financial reasons.

> **&** At the beginning of the twentieth century there was a suggestion that a high-speed (over 100 mph) monorail line should be built linking Manchester and Liverpool. In 1966 there was another proposal for a monorail between Manchester Airport and Middleton, via the city centre.

> 20 THE GUARDIAN Friday January 21 1966
>
> ## Study of £21m. monorail's feasibility proposed
>
> # 16-mile line may follow
>
> By GEOFFREY WHITELEY
>
> MANCHESTER CITY COUNCIL is to be asked to agree to an intensive feasibility study of a scheme for a £21-millions monorail sytem for the city.
>
> The study, which would itself cost £28,000, would answer the engineering and planning problems involved. The city could then seek substantial Government support for the scheme, which corporation officials believe could solve the problems of public transport in a congested area and could eventually form the hub for a monorail network serving the Greater Manchester area.
>
> **Paying third**
>
> The scheme that would form the subject of the feasibility study is for a 16-mile line extending from Manchester Airport, in
>
> A monorail such as this suspended system developed in France could operate in Manchester. Complete enclosure of tracks and working parts within a hollow gantry allows all-weather operation and the use of rubber tyres means relatively quiet running.

Buses

The first bus service in Britain began on 1 January 1824 when a regular horse-drawn service was established by John Greenwood. It ran three times a day between Market Street, Manchester and Pendleton. It held eight passengers and cost 6d (2½p) for three miles. Double-deckers, pulled by three horses and capable of carrying forty-two people, were introduced in the 1850s. In 1865 the Manchester Carriage company was formed to operate horse-drawn buses in the area.

The first motor buses started operating in 1906; horse-drawn buses had stopped running in that year but were reinstated in 1914 when Manchester Corporation's motor-buses were requisitioned for the war effort. The following year female conductors (or conductresses) were employed for the first time as many of the male employees had gone to war.

This photograph, taken in 1930, shows one of a fleet of motor-cycles which were used to lead buses through the streets in fog and smog.

Trams

Horse trams were introduced on 17 May 1877; the first line to be opened was between Bury New Road and Deansgate. Manchester Tramways had 5,000 horses.

A horse-drawn tram in 1910

The first electric trams in the city centre began in 1901 between Albert Square and Cheetham Hill and horse trams finished operating two years later. A night service was begun in 1913. The last 'old' tram left Piccadilly in 1949, but in 1992 they made a comeback and Manchester now has the largest tram network in the UK.

Trolley Buses

Manchester trolley buses ran between 1938 and 1966. The first route was along Ashton Old Road.

Cars

When it comes to cars, the city is best remembered as the meeting-place of the Hon. Charles Stewart Rolls and (Frederick) Henry Royce. Royce became a railway apprentice at the age of 14 and seven years later he set up his own electrical business, Royce Ltd, in Hulme. In 1904 he built his first car. The following year he met Rolls in Manchester's Midland Hotel and the Rolls-Royce, priced 'from £375' was born. Rolls was killed in a flying accident when he was 32; Royce died at the age of 70.

Manchester had its fair share of British car manufacturers in the first decades of the twentieth century, none of which survive today. There was also a branch of the American Ford Motor Co. in Trafford Park which produced 302,000 cars between 1911 and 1927, when the factory closed. During the Second World War, Ford returned to Manchester; they built a new plant and employed 17,000 workers who turned out 34,000 Rolls-Royce Merlin engines for the RAF.

Chapter 12

The Press

Manchester's first 'real' newspaper was the *Manchester Weekly Journal* which was published from 1719 to 1726 and cost one penny. In 1752 the *Manchester Mercury* appeared; it cost 3½d and ran for 78 years.

This somewhat biased account of the Peterloo Massacre appeared in the right-wing *Manchester Mercury* on 17 August 1819.

Various other newspapers were published in Manchester during the latter half of the eighteenth century; some ran for decades (such as the *Manchester Chronicle* from 1781 to 1838) and others were very short-lived.

One anonymous visitor to Manchester in 1821 sent a poem to the 'Chronicle':

> I arrived in a shower, in the rain now set off,
> Eight days in the place I remained:
> Seven days, seven nights and a quarter, I vow,
> By Jove! It incessantly rained.

In 1792 the first edition of the *Manchester Herald* was published. This was the first newspaper owned and published by and for those calling for parliamentary reform. Needless to say, the authorities were somewhat alarmed by this, fearing that the paper was promoting revolution (just after the French Revolution in 1789) and within a short space of time they had engineered riots, repeatedly taken legal action for sedition and finally destroyed the premises, forcing the business to close.

To Quote:

'The great cause of liberty demands the steady support of the brave, the just, and the philanthropic - for should oppression triumph, the vengeance of power will know no bounds; racks and tortures, Bastilles and Inquisitions, will be the punishment of those who have dared to avow themselves the Friend of Liberty.'

from the *Manchester Herald* (28 April 1792)

In 1795 the *Manchester Gazette* was founded by William Cowdray and printed at his home on St. Mary's Gate. Following the demise of the *Herald*, the *Gazette* was the only non-Tory paper in the town. It contained unpaid contributions from two young clerks – John Edward Taylor and Archibald Prentice. This was one of the first 'quality papers' and was regarded by many as the best newspaper in Manchester. Following the Peterloo Massacre in 1819, the reporter from *The Times* was arrested, but Taylor and Prentice dispatched full reports of the atrocity to London by coach and horses. Two years later Taylor founded the *Manchester Guardian* and Prentice went on to establish the *Manchester Times*.

Another victim of persecution by the authorities was James Wroe, editor of the *Manchester Observer*. Wroe was sued for libel many times and was imprisoned for printing articles critical of the government. After his report on the Peterloo Massacre, a term he had coined, he was again arrested and charged with sedition; he was sent to prison for one year and fined £100. The newspaper shut down in 1820 following constant police raids. Wroe became a bookseller at 42, Great Ancoats Street, where he sold radical books and newspapers.

On Saturday, the 5th of May, 1821, will be Published,
Price Seven-pence,
No. 1 of a New Weekly Paper,
TO BE ENTITLED
The Manchester Guardian.

PRINTED AND PUBLISHED BY J. GARNETT, MANCHESTER.

The PLACE of Publication will be announced when the necessary arrangements are completed; and, in the mean time, Orders, Advertisements, and Communications, will be received by MR. SOWLER, Bookseller, St. Ann's Square, Messrs. ROBINSON AND ELLIS, St. Ann's Place; and MR. JOHN FORD, Market-street.

PROSPECTUS.

IT may safely be asserted, that no former period, in the history of our Country, has been marked by the agitation of questions of a more important character, than those which are now claiming the attention of the public. To any one, who regards, for a moment, the conflicting views and wishes of the Commercial and Agricultural Interests,—the considerations which may arise out of the existing Laws for the regulation of our Currency,—the present and the anticipated pressure of the National Debt and of Taxation,—this statement will be sufficiently apparent.

The first edition of the *Manchester Guardian* appeared on 6 May 1821; it was founded by John Taylor, cost 7d, and was advertised as 'a backer of the Liberal cause'. Originally a weekly paper, it was printed and published from a large building on the corner of Market St. and Cross St. In 1836 a Wednesday edition was introduced and following the abolition of stamp duty on newspapers it became a daily paper and the price was reduced to 2d. In 1907 Charles Prestwich Scott (better known as C.P. Scott) who became editor of the newspaper in 1872, aged just 25, bought the paper and remained editor until his death on 1 January 1932. He famously wrote, 'Comment is free, but facts are sacred. The voice of opponents no less than that of friends has a right to be heard.' The newspaper lost 'Manchester' from its title in 1959 and five years later, its headquarters moved to London.

The *Manchester Evening News*, which became Britain's biggest-selling regional newspaper, began in 1868 as an election hand-out by Mitchell

Henry, merchant and would-be Liberal MP. He lost! Following his defeat, his interest in the paper waned and he sold it to John Taylor Jnr. (son of the *Manchester Guardian*'s first proprietor) and Peter Allen. Following this it became an independent newspaper costing ½d. From its humble beginnings in a small dingy office on Brown Street, it moved in 1879 to share premises with the *Manchester Guardian* on Cross Street. The M.E.N. was the first newspaper in Britain to announce the end of the Second World War.

By the beginning of the twentieth century Manchester was an important centre in newspaper production and what is now the Printworks was the largest printing house in Europe.

The offices of the Manchester Guardian and the Manchester Evening News

Chapter 13

Entertainment

Hostelries

Two of the oldest inns in Manchester were demolished in the twentieth century: both had been standing for over 600 years.

The 'Seven Stars'

This hostelry on Withy Grove claimed to be 'the oldest licensed house in Great Britain' and did, in fact, date back to the 1300s. It was traditionally believed that the workmen who built the Cathedral were paid a penny a day plus free meals in the Seven Stars.

> In his novel *Guy Fawkes,* published in 1842, the Manchester author William Harrison Ainsworth has the Gunpowder Plot being hatched in the Star Chamber of Ordsall Hall in Salford. Guy Fawkes is said to have evaded capture through an underground tunnel which led to an inn near Manchester Cathedral. This is thought to refer to the Seven Stars on Withy Grove where Guy Fawkes and Robert Catesby are reputed to have stayed in 1605. (One of the rooms in the inn was named 'Ye Guy Fawkes Chamber' to add authenticity to the claim.) Though the story is more fiction than fact, it could be true. The Radclyffes of Ordsall Hall were devout Roman Catholics and knew the Catesby family, one of whom was Robert Catesby, Fawkes's co-conspirator.
>
> Legend has it ...

There was certainly one underground passage from the Seven Stars; it led to the Collegiate Church. Records exist of a priest sneaking out during a service and popping along the passage for a quick beverage (or two).

When the New Bailey Prison was demolished in 1872, the inn acquired and displayed some 'souvenirs' of the place, including leg irons and the doors of the condemned cell.

This postcard shows a policeman on duty outside the Seven Stars at the beginning of the twentieth century.

'Ye Olde Rover's Return Inn'

This building had stood on Shudehill since 1306 and was at one time home to Ye Olde Rovers Return Inn (commemorated in *Coronation Street*). It is thought that the building was once part of Withingreave Hall estate, home of William Hulme. In a 1906 book, *The Old Inns of Old Manchester*, the building is described as 'a tottering, crazy-looking tavern'. In the 1920s the inn became home to a café and antique shop.

The building was demolished in 1958.

'The Old Wellington Inn'

One of the oldest surviving buildings in Manchester is the Old Wellington Inn which dates back to at least 1552. To put this in context, it was the age of the Tudors. Henry VIII had died five years earlier and Edward VI was now on the throne. The building has had an interesting journey and is now in its third location. It was originally situated in the Shambles area of the town, near the main road from London to Carlisle and so in an ideal location to attract passing trade. In 1554 the Byrom family moved in, living above their drapery business which occupied the ground floor. The Byroms had a long association with Manchester and the building remained in their family for the next 250 years. A third storey was added to the building and in 1692 it was the birthplace of perhaps the most famous member of the dynasty: John Byrom. In 1830 the building was granted a licence and the 'Vintners' Arms' and later the 'Kenyon Vaults' occupied the building. In 1865 the name was changed again, this time to 'The Wellington Inn' which was a pub downstairs and a workshop for optical instruments upstairs.

A building with a long and colourful history

At the end of the nineteenth century Will Chambers used the upper floors for his fishing rod and fly business.

During the 1940 Christmas bombings of Manchester by the German Luftwaffe, the Old Wellington Inn, although slightly damaged, remained more or less in one piece despite the devastation all around. In 1974 the pub was raised by 4 feet 9 inches and moved to its new home – an unprepossessing place, hidden away among soulless modern concrete blocks. This was in order to make way for the Arndale Centre. In 1996, the building suffered bomb damage yet again when an IRA bomb exploded nearby. After renovation the pub was once again moved to a different location – this time near Manchester Cathedral where it can now be seen and appreciated in all its glory.

The 'Sun Inn' (Poets' Corner)

By the mid-nineteenth century the Sun Inn, a gabled timber-and-plaster building, had been standing on Long Millgate for centuries. In the early 1840s the landlord of the inn was Mr. William Earnshaw who was a lover of all things literary. It was during his tenure that the inn became the haunt of a group of local poets and writers, the most notable of whom were John Critchley Prince, Samuel Bamford, Isabella Varley (later Mrs. G. Linnaeus Banks) and Robert Rose. It soon became known as Poets' Corner, a name which was still used long after poets and inn had gone. The *Festive Wreath*, published in 1842, is an anthology of works by the Sun Inn poets.

> One of the aforementioned scholars, Robert Rose, was a wealthy West Indian Creole, born in 1808 and known as the 'Bard of Colour'. He lived in Salford and was a prominent member of the Sun Inn group.

The Sun Inn lost its licence in the 1870s and the building morphed into 'Ye Olde Curiosity Shop', owned by M.J. Davis, an antique dealer. For a time, it shared the premises with a tuck shop, popular with the boys from Manchester Grammar School which was situated across the road. The inn was pulled down in the 1920s.

'John Shaw's Punch House' ('Sinclair's Oyster Bar')

This inn was located in the Shambles area of Manchester and was a meeting place for 'High Tories', becoming the first Gentlemen's Club in the town. As the name suggests it was renowned for its punch, a popular beverage at the time; the eccentric John Shaw was known for always carrying a silver spoon in his pocket which he used to mix the punch which was served in china bowls. A shilling bowl was called a P and a sixpenny bowl a Q. The rule of the house was that if a customer were alone he would order a Q, if in company a P. It has been speculated that this is where the expression 'to mind one's Ps and Qs' comes from.

John Shaw, having served in the army, was a strict disciplinarian and closed his hostelry every evening at 8 o'clock sharp. He would announce closing time accompanied by a crack of his horsewhip (not at, but very near his customers). No matter who or of what rank, any customer trying to flout this rule would be met by the servant, Molly, with her mop and bucket. She would begin slopping water about, forcing the loiterers to leave with wet feet.

Shaw ran the pub successfully for fifty-eight years. After his death in 1796 at the age of 80, the Punch House became 'Sinclair's' and in 1845 when oysters were added to the menu, it became Sinclair's Oyster Bar. Now considered by some to be a (not so cheap) delicacy, pickled oysters were at that time part of the diet of the poor. There are currently two pub signs attached to the building: one depicts John Shaw and the other the mop-wielding Molly.

> A regular customer at Sinclair's Oyster Bar was known as Lady Spittlewick; she apparently ate forty oysters every day. One day, mid-oyster, the poor lady had to be rushed to hospital but alas, it was too late; she had choked to death on a pearl!
>
> **Legend has it ...**

'Circus Tavern'

Though many pubs lay claim to having the 'smallest bar in Britain', the Circus Tavern on Portland Street goes one better and claims to have the 'smallest bar in Europe'. Whether this is true or not, it is surely a contender. The tavern itself is tiny, but the bar was described by one visitor as 'more of a walk-in drinks' cabinet than a bar'.

The building dates back to around 1790 when it was a weaver's cottage. It became a pub in 1840 and was frequented by travelling entertainers and performers from the nearby Hardy's Equestrian Circus Hall, from which the hostelry is reputed to have taken its name. (Circus Street marks its location.) Mr. Hardy's Equestrian Circus embarked on an ill-fated tour to Dublin, aboard the *Viceroy*. A violent storm blew up in the Irish Sea and the boat was lost along with the performers, their children and twenty horses. Mr. Hardy, who was due to follow on a later boat, escaped the same fate and retired soon after the tragedy.

The 'Oxnoble'

On Liverpool Road in Castlefield, the Oxnoble is (almost) certainly the only pub in Britain to be named after a potato. It was established in 1804, making it one of the oldest pubs in Manchester. It was originally called the 'Coopers' Arms' but changed its name in the 1840s when the men working at the nearby Potato Wharf would pop in for a pint. The potatoes would arrive by canal boat from the fields of Lancashire and Cheshire and were then unloaded and transported to the local potato market.

In an 1847 list of potato varieties, the oxnoble (now extinct) comes under the heading of 'Varieties grown exclusively as food for livestock' and is described as 'large, yellow without and within, very prolific, not fit to eat'. Conveniently, this was ignored as this 'inedible' potato was the one advocated by some of Manchester's leading doctors as 'cheap, filling and a good substitute for wheat' – ideal for the working-classes!

'Peveril of the Peak'

Built c.1830, this is certainly a unique pub, from its shape (like a wedge of cheese) to the unusual mustard and green tiled exterior (an addition made by the Manchester Brewery Company around seventy years later). Even more unusual is the fact that it survived the surrounding redevelopment. The pub is thought to have been named after the famous 'Peveril of the Peak', a horse-drawn stagecoach which ran between Manchester and London at a rattling speed of around ten mph: a journey of two days. Pulled by four piebald horses, the 'Pev' left the Peacock Office located at 105, Market Street at noon and travelled via Derbyshire, calling at Buxton, Matlock and Derby. The stagecoach itself probably took its name from a novel of the same name by Sir Walter Scott; the ruins of the medieval Peveril Castle near Castleton provided the setting of Scott's novel.

'Tommy Ducks'

Originally named 'The Prince's Tavern', this legendary Manchester pub changed its name in the 1860s when the landlord was Tommy Duckworth. Whether fact or fiction, the story goes that Mr. Duckworth wanted his own name writ large on the outside of the hostelry. The signwriter, having got as far as Tommy Duck, realised that he had run out of space and with room for only one more letter, he added an 's'. Tommy Ducks was born and remained in business for well over a century.

In later years, the pub was noted for its unusual taste in décor; some of the tables were glass-topped coffins (one actually contained a skeleton) and the ceiling was decorated with ladies' knickers; on arrival, women were asked for donations.

By the late 1980s the pub, which in the past had been hemmed in on all sides by houses and factories, now stood in what had become a wasteland. Developers wanted to buy the land and the brewery wanted to sell it, but the locals were up in arms and persuaded the council to put a temporary preservation order on the building. This order was renewed several times until 1993 – the preservation order lapsed on a Sunday and couldn't be renewed until the following day. In just a few hours during the night, Tommy Ducks was reduced to a pile of bricks. The brewery was fined £150,000, probably a fraction of what it received for the land.

'Lass o' Gowrie'

This is a Victorian pub which was the site of Manchester's oldest *pissotière* (a public urinal for men) which presumably dispensed its contents into the gently flowing River Medlock below. Nice!

****

Poison in Beer.

EVERY Band of Hope boy and girl knows that there is always one poison in beer, and that it is ALCOHOL. Lately there has been a scare in the Manchester district because another poison has been found in beer, ARSENIC. Moral: Never take any drinks which contain any poison at all— then two dangers will be avoided.
   Mr. F. R. Docking, of Croydon, has done a good thing by publishing a big poster containing these words:—

POISONED BEER.

ARSENIC IS POISON !

ALCOHOL IS POISON!

ARSENIC IS PRESENT NOW
By accident (in some Beers),
ALOOHOL IS ALWAYS PRESENT
By intent in **ALL** Beers, and a larger proportion in
Whiskey, Brandy, Gin, and Rum.

DRINKERS, BEWARE !

&

Manchester, influenced by the 1850s U.S. Maine Law which introduced the prohibition of alcohol, was the home of many temperance hotels and 'bars'. Maine Road, former home of Manchester City's ground, was named after the American state.

Drinkers did indeed need to beware when a very different kind of poison was found in their beer.

What's Your Poison?

This question took on a whole new meaning at the beginning of the twentieth century. Doctors in and around Salford and Manchester had noticed a growing number of both men and women complaining of weakness, pain in the limbs, pins and needles in the hands and feet and, in the most severe cases, paralysis of the limbs. The common thread linking all these patients was their partiality for a glass (or two, or three …) of beer. At first, their symptoms were thought to be caused by over-indulgence, but it soon became clear that something more sinister was to blame.

In December 1900, the Salford Health Committee held a meeting in which it was disclosed that in the previous four months 41 people had died from neuritis (a painful disease affecting the nerves and eventually causing paralysis) and 66 from alcoholism, way above the average for a four-month period. The committee concluded that the beer must have been contaminated and when it was analysed, it had indeed - with arsenic! The poison was found in the sugar used in the brewing process. Sugar had been stripped from the cane with sulphuric acid which is normally made from pure sulphur. However, as sulphur had become so expensive, pyrites (iron sulphide which contains arsenic) had been substituted and so had contaminated the sugar.

The brewers, Groves and Whitnall, in a damage-limitation exercise made a great show of emptying their entire stock of beer into the River Irwell. Needless to say, this seemed like manna from heaven for some who tried to collect the beer in whatever container came to hand.

In all, the 'beer scare' lasted over a year and claimed 115 victims.

In 1896 the ratio of public houses to the population in Manchester was one pub to 168 people. In the same year in London, the ratio was one pub to 1,395 people.

Ben Lang's Music Hall

A Manchester magazine of the mid-1860s, *How Manchester is amused*, described the city's three main music halls which provided 'facilities for obtaining beer with the music' and a 'lower class of music hall which simply throw in music with the beer'. Ben Lang's Music Hall (later renamed Victoria Music Hall) was one of the latter and was able to (and frequently did) pack in 'incessant crowds of the matter-of-fact sons and daughters of John Bull'. The Hall, which was one of the first music halls to be established in the town, was a five-storey building situated by Victoria Bridge, overhanging the River Irwell and close to the Cathedral. It became one of the most popular working-class venues with its mix of audience participation and entertainers such as comics, singers, jugglers and magicians. The building's flat roof was later covered over and used as a dance hall. All this, for just tuppence! After several warnings, Ben Lang had his licence to sell spirits withdrawn, but he was still able to sell beer and Mrs. Lang's coffee, described as 'moderate in price and unequalled in quality'.

On 31 July 1868, Ben Lang's was the scene of Manchester's worst 'theatre' disaster; there was an 'incident' with a gas chandelier and a false alarm of fire was given. This was followed by a stampede down the stairs and out of the doors; 23 people, most of them teenagers, were crushed to death and many more were injured. This tragedy (amongst others) led to stricter regulations around fire safety in theatres and other places of entertainment where large numbers of people gathered.

One act who often appeared at Ben Lang's was Joseph Bryan Geoghegan who was born in Salford in 1816 to an Irish father and an English mother. He was a travelling 'Comic Vocalist and Author of numerous Popular Songs' and appeared in music halls around the country. On his travels he did more than sing! He led a double life, having two 'wives' who between them had twenty-one children.

Ben Lang also owned rowing boats for hire and four passenger steamers which ran trips down to Pomona Gardens (though why anyone would want a trip on a river nicknamed 'Sewage Canal' is a mystery).

Theatre

The earliest theatre in Manchester was located on Marsden Street from 1753 to 1775 when an Act of Parliament was passed to open the first licensed theatre in the town; this was the Theatre Royal which stood at the corner of Spring Gardens and York Street. Before this, theatrical performances and other types of entertainment took place in temporary wooden structures or in the first Exchange building. Parish records show that a 'commedian' and a 'player' were buried in Manchester as early as the 1740s.

A bridge too far

Some entertainers will go to any lengths to ensure that their show is a success, but maybe none more so than the members of the theatrical companies from Drury Lane and Covent Garden who, legend has it, in 1761 actually built a narrow wooden footbridge over the River Irwell so that the good folk of Manchester could more easily visit the theatre in Water Street, Salford where they were performing. They gave it the name Blackfriar's in ironic homage to the grand bridge of the same name being built in London at that time.

> In the years seventeen sixty and sixty and one,
> The town by the players was well play'd upon;
> Old Whiteley possession had got of the town,
> And the two London houses join'd force and came down,
> And no place being vacant that was near to the centre,
> They determined in Salford to try their adventure;
> Erected a building, erected a stage,
> To act o'er the passions of man and the age;
> And to tempt the Mancastrians, made steps down the ridge,
> And over the river threw Blackfriar's Bridge.

The 'Old Whiteley' mentioned in the rhyme (from *The Metrical Records of Manchester* by Joseph Aston) was the proprietor of a rival theatre on the Manchester side of the Irwell.

The old wooden Blackfriars Bridge

In 1820 the wooden bridge was replaced by the more substantial stone arch bridge which still stands today.

****

For almost 250 years Manchester has been home to many theatres which have been host to the leading lights of stage and screen.

Theatre Royal

The first Theatre Royal was abandoned in 1807 and a theatre of the same name was built on Fountain Street. In 1844 this second Theatre Royal burned down. The new (third) Theatre Royal, built on the site of the Wellington Hotel and Brogden's Horse Bazaar on Peter Street, opened in 1845. Following the destruction of many theatres by fire, a tank capable of holding 20,000 gallons of water was added to the roof. Though it ceased to operate as a theatre in 1921, it is the oldest surviving theatre building in Manchester.

During the first half of the nineteenth century there were many unlicensed entertainment venues. 'Penny theatres' or 'penny gaffs' as they were more commonly called were a very cheap and therefore popular night out for many.

The London Music Hall/Queens Theatre

In 1862 Hayward's Hotel on Bridge Street was converted into the London Music Hall which a few years later became the Royal Amphitheatre and Circus.

Poster from 1864

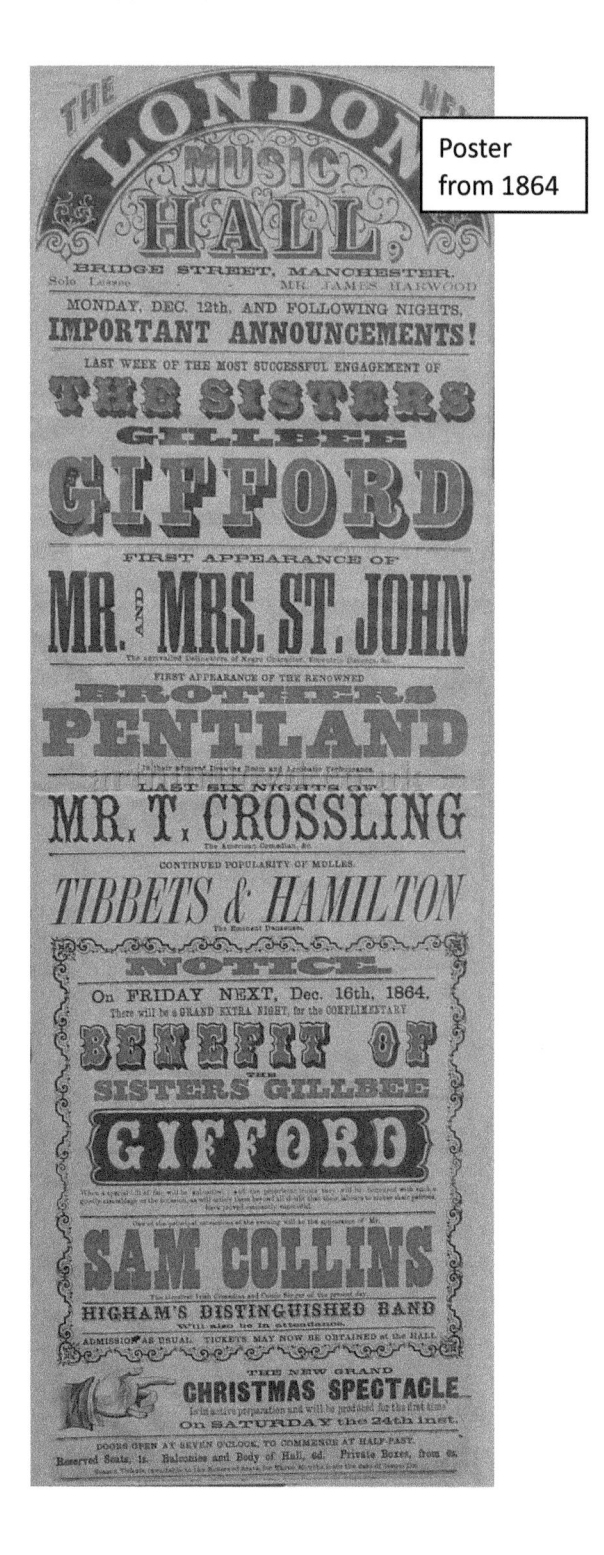

> Following demolition of the old building, the Queen's Theatre was built on the site. This was in operation until 1911 when the site was cleared and the art deco Masonic Hall was built.

Palace Theatre

The Palace Theatre opened in 1891 as the Manchester Palace of Varieties. The theatre was rebuilt following a direct hit in the Manchester Blitz of 1940. In 1949 Danny Kaye performed there; when the tickets went on sale, there were around 25,000 people queuing up around the block. Judy Garland, Noel Coward and Laurel & Hardy are just a few of the famous names that appeared here. Earlier performers included Charlie Chaplin and Harry Houdini.

Manchester Hippodrome

The Hippodrome Theatre, a grand building on Oxford Street, opened in 1904 as a variety theatre playing host to music hall, circus performances and (in a tank containing 70,000 gallons) water spectaculars. It was the work of Frank Matcham, one of the great theatre designers of the age; he was also responsible for Blackpool Tower Ballroom and the London Palladium. In the basement was a lions' den plus stables for 100 horses. It closed in 1935 and was demolished to make way for the art deco Gaumont Theatre, then Cinema. The Ardwick Empire Theatre then became the Manchester Hippodrome.

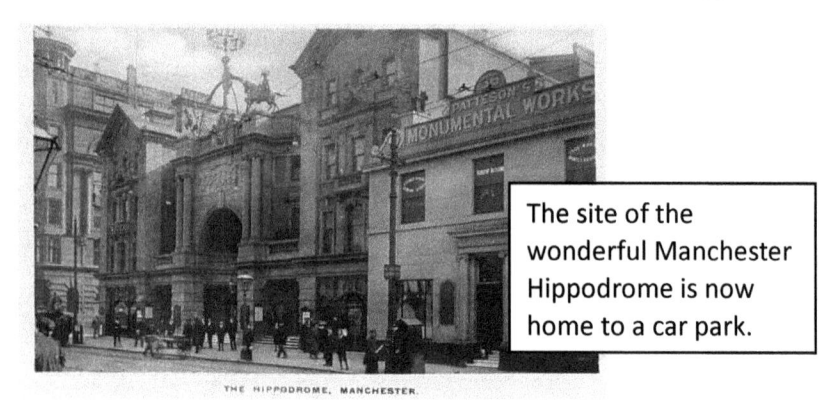

The site of the wonderful Manchester Hippodrome is now home to a car park.

Annie Horniman

Annie Elizabeth Fredericka Horniman was a lady way ahead of her time. After studying art and cycling alone around Europe, she inherited money from her grandfather (founder of the famous Horniman's Tea Company) which she used to establish a theatre company which initially performed at the Midland Hotel Theatre. She then bought the Gaiety Theatre on Peter Street, for £25,000, where in 1908 she founded the first repertory theatre in Britain. She staged over 200 plays and encouraged local writers such as Harold Brighouse (*Hobson's Choice*), Stanley Houghton (*Hindle Wakes*) and Allen Monkhouse, all members of what came to be known as the 'Manchester School of Dramatists'. Her aim was to make theatre available to all, including the working classes. George Bernard Shaw credited her with starting the 'modern theatre movement'.

Miss Horniman delighted in shocking the establishment and would often appear wearing a monocle and smoking a cigar. She also dabbled in the occult and would consult Tarot cards before making any decision.

Opera House

Originally named the New Theatre, which opened on Boxing Day in 1912, it became the Opera House in 1920. Apparently, on opening night, when *Kismet* was being performed, the audience was treated to a plague of rats running around their feet. The theatre closed in 1979 bur reopened five years later (with *Barnum*) after being restored.

Cinemas

Oxford Street was well-known for its theatres, dance halls and later cinemas. Before the Second World War, cinemas and other entertainment venues remained closed on Sundays. However this rule was relaxed for the duration of the war. Post-war, Sunday opening continued, despite calls from some religious groups to reinstate the ban. In 1947 a ballot was held with the overwhelming majority voting for cinemas to stay open on Sundays.

There were many cinemas in the city centre. Some of the buildings remain, but are used for other purposes. The 'Moon under Water' pub was once the Deansgate Picture House (later the ABC) which opened in 1914. Another gem of a building is the former Grosvenor Picture Palace on Oxford Street. At one time this was the largest picture house in Manchester, with 1,000 seats.

It's a Northern Thing!

A famous quotation by writer and broadcaster Mark Radcliffe states, 'Manchester is a city that thinks a table is for dancing on.' This is nothing new; for centuries Manchester folk have been fond of 'a bit of a do'!

Wine on tap

In 1661, to celebrate the coronation of King Charles II, the water conduit which was situated in the Market Place ran with claret. In the *History of the Collegiate Church, Manchester* the event is described so: 'The gentlemen and officers then drank his Majesty's health in claret running forth at three streams at once out of the said conduit, which was answered from the soldiers with a great volley of shot, and many great shouts, saying God save the King; which being ended the gentry and ministers went to dinner, attended with the officers and music of the town ... During the time of dinner, and until after sunset, the said conduit did run with pure Claret, which was freely drunk by all that could.'

****

Say 'Wakes Week', 'Whit Walks' and 'Rush carting' to people outside the North-west (and even many young people in the North-west) and the result is likely to be an uncomprehending look.

Whit Walks

The history of Whit Walks goes back over 200 years. The first procession can be traced back to Manchester in 1801 when children from Church of England Sunday schools walked from St. Ann's Church to Manchester Cathedral. This started a tradition which continues to this day, though not on the same scale. At a time when many children had to work long hours, six days a week, in appalling conditions, Sunday schools tried to protect them from the prevailing working-class culture of drinking and gambling.

For decades, in towns and cities across the region, thousands of people would take part in Whit Walks and thousands more would line the streets to cheer them on. Each church was led by a brass band, followed by a banner and the church dignitaries. Then came the scholars (as the walkers were called). In the nineteenth century the procession would have provided a rare burst of colour as it passed through streets lined with soot-blackened mills, factories and drab-looking houses. In later years it became the fashion for those walking to have new clothes for the occasion, especially the young girls who wore new white dresses and white shoes and socks. As the Walks became more popular, the meeting-place moved to Albert Square. One commentator of the time, W.H. Shercliff, described the centenary procession of 1901: 'The scene in Albert Square this morning was one of exceptional beauty... the music of a dozen bands proceeded from all corners of the square... There was a free mingling of colours... nearly 30,000 young voices sang the Old Hundredth... The schools marched out of the square... At every point on the route were gathered large crowds of sightseers.'

Whit Week became the 'Great Manchester holiday': a time not only of walks, but of celebrations such as the Whit Fair (also referred to as 'Whitsun Ales') – a time to have fun in what was for many an otherwise drab and gruelling existence. There were race meetings on Kersal Moor every Whitsuntide for 102 years which were visited by thousands; after the races there would be cockfights which would be cheered on by both men and women (who were accommodated in a separate ladies' stand). In addition to the races and the ever-popular cockfights there would be a fairground, Punch & Judy shows, 'freak' shows, music, dancing and drinking. These events went ahead despite fierce opposition from some, who believed that such activities led to 'immoral tendencies'. Men would frequent the races at the weekend and many women would go window-shopping in the town on what came to be known as 'Gaping Saturday'.

Wakes Week

The original 'Wakes' referred to a religious festival when a fête would be held in each town or village to celebrate the life of the saint to whom the local church was dedicated. The name was later adopted and Wakes Weeks became a feature of (mainly) the 'industrial north', a tradition which, in some places, continued into the late twentieth century. All the mines, mills and factories in a particular town would shut down for the same week, giving the workers a well-deserved (though unpaid) holiday and the employers a chance to have maintenance work on their machinery carried out. Previously, the only 'holidays' a worker would have had during the year were Sundays, Christmas Day and Good Friday. After many mass protests, demonstrations, strikes and the rise of trades unions, various Factory Acts were passed and conditions very slowly began to improve. What had once been viewed as unthinkable by employers, i.e. giving the workers a whole week off, was gradually accepted, though it would be many years before paid holidays became the 'norm'. The 1871 Bank Holiday Act introduced the idea of paid holidays and four more days were added to the meagre list of one day for Christmas and one at Easter. A law was passed in 1939 ensuring that all workers had one week's paid annual leave; by the 1950s this had risen to two weeks and in 1980 it was four weeks. In 1830 the average working week in the town's mills and factories was 69 hours, in 1900 the average working week was 54 hours and by the 1980s this had been reduced to 39 hours.

With the advent of the railway, the opportunity arose for working-class people, for the first time ever, to make day-trips to the seaside; Blackpool was the destination of choice for most Mancunians. However, it would still be many decades before most working people could afford to take week-long holidays and so people attended entertainments closer to home.

> There is a merry, happy time,
> To grace withal this simple rhyme:
> There is jovial, joyous hour,
> Of mirth and jollity in store:
> The Wakes! The Wakes!
> The jocund Wakes!

(from 'The Village Festival' by the Droylsden poet Elijah Ridings)

Fairs and other forms of entertainment were held in various places in the Manchester area during Wakes Week. There would have been a variety of activities for both spectators and participants, including the usual sack and running races plus the not-so-usual –

- Bolting of hot porridge,
- Swarming the greasy pole,
- Gurning (pulling funny faces) through a horse-collar,
- Apple dumpling eating,
- Catching a 'soaped' pig,
- Bull-baiting, or occasionally even bear-baiting. The bull-ring was fenced so that

> The timid, the weak, the strong,
> The bold, the brave, the young,
> The old, friend, and stranger,
> Will be secure from danger.

Records exist of an incident of bear-baiting in 1749 which took place in the open street in front of the Old Boar's Head (now the site of the Printworks). The bear was tethered by a short rope from its nose to a stake in the ground and was then be teased by the public prodding it with pigs' bladders on sticks.

- Cockfights

At one time cockfighting was a very fashionable and popular 'sport' enjoyed (?) by all classes of society (including royalty) and Manchester had its fair share of 'cock-pits', one of which stood at the junction of Market Stead Lane (Market Street) and Old Mill Street (roughly where M&S now stands). A 1650 plan of Manchester shows a cock-pit at its centre. Bets were placed and much alcohol was consumed at these events. Thankfully, the days of public cockfights came to an end and an Act of Parliament of 1835 banned the practice, though illegal fights did continue. As late as 1896, the landlord of the 'Black Boy' public house on Tib Street was convicted of staging organised cockfights.

Rush carting

Until the 1400s people were expected to stand during church services. The floors were made of slabs of stone or just packed earth and standing and kneeling on them was cold and uncomfortable, especially in the winter. The practice of laying rushes on the floor was introduced and the cutting and the gathering of the rushes came to be an annual event, developing into a pageant which became known as rush bearing or rush carting; the event was accompanied by music, dancing, street entertainers and drinking. As the rushes had to last a year before being replaced, it's small wonder that the clean, fresh rushes were something to celebrate! Small towns and villages would compete to make the biggest and best cart on which the rushes would be taken to the church. The rush-carts were highly decorated with ribbons, flags, foliage, etc.

> Behold the rush-cart, and the throng
> Of lads and lasses pass along:
> Now, view the nimble morris-dancers,
> The blithe, fantastic, antic prancers,
> Bedeck'd in gaudiest profusion,
> With ribbons in a sweet contusion
> Of brilliant colours, richest dyes,
> Like wings of moths and butterflies.

(from 'The Village Festival' by the Droylsden poet Elijah Ridings)

The tradition of rush-carting continues and in some towns and villages in Lancashire and Cumbria, for example in the Saddleworth area, the festival is still celebrated in style (and pubs).

Knott Mill

Knott Mill fair was an annual event which took place at Easter. Highlights were Wombwell's menagerie, an equestrian show and circus, plus a bazaar and food stalls. The *Manchester Guardian* of 18 April 1846 described the nefarious goings-on, 'Nearly thirty of the itinerant nut vendors were convicted yesterday at the Borough Court for having defective measures, apparently pints and half pints, many of them from a third to nearly half deficient, and having false sides, and some false bottoms!'

May Day

> Happy the age, and harmless were the days
> When every town and village did a May-pole raise.

Beltane was a Celtic festival marking the first day of summer. (Beltane is the Irish word for May.) The Romans celebrated the festival of Floralia in honour of Flora, the goddess of flowers; it began on 28 April and lasted for several days. It was a time to celebrate the long-awaited return of spring. Both these festivals were accompanied by certain festivities and traditions, some of which continued and became incorporated into the later May Day holiday. The festival is still celebrated in many countries across the northern hemisphere.

The maypole is mentioned in historical texts as early as the fourteenth century. There is even mention of one in a will made in Pendleton, Salford in 1373. Some sources suggest that the maypole was first introduced to indicate the meeting place of the festivities, others that it was a symbol of fertility, a welcoming of new growth and new life. Many maypoles were painted with red, white and blue stripes and decorated with foliage, flowers and brightly-coloured ribbons attached to the top of the pole, around which the children, both boys and girls, would dance in intricate moves, winding the ribbons in a pattern around the pole.

In 1652, during the 'reign' of Oliver Cromwell, the maypole, along with many other traditions and celebrations (including Christmas) were banned as 'heathenish vanities' and hefty fines were imposed on towns and villages which failed to destroy their maypole.

On May Day in the centre of Manchester there was a grand procession made up of newly-painted stagecoaches with the coachmen and guards in new uniforms and the horses with shining coats, cockades and nosegays about their heads. Following them were wagons, drays, milk-carts, etc. all decorated with ribbons and flowers. Itinerant musicians and minstrels would travel from town to town singing songs about the 'merry month of May'. The crowning of the May Queen, to represent the Roman goddess Flora, was also an important ritual in the celebrations. Another custom was for the young men to place boughs above the doors of any marriageable young ladies.

Other May Day traditions included girls dressing up in a white curtain and carrying a decorated broomstick to represent a maypole. The boys would paint their faces and wear brightly-coloured girls' clothes; these were known as 'molly dancers'.

The boys and girls would then knock on doors singing 'Molly Dancers kicking up a row, kicking up a row, kicking up a row. Molly Dancers kicking up a row, my fair lady'; they would then hope to receive a few pennies or sweets in return for their singing (or, more likely, in return for their leaving). 'Up the molly dancers!' seems to have been a popular saying in the Manchester area, meaning 'Go upstairs to bed!'

May Day was a secular festival, unrelated to the Church. As such, it was regarded as the day for 'ordinary' working people. For this reason, it became linked to socialism and the Labour Party, a day to highlight the campaign for workers' rights. Even now, the holiday is called 'Labour Day' in many countries.

In 1978, for the first time in over 300 years, the Labour government reinstated May Day as a national holiday in England.

> A 'molly' was once used as a term for an effeminate man and in the eighteenth and nineteenth centuries 'molly houses' were cafés, taverns, etc. where gay men would meet. It was only in 1861 that the death penalty for homosexual acts was abolished and these houses were often raided by the authorities.

> 'Molly House' is a café & bar in Manchester's Village; one side of the building is adorned with this large mural of 'gay icons'.

Pleasure Gardens
Belle Vue
Maharaja

If you visit Manchester Museum it is hard to miss the skeleton of the Indian elephant Maharajah who was one of the star attractions at Belle Vue Zoological Gardens at the end of the nineteenth century. He was bought (along with other exotic animals) at a menagerie auction at Waverley Market in Edinburgh by the owners of Belle Vue at a cost of £680. After causing a bit of a commotion at the station and smashing the railway carriage in which he was due to travel, the elephant, normally a calm and friendly animal, and his keeper Lorenzo Lawrence (erstwhile lion tamer) had to walk all the way to Manchester, a journey of 220 miles which took ten days. At over seven feet tall and with tusks measuring 22 inches, he must have presented quite a spectacle. Whether this was part of a cunning advertising ploy is unknown, but the journey certainly earned Belle Vue lots of free publicity (and money from the crowds he attracted along the way). A great celebration was prepared for their arrival at Belle Vue which was attended by thousands of people (including many from the press) and Maharaja and Lorenzo received a hero's welcome. The adventures of Maharajah were recounted in the book *The Elephant Who Walked to Manchester* by David Barnaby.

Lorenzo 'the Lion Tamer' Lawrence

Photograph: Courtesy of Chetham's Library

A myth soon arose around the journey and it became the subject of several paintings, one of which is 'The Disputed Toll' by Heywood Hardy. The story goes that there was a contretemps between Lorenzo and an officious toll-keeper regarding the toll that should be charged for an elephant. Maharaja, obviously fed up with waiting, lifted the gate off its hinges with his trunk and plodded on his way.

Maharaja in 1880

Maharajah stayed at Belle Vue for ten years, taking young visitors for rides around the Gardens.

> In the zoo's early days, crowd control could sometimes be a problem. Once, six policemen had to be employed when an orangutan, billed as the 'Wild Man of Borneo' caused a sensation, leading to a mad crush by those wanting to see the animal.

&

The 'Bobs'

The Bobs, a roller coaster at Belle Vue, was so named either because it cost a bob (i.e. a shilling/5p) to ride it or, which seems more likely, because it resembled a bobsleigh ride. The Bobs was a wooden structure (a 'woodie' in roller coaster speak!) designed by Fred Church, a Canadian engineer who is apparently a bit of a legend in the roller coaster world, and it was made by Harry Traver. Its ten-car trains reached a height of 80 feet, dropped at an angle of 45 degrees and travelled at a speed of 61 mph. At the time, it held the record as the world's fastest gravity ride. It was bought for £20,000 from Buffalo, USA, and its inaugural ride at Belle Vue took place on 20 May 1929 (Whit Monday and a Bank Holiday) with crowds of people queuing up for the privilege of being the first riders. On the opening day and for the following few years, the price of a ride was 6d (sixpence and only half a bob!) but it was later increased to a shilling. The last ever ride was on 31 October 1970 by which time the price had risen to half-a-crown (2s/6d or 12½p). The 'Bobs' were demolished in 1971; following the demolition, which took four months, little pieces of it were sold off to souvenir hunters.

In 1967 Vance Tutton, a 20-year-old student, set a world record by riding the 'Bobs' continuously – 325 times!

The Bobs dominated the skyline for over 40 years.

A Grand Balloon Ascent

> In addition to these novelties, and with the especial view of gratifying Whitsuntide visitors, arrangements have been made for
> A GRAND BALLOON ASCENT,
> On the evening of Wednesday, 2d June, by Guiseppe Lunardini, the celebrated Spanish aeronaut, from the Cremorne Gardens, London, for whom a new balloon has been constructed expressly for this occasion, and which will be inflated by gas produced on the premises. This ascent, however, will only take place in the event of favourable weather on the previous day and on the day announced, in consequence of the impossibility of filling the balloon during rain. And to meet this uncertainty, it will be seen, from the terms of admission, that no extra charge is made on this occasion. The ascent will take place precisely at seven o'clock.

Even in 1852, promoters weren't averse to a tad of exaggeration! Signor Giuseppe Lunardini was in fact not a 'celebrated Spanish aeronaut', but a James Goulston, owner of an oil-cloth factory in the Old Kent Road, London. It was there that he had made the balloon especially for the ascent at Belle Vue. It was 40 feet high, 33 feet in diameter and held 23,000 cubic feet of gas.

Despite the assertion in the advert, the weather on 21 June was not at all favourable and yet the ascent went ahead as planned. A huge crowd had gathered to witness the spectacle but after only a few minutes the balloon had disappeared into thick black clouds.

Goulston had already made fifty balloon flights but this was his first solo ascent as on this occasion his son had been unable to join him. Apart from the pouring rain, there was also a strong wind which blew the balloon straight towards the Saddleworth area. As he began his descent, Goulston struggled to release the gas and threw out a grapnel (a kind of anchor); this, combined with a sudden gust of wind, jolted the basket causing him to fall out, his feet becoming entangled in the netting. He was carried, upside down, over hills, fields and villages until another gust blew him against the side of a house on which he struck his head. Some villagers eventually managed to catch hold of the ropes and pull down the balloon, but it was too late; 'Signor Giuseppe Lunardini' had made his last balloon flight!

Ice lolly, anyone?

Another unfortunate incident occurred at Belle Vue when someone had the bright idea of making ice lollies with water from the ornamental lake;

water which came directly from the (somewhat polluted) Stockport Canal. They were advertised with the more upmarket-sounding name 'water ices'. Needless to say, the result was a nasty outbreak of food-poisoning!

Escape!

During the Second World War, with the threat of aerial bombing and escaping animals, the zookeepers, accompanied by soldiers, had to patrol the grounds carrying rifles and a machine gun. A list was drawn up of those animals which would present the most danger if let loose – top of the list were 13 lions, 6 tigers, 2 leopards and 1 cheetah.

Belle Vue was not the location of the first Pleasure Gardens in the Manchester area, nor was it the only Zoological Gardens:

Vauxhall Gardens

Robert Tinker was the proprietor of the 'Grape and Compass Coffee House and Tea Gardens' in Collyhurst (still largely rural at the end of the eighteenth century). He recognized the potential of extending his business down to the banks of the (then) pleasant and clean River Irk. He opened the new 23-acre Pleasure Gardens in 1796 and called it Elysian Fields, changing its name again in 1814, this time to Vauxhall Gardens (after the famous Vauxhall Gardens in London). However, it was always known to the locals as 'Tinker's Gardens'. One poster advertised the Gardens as being 'so happily disposed by nature as to form a complete amphitheatre'. The Gardens had an unusual claim to fame which was advertised as 'the greatest curiosity of its kind Nature ever produced in the kingdom'. The 'curiosity' was a cucumber measuring 7 feet and 8 inches long! As if that wasn't sufficient to keep the crowds entertained, there were also other attractions: roundabouts, swings, a bandstand, a café, firework displays, balloon ascents and dancing on the lawns. It was THE place to see and be seen! For over fifty years, the gardens attracted people from all walks of life. However, there were some occasions when the entrance fee was beyond the pocket of many; one such was the celebration of Wellington's 1815 victory over Napoleon. The gardens were decorated with a display of 3,000 coloured lights, accompanied by musical entertainment – all for the cost of 1s 6d (7½p). As the area around Vauxhall Gardens became more industrialised and the Irk became increasingly polluted and noxious, a decline set in; the Gardens, once described as 'th' grandest place i' th' nation' closed in 1852.

Manchester Zoological Gardens

The Manchester Zoological Gardens were opened in May 1838 in Higher Broughton, Salford; they were not intended to be just a visitor attraction, but also an opportunity for a true scientific study of the animals and plants and an educational resource for the town; experts in the field of zoology and horticulture were hired to run the Gardens. Initially, they were popular as people flocked to see the huge variety of exotic animals (including polar bears) on display there. In fact on one occasion there was such a crush outside the lions' enclosure that one unlucky chap was forced against the bars of the cage and had his arm mauled by a lion; the arm later had to be amputated.

However, the entrance fee was one shilling, a price which would have excluded a large proportion of the working population and, unlike Belle Vue, there were few other attractions at the Manchester Gardens. In what very little free time most workers had, they wanted to be entertained rather than educated; as Belle Vue prospered, the Manchester Zoological Gardens plunged into financial difficulties and after only a few years was declared bankrupt. When it closed down in 1842, many of the animals were sold to Belle Vue Zoo.

Pomona Gardens

> Now I'm going to sing of a nice young Lady Fair.
> I met some time ago at the corner of Albert Square.
> She had jet black eyes, I thought I'd like to own her.
> In a voice so sweet she asked of me the way down to Pomona.
>
> We met in Albert Square that night. I'll never forget.
> Her eyes shone like diamonds and the evening it was wet.
> Her hair hung down in curls, that lovely little Donah.
> We rode that night, in great delight: away down to Pomona.
>
> My heart beat like a drum, as I answered her with pride,
> Yes, and if you have no objections, I will take you there beside.
> She blushed and answered yes, then I fell in love all over,
> For a cab I sent and off we went, away down to Pomona.
>
> We had scarce got in the cab; when she asked of me my name.
> Of course I gave it to her and asked of her the same.
> She lifted up her veil, for her face was covered over.
> And upon my life it was my wife I was taking down to Pomona.

She said, 'Do you know me now, for we are not in the dark?'
Of course, I answered, 'Yes, but it was only a lark.'
'Then for your larking pay, forgetting your lonely Donah.
You've had your say and now you'll have to pay
For taking your wife down to Pomona.

(Donah is an old slang word for woman, especially a sweetheart.)

The Gardens, originally called Cornbrook Strawberry Gardens, were opened in 1845 on land leased from the de Trafford family. The name was changed to Pomona (the Roman goddess of fruitful abundance) to reflect the rural nature of the area and the surrounding orchards. In 1868 the Gardens were sold and the new owner, James Reilly, built the grand Royal Pomona Palace in the grounds; it had a 100-foot-tall clock tower, a 100-person orchestra pit, the largest ballroom in Britain and capacity for 20,000 people. The dining hall ceiling was painted à la Sistine Chapel (well, almost) with Roman gods and goddesses including Mars, Venus, Neptune and, of course, Pomona. The Palace was put to many uses, including dancing and political rallies during which it played host to some famous names, including Prime Minister Benjamin Disraeli.

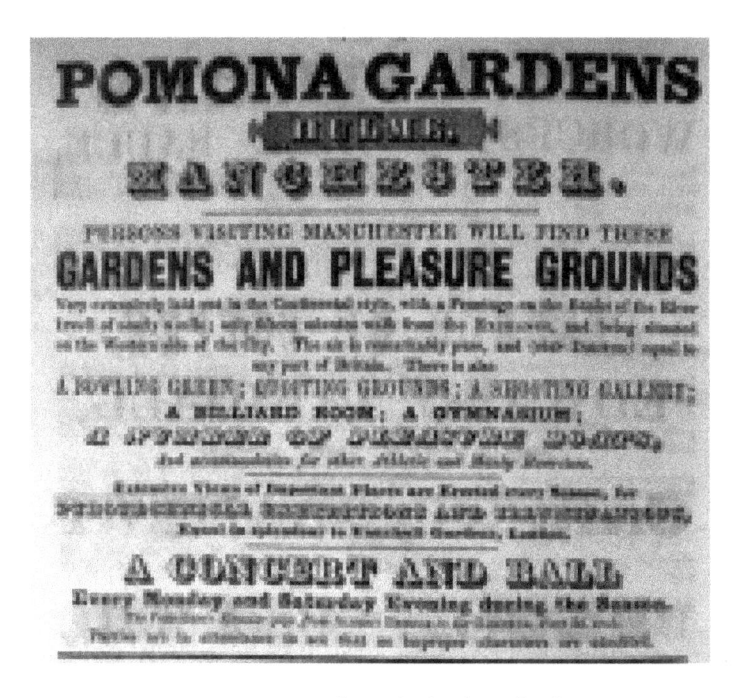

Pomona Gardens in its heyday!

The grounds were used for a variety of shows – dogs, horses, chariot races and circuses, plus the usual entertainments – fairground rides, a maze, shooting gallery, bowling green, and Remington Scott's 'Magic Bridge – the greatest scientific wonder of the world'. It was also host to an 'Ethnological Show' (in other words, a 'human zoo') which featured natives of Africa, Ceylon (and other outposts of the British Empire) in their national dress, performing traditional dances, singing and charming snakes.

People would travel to the Gardens by boat from the landing stage at Cathedral steps. Considering the toxic quality of the River Irwell, surely this was an increasing health hazard with every passing year!

The area around Pomona Gardens gradually became more industrialised and a decline set in. Then in 1887 the nearby Roberts and Dale's Chemical Works exploded, taking parts of the Gardens and Palace with it. There were two explosions, the first of which was fairly small but resulted in a fire. One of the employees, James Martin, was killed; as he attempted to put out the fire a second, this time massive, explosion occurred. The Gardens finally closed in 1888 and the land was used to create the Pomona Docks on the Manchester Ship Canal.

Pomona Palace – past its heyday!

The Royal Botanical Gardens

Old Trafford was at one time known for something other than football and cricket. It was also home to the magnificent Botanical Gardens which were opened in 1831. This site was reputed to have been chosen when one of the most eminent and distinguished scientists of the day, the chemist John Dalton, was asked to find the best location for the Gardens. Which great scientific methods did this genius use? Apparently he travelled around the suburbs of Manchester and wiped leaves with his white handkerchief to look for signs of smoke and dirt. Apparently Old Trafford was the place with the cleanest leaves.

The Gardens were later the site of the 1857 Art Treasures Exhibition and in 1887 the Royal Golden Jubilee Exhibition was also held there.

The very elaborate Palm House in Manchester's Royal Botanical Gardens

Towards the end of the century the Gardens got into financial difficulties as the wealthier middle-class moved out of the area into the leafy villages of Cheshire. The site was finally sold in 1907 and the land became home to White City Amusement Park. Sadly, the only reminder of the area's former glory is the impressive gateway.

The Royal Jubilee Exhibition

This Exhibition was held in 1887 to celebrate the Golden Jubilee of Queen Victoria. The event lasted for 166 days and received around 4½ million visitors in a huge purpose-built exhibition hall constructed of iron and glass; it was set on an area of forty-five acres and was designed by Maxwell and Tuke (who also designed Blackpool Tower). The Exhibition was dedicated to the progress made in art, science and industry during Victoria's reign. It included a 32-foot model of the Manchester Ship Canal, a project which began the day after the Exhibition closed.

There was also a full-scale reconstruction of streets and buildings from Manchester and Salford's past which received rave reviews. One observer enthused, 'It is as splendid a display as any the world has ever seen.' In the *Observer*, one reporter wrote, 'Old Manchester ... is carried out upon so large a scale and to such perfection that when passing through, it is difficult to believe we are living in the nineteenth century.'

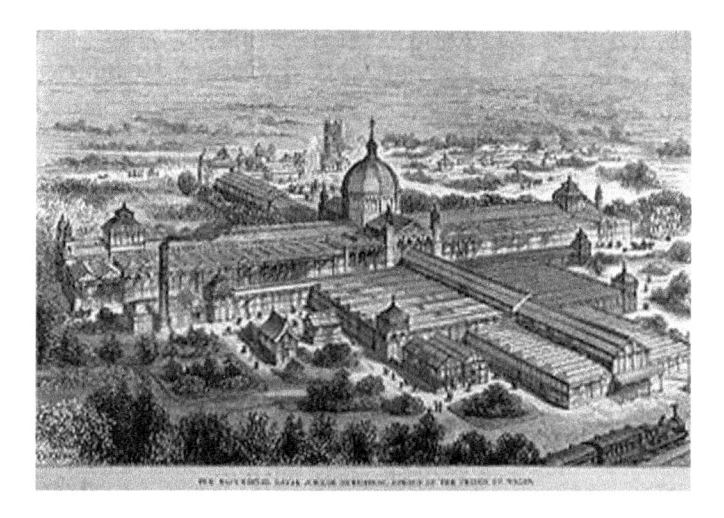

The dome was almost the same size as that of St. Paul's Cathedral.

Actors were used to set the scene of times past in Manchester and Salford.

Chapter 14

Creative Manchester

Literature

Manchester has a long tradition of producing novelists, poets and dramatists. It also has a long history of publishing. The first book published in Manchester was *Jackson's Mathematical Lectures* in 1719.

John Byrom (1692–1763)

John Byrom was born at 1, The Shambles, now the Old Wellington Inn, which at that time was a prosperous draper's business owned by his father. Byrom was a religious man and a scholar; he was renowned as a writer, poet and inventor of a new system of shorthand. He is perhaps best remembered for the hymn 'Christians Awake' which he wrote for his daughter Dolly as a Christmas present.

He also expressed opinions on political matters of the day. The inhabitants of Manchester were becoming increasingly indignant over the monopoly which the mill owners exerted; people in the town were still compelled to use (for a charge) only the mills owned by the Lords of the Manor. John Byrom penned,

> Bone and Skin two millers thin,
> Would starve the town or near it;
> But be it known to Skin and Bone
> That Flesh and Blood can't bear it.

He is maybe less known for writing an epigram in which two characters make their 'literary debut', long before appearing in Lewis Carroll's *Through the Looking Glass and What Alice Found There*. Byrom was referring to the frequent disputes between the two composers Handel and Bononcini when he wrote,

> Some say, compar'd to Bononcini
> That Mynheer Handel's but a Ninny
> Others aver, that he to Handel
> Is scarcely fit to hold a Candle
> Strange all this Difference should be
> 'Twixt Tweedle-dum and Tweedle-dee!

The names came to describe, not in a flattering way, two people who look and act in an identical way, but continually fight.

John Byrom's son, Edward, built St. John's Church (off Deansgate) in his father's memory. It stood on the site now occupied by St. John's Gardens on Byrom Street.

John Byrom

> Another member of the illustrious Byrom family was Margaret Byrom who achieved notoriety when, in 1594, she was pronounced to be suffering from demoniacal possession. Edmund Hartley, a travelling 'magician' was accused of 'breathing the devil' into her and several others. He was arrested and, being unable to recite the Lord's Prayer, was tried and convicted of witchcraft; he was then hanged.
>
> ****
>
> The last of the Byroms died in 1870. Eleanora Atherton was a well-known figure in Manchester where her old servants would carry her around town in a sedan chair.

Peter Mark Roget (1779–1869)

Peter Mark Roget was born in London; his father was a Swiss clergyman who had died when his son was just 4 years old. Roget had a turbulent early life; in addition to his father's early death, there was a strain of mental instability in his maternal family and both his mother and his sister spent time in mental institutions. His uncle committed suicide by slashing his throat in Roget's presence, dying in his nephew's arms. Little wonder then that he suffered from depression for most of his life and already by the age of 8 he had begun compiling lists as a means of establishing some kind of order in his chaotic life. List-making was to be a life-long obsession and culminated in *Roget's Thesaurus of English Words & Phrases* which was first published in 1852 and has remained in print ever since.

However, there was much more to Roget than his Thesaurus. He studied Medicine at Edinburgh University, graduating as a doctor when he was just 19. He then worked as a tutor to two sons of a wealthy Manchester merchant. In 1805 he was appointed physician at Manchester Infirmary, becoming the co-founder of the town's Medical School. He also invented a slide rule and propounded the theory of the persistence of vision (a concept which eventually led to moving pictures).

He was the first secretary of the Portico Library where he began compiling his Thesaurus and vice-president of the Manchester Lit. & Phil. Society.

Thomas de Quincey (1785-1859)

Thomas Quincy was born in Manchester, the son of a wealthy linen merchant; the family later added the aristocratic 'de' to their name. He attended Manchester Grammar School from 1800; he described his time there as 'miserable' and ran away to London after only eighteen months. Here he was homeless and practically penniless for a time before being reconciled to his family.

He then went to Oxford University but made frequent trips to London where, initially for pain relief, he began taking opium. He wrote, 'Here was the secret of happiness, about which philosophers had disputed for so many ages, at once discovered: happiness might now be bought for a penny, and carried in the waistcoat pocket.' He inevitably drifted into addiction; from taking opium once every few weeks, it became every Saturday night, then daily, then almost hourly. He married, had eight children and turned to journalism in order to support them.

He is best remembered for his book *Confessions of an Opium Eater*.

Charles Swain (1801–74)

Born on Every Street in Ancoats to an English father and French mother the poet Charles Swain remained in the Manchester area all his life; he was nicknamed the 'Manchester Poet' and was a regular member of the 'Sun Inn' group. He was also the honorary president of the Manchester Royal Institution. Though now largely unknown, even in his home city, Swain's friend Robert Southey, who was Poet Laureate for thirty years, wrote, 'If ever man were born to be a poet he was; and if Manchester is not proud of him yet, the time will certainly come when it will be so.'

He is thought to have written his poem 'Mortality' about the old prison building on Hunt's Bank:

> The house is old, the house is cold,
> And on the roof is snow;
> And in and out and round about
> The bitter night-winds blow:
> The bitter night-winds howl and blow —
> And darkness thickens deep, —
> And oh, the minutes creep as slow
> As though they were asleep!

Old visions haunt the creaking floors —
Old sorrows sit and wail; —
While still the night-winds out of doors
Like burly bailiffs rail!
Old visions haunt the floors above:
The walls with wrinkles frown;
And people say, who pass that way,
'Twere well the house were down.

William Harrison Ainsworth (1805-82)

William Harrison Ainsworth was born in King Street, Manchester, at that time an affluent, highly-desirable residential street of three-storey Georgian houses. His father, Thomas Ainsworth, was an eminent lawyer, and his mother, Ann Harrison, was the daughter of a minister at the Cross Street Chapel. Ainsworth's birthplace later became the site of the York Hotel.

At the age of 12, having previously been tutored at home, Ainsworth began attending Manchester Grammar School. He was a voracious reader and writer from an early age; he and his brother created a theatre in the basement of their home where they would act out William's plays and stories. His first published writing appeared in 1821 when he was just 16 (initially under the name of Thomas Hall). Although Ainsworth wanted to pursue a literary career, he was expected to follow in his father's footsteps and become a lawyer. He complied, but continued to spend much of his time reading and writing. When his father died in 1824, William was left to carry on the family law firm; he moved to London to continue his studies and became a qualified solicitor.

Ainsworth's first major novel was *Rookwood* which featured the highwayman Dick Turpin as its central character. Following the success of his book, he gave up the law to become a full-time writer. In addition to writing, he spent his time travelling and socialising with the literary elite of the day, including Thackeray and Dickens. He continued to write many more historical novels, including *Guy Fawkes* and *The Manchester Rebels*.

After his death, the works (forty novels) of this prolific writer became largely forgotten. Although he had left his Manchester home long ago, many of his stories were set in and around Lancashire. William Harrison Ainsworth's most remembered and, according to many critics, best novel is *The Lancashire Witches* – a story about the witches of Pendle.

Elizabeth Gaskell (1810–65)

Elizabeth Cleghorn Gaskell (née Stevenson) was the daughter of a Manchester clergyman. She was born in London, but following the death of her mother a year later she was sent to Knutsford to be brought up by an aunt. Knutsford was the setting of perhaps her most well-known novel *Cranford*.

In 1832 she married William Gaskell, a Unitarian minister at the Cross Street Chapel. They had six children, four of whom survived. It was after the death of her only son, William, from scarlet fever that she began writing. Her first novel *Mary Barton* had the sub-title *A Tale of Manchester Life*. The book details the horrendous living and working conditions of many of the city's inhabitants and the greed and exploitation of many of their 'masters'. Both the Gaskells were active in the cause of social and political reform and this is often reflected in her novels.

Creative Manchester 181

The Gaskells, together with their four daughters, lived at 42, Plymouth Grove where they played host to many illustrious visitors including Charles Dickens, Charlotte Brontë and Charles Hallé. Elizabeth died in 1865 but her family continued to live there until 1913.

After many years of falling into decay, the former Gaskell house, a stunning Victorian villa, has been beautifully restored.

Elizabeth Gaskell died from a heart attack while writing the final chapter of *Wives and Daughters*; she was 55. She is considered to be one of the most important authors of the Victorian era.

> Charles Dickens paid many visits to Manchester and was a great admirer of the city. He was fascinated by the increasing industrialisation he saw and the effect it was having on society. One of his sisters lived in Ardwick where he would often stay on his frequent trips to the city. He used the Grant brothers (William & Daniel) who were wool and linen merchants of 3, Cannon Street as models for the Cheeryble brothers in *Nicholas Nickleby*.
>
> His sister Fanny married Henry Burnett of Rusholme; their son Harry is thought to have been the model for Tiny Tim. Dickens once read *A Christmas Carol* at the Free Trade Hall.

&

Geraldine Endsor Jewsbury (1812–80)

> Born into a wealthy middle-class family, Geraldine Jewsbury was a (now largely forgotten) Victorian novelist. She moved to Manchester when she was 6 and remained in the town for many years. Her works were fairly controversial at the time, exploring issues such as religious scepticism and the role of women in society, questioning the role of wife and mother as the only acceptable option for a middle-class woman. She outraged society by wearing men's clothes, smoking and swearing in public.

Charlotte Brontë (1816-55)

In August 1846, Patrick Brontë and his daughter Charlotte travelled from their parsonage home in the village of Haworth to Manchester in order to consult an eye specialist. Patrick had cataracts and his eyesight was rapidly deteriorating; the renowned oculist William Wilson subsequently performed a successful operation (which lasted fifteen minutes and was witnessed by Charlotte). However, Patrick and Charlotte had to remain in Manchester for a month while Patrick convalesced. During this time they boarded in a house just outside town; Charlotte's friend and biographer Elizabeth Gaskell later wrote about the Brontës' stay in Manchester and described their lodgings 'in those grey, weary, uniform streets... of small, monotonous-looking houses'.

It was here that Charlotte learned that her first book *The Professor* had been rejected. Undaunted, she began to write what was to become one of the greatest novels in the English language: *Jane Eyre*.

> William James Wilson was a surgeon at the Infirmary (then located in modern-day Piccadilly). He also had a private practice at 72, Mosley Street. In 1814 he helped to found the 'Manchester Institution for curing the Diseases of the Eye'.

> This plaque is on the outside of the Salutation Hotel on Boundary Street, which stands opposite the site of the (long-since demolished) house where Patrick and Charlotte Brontë stayed and where *Jane Eyre* was born. *Jane Eyre* was published the following year to great acclaim and remains Charlotte Brontë's most popular novel.

CHARLOTTE BRONTË (1816-1855)

In 1846 The Revd. Patrick Brontë came to Manchester for a cataract operation accompanied by his daughter Charlotte. They took lodgings at 59 Boundary Street West (formerly known as 83 Mount Pleasant). It was here that Charlotte began to write her first successful novel *Jane Eyre*.

2005

Mrs. G. Linnaeus Banks (1821–97)

> Isabella Varley was born at 10, Oldham Street where her father James ran his pharmacy. James and his wife Amelia were both active in politics, James being an alderman and a magistrate. Isabella took a great interest in the history of her town and began writing stories and poems at an early age.
>
> She married the journalist and lecturer George Linnaeus Banks in 1846. She wrote many novels and was a member of the group of writers and poets which met at the Sun Inn (Poets' Corner). She was also a campaigner for women's rights and an active supporter of the Anti-Corn Law League.

Creative Manchester 185

In 1876, what is almost certainly the most famous novel about life in nineteenth century Manchester and the work for which she is remembered, *The Manchester Man*, was published. It is the rags-to-riches story of its principal character, Jabez Clegg and covers the social and political issues of the day such as the Peterloo Massacre and the Corn Law riots. She also introduces real characters into the story, for example, Joshua Brookes.

> Mutability is the epitaph of worlds
> Change alone is changeless
> People drop out of the history of a life as of a land
> though their work or their influence remains
>
> The Manchester Man
>
> G Linnaeus Banks 1876

A quotation from *The Manchester Man* is the epitaph on Tony Wilson's grave in Southern Cemetery.

&

Frances Hodgson Burnett (1849–1925)

Frances Eliza Hodgson was born in 1849 in the Cheetham Hill district of Manchester, the middle of five children. Her father owned an ironmongery business in Deansgate and the family lived comfortably, employing several servants. However, their happy comfortable life was short-lived and came to an abrupt end when her father died of a stroke in 1852. While her mother took over the running of the business, Frances and her siblings were looked after by their grandmother. It was during this time that Frances developed a life-long love of books as she began reading and acting out stories. The family made several moves over the next few years, one of which took them to the outskirts of Salford, close to one of the poorest and most deprived areas of the city. The fortunes of the family declined even more during the American Civil War: the supply of cotton, the lifeblood of Manchester, began to dry up and her mother was forced to sell the ironmongery business.

In 1865, when Frances was 16, she and her family emigrated to America to join her mother's brother in Tennessee. Frances was determined to escape what she considered to be her life of poverty and so she began writing and selling short stories to magazines as a way to support her family. Within a few years she had made enough money to move them to a bigger and better house. In 1870 her mother died and two years later Frances married Swan Burnett, a medical doctor. They later moved to Washington DC with their two young sons and in 1877 Frances's first book *That Lass o' Lowries* (set in a Lancashire mining town) was published. The novel was well received, but it was *Little Lord Fauntleroy*, published in 1886, which made her reputation as a children's author (although she also wrote many novels for adults). It became a best-seller in America and in Britain and was translated into twelve languages. When her two sons Lionel and Vivian were young, Frances would make their clothes herself – velvet suits with lace collars. She also let their hair grow long and would curl it every day. (Apparently she had wanted a daughter.) The central character of the story, Cedric, was based on her youngest son Vivian.

Despite suffering from bouts of depression (one of which followed the death of her son Lionel from consumption in 1890), Frances enjoyed socialising and had an extravagant lifestyle. She divided her time between the USA and England.

> Burnett lived at Great Maytham Hall in Kent for several years; it had various walled gardens, including a rose garden and it was here that she had the idea for one of her most popular stories, *The Secret Garden,* published in 1911. However, part of this book was actually written in Buile Hill Park in Salford during one of her visits to the city.

In 1898 she divorced Swan Burnett to live with and later marry Stephen Townsend (a would-be actor).

> **To Quote:**
>
> The *Washington Post* attributed the divorce to her **'advanced ideas regarding the duties of a wife and the rights of women'.**

It was an unhappy and ill-conceived marriage which lasted barely two years. In 1907 she returned permanently to the USA, eventually settling in Long Island where she died in 1924.

Harold Brighouse (1882-1958)

Harold Brighouse was born in Eccles; his father was manager of a cotton-spinning business and his mother a headmistress. On leaving Manchester Grammar School, Brighouse worked in a shipping merchant's office before becoming a full-time author, playwright and theatre critic.

One of his earliest works, *The Doorway*, was a one-act play which was performed in 1909 at Annie Horniman's Gaiety Theatre on Peter Street. In the First World War he worked in the Air Military Intelligence Service and it was during this time that he wrote his most famous and enduring play *Hobson's Choice – A Lancashire Comedy*. Owing to the success of this play, Brighouse later described himself as a 'one-play man', though he was in fact anything but. He was a prolific writer of novels, plays and newspaper articles; he continued to contribute to the *Manchester Guardian* until 1949.

Brighouse was one of the first playwrights to portray the harsh reality of working-class life in an industrial city. In the early twentieth century he was a prominent member of what became known as the 'Manchester School of Dramatists', together with Stanley Houghton and Allan Monkhouse.

(Brighouse also adapted Houghton's play *Hindle Wakes* into a novel.) Other plays by Harold Brighouse include *Zack*, *The Game* (about football, what else?) and *The Northerners*.

> **Hobson's Choice** is a comic story set in a cobbler's/boot & shoe shop in a grimy, industrial Salford in the 1880s. The play has a familiar theme; three daughters - two are frivolous and selfish, the other sensible and hard-working. Unlike the finale in *King Lear*, *Hobson's Choice* has more of a *Cinderella*, happy-ever-after ending.

> In 1953 *Hobson's Choice* was made into a classic film starring Charles Laughton, Brenda De Banzie and John Mills.

> **Hobson's choice** &
>
> The expression 'Hobson's choice', meaning no choice at all, was coined at the turn of the seventeenth century. Thomas Hobson ran a livery business in Cambridge hiring out horses, mainly to students from the university. He wouldn't allow the customer to choose his own horse; Hobson would choose the horse himself, always the one nearest the stable door. So it was a case of 'this horse or none'.

(Robert) Howard Spring (1889-1965)

Born in Cardiff, Howard Spring was the son of an Irish odd-job gardener. After his father's death the young Howard and his eight siblings, all living in a tiny two-bedroomed house, had to earn money by selling firewood and rhubarb. Their mother would make ends meet by taking in washing and cleaning the neighbours' doorsteps. Howard worked in a greengrocer's shop on Saturdays (a sixteen-hour day) and when he reached the age of 12 he had to leave school and take a job as a butcher's boy. However, he had his sights set on higher things and became a messenger on the *South Wales Daily News*. He wanted to be a reporter and spent his spare time learning shorthand and studying at night school; he gradually worked his way up from being a messenger to a journalist on the paper. In 1915 he joined the *Manchester Guardian* where he remained until 1931 working as reporter, theatre critic and book reviewer (apart from a stint working for Military Intelligence during the First World War). During his time in Manchester he and his wife lived in a house in Didsbury, now adorned with a commemorative blue plaque. In 1931 he was offered and accepted a job on a London newspaper and shortly afterwards, at the age of forty-something, he began to write novels.

His first novel *Shabby Tiger* and its sequel *Rachel Rosing* were moderately successful, but when *My Son, My Son!* was published in 1938, it was both a critical and a financial success. When Howard Spring learned that his book had reached the best-seller list, he packed his bag, picked up his pen and left his office for good.

> For around three decades Howard Spring remained on best-seller lists and his novels were hugely popular both in the UK and abroad. He was a very disciplined author; he wrote 1,000 words a morning, five days a week and all with a 'twopenny pen' –
> 'no gimmicky things like typewriters or tape recorders for me'

Howard Spring died in 1965. His wife donated the manuscripts of his novels to the John Rylands Library.

Louis Golding (1895–1958)

Though now largely forgotten, Louis Golding was a prolific and popular writer in his day; not only a novelist, he was also a poet, journalist and Hollywood screenwriter. He was born to poor Ukrainian-Jewish refugee parents; his father was a struggling teacher of Hebrew. The family lived on Sycamore Street in the deprived working-class area of Hightown and Yiddish was the language spoken at home. Golding won a scholarship to Manchester Grammar School and then studied Classics at Oxford University. His studies were interrupted by the outbreak of the First World War. Declared unfit for active service, Golding spent much of the war in Salonika, volunteering in the YMCA.

It was during his time at Oxford that his first novel *Forward from Babylon* was published.

Golding's Manchester upbringing had a great influence on his work. Many of his novels are set in the fictional city of Doomington (based on Manchester). His most successful novel was *Magnolia Street*, published in 1932 and an immediate best-seller; it sold over 1,000,000 copies and was translated into twenty-seven languages. Partly autobiographical, the story is based on the Hightown area of Manchester in the early part of the twentieth century. *Magnolia Street* is the story of a street divided, Gentiles living on one side of the street and Jews on the other (as was the case on Sycamore Street). The novel explores the themes of conflict and assimilation.

Dodie Smith (1896-1990)

Dorothy 'Dodie' Gladys Smith was born in Whitefield, Bury. When she was almost 2 years old, her father died and she and her mother went to live at her grandparents' house on Stretford Road in Old Trafford; this is where she remained until 1910 when her mother remarried and they moved to London.

She later went on to study at RADA (the Royal Academy of Dramatic Arts) and although she landed some minor roles in touring theatre companies, it was difficult to find steady employment. She went to work at Heal & Sons furniture store where she became a toy buyer (and, allegedly, the mistress of the chairman, Ambrose Heal). It was also where she met her future husband.

Dodie Smith had been writing stories and plays since the age of 10, but it was not until 1931 that she found success as a writer with her play *Autumn Crocus* (written under the pseudonym C.L. Anthony). This was followed by several more well-received plays.

With war brewing in Europe, she and her husband, Alec Macbeth Beesley, moved to America; he was a conscientious objector and felt that staying in the UK would be problematic. Dodie Smith was homesick for England and it was at that time that she began to write one of her most popular novels, *I Capture the Castle*.

> & Alec Macbeth Beesley was the son of Lawrence Beesley, a survivor of the *Titanic* and author of *The Loss of the SS Titanic,* which was published just nine weeks after the disaster.

Dodie Smith's best-known work is, of course, *The One Hundred and One Dalmatians* which began as a story in a magazine with the title *The Great Dog Robbery*. She later reworked the story into a novel which was adapted into an animated film by Walt Disney. 'Pongo', one of the main characters in the novel was named after her own pet Dalmatian. (She had nine of them.) She got the idea for the story when a friend remarked, 'Those dogs would make a lovely fur coat!' She also wrote a sequel to the story – *The Starlight Barking* – which was published in 1967.

> *101 Dalmations* featured in the top 100 best-loved novels of all time, voted for in the BBC's *The Big Read* in 2003. It was also made into a film the same year.

The first part of Dodie Smith's autobiography is titled *Look Back With Love: a Manchester Childhood* and was published in 1974.

Anthony Burgess (1917–1993)

John Anthony Burgess Wilson was born in Harpurhey; his father was a bookkeeper and part-time pianist and his mother a dancer and musician. He had a tragic beginning to his life: as a toddler he was found in bed with his mother and sister lying beside him – both of them were dead, victims of Spanish flu.

Burgess studied English at Manchester University before spending six years as a soldier during the Second World War. After the war he became an education officer in Malaya and Brunei. In 1959 he was diagnosed with a terminal illness and so returned to Britain. He turned to writing in order to leave some financial security for his wife. Fortunately, he had been misdiagnosed; he went on to write more than thirty books, the most famous of which is *A Clockwork Orange* made famous by the Stanley Kubrick film of 1971.

Burgess lived in Monaco until his death in 1993.

Maurice Procter (1906–73)

Maurice Procter was born in 1906. After serving as a policeman for many years, he turned his hand to writing. His most famous works were a series of crime novels featuring DCI Harry Martineau of the Granchester City Police (a fictional 1950s Manchester). *Hell is a City* is probably the best-known book in the series. In 1959 it was made into a film which has since become something of a cult 'film noir'. Filmed in and around Manchester (in black & white) it is a glimpse of a greyer, post-industrial city, now all but vanished. The world premiere of *Hell is a City* was held in 1960 at Ardwick Apollo, then a cinema.

Visual Art

The Art Treasures Exhibition

The 'Exhibition of the Art Treasures of the United Kingdom' was opened by Prince Albert on 5 May, 1857 just four years after Manchester was given city status. It lasted for 142 days and was visited by over 1,330,000 people. This was around four times the population of Manchester at that time and a new railway station was built near the venue to cope with the number of visitors. (The exhibition made a profit of just over £300 while the railway company made around £50,000.) It showed the world that there was more to Manchester than dark, satanic mills; to this day it remains one of the world's largest art exhibitions ever staged.

A temporary structure of iron and glass, inspired by Crystal Palace, was erected on a site adjacent to Manchester Botanical Gardens in Old Trafford on land owned by Sir Humphrey de Trafford. Though temporary, the cost of constructing the building was £25,000 (equivalent to over £40 million today). Over the entrance to the exhibition was a quote from John Keats – 'A thing of beauty is a joy for ever' and above the exit was a quotation from Alexander Pope – 'To wake the soul by tender strokes of art'. In addition to the grand exhibition room there were two refreshment rooms – first and second class – and a royal reception room.

The exhibition boasted 16,000 works of art, arranged chronologically to chart the history of art through the ages. Most items were on loan from private collectors, including many works from the Royal Collection. However, the Duke of Devonshire replied to a request for a contribution with, 'What in the world do you want with art in Manchester? Why can't you stick to your cotton spinning?' Despite this condescending reply, the Exhibition had its fair share of 'celebrity' visitors – Queen Victoria, Florence Nightingale and Charles Dickens, to name but a few. Music was provided by Charles Hallé and his orchestra.

One of the main attractions was an unfinished work which had only recently been attributed to Michelangelo; the painting, 'The Virgin and Child with Saint John and Angels' from c.1497, has since been known as 'The Manchester Madonna' and hangs in the National Gallery in London. It returned to Manchester, briefly, for the Exhibition's 150th anniversary celebration in 2007.

The Manchester Exhibition left a lasting legacy; it heralded the beginning of public art, something that could be accessible to everyone. Civic art galleries began to appear in all major towns and cities across the country.

The temporary Exhibition Hall

City Art Gallery

The Grade I listed building which is now home to the City Art Gallery was erected in 1824 and designed by Charles Barry (architect of the Houses of Parliament). It was originally built as the Royal Manchester Institution which was intended to promote literature, science and the arts. Following the success of the Art Treasures Exhibition, the building was bought by Manchester Corporation in 1882.

In the early twentieth century plans were afoot to build a new gallery in Piccadilly, on the site of the old hospital, but owing to lack of funds following the Second World War, the plans were scrapped.

The Gallery is particularly noted for its collection of Pre-Raphaelite paintings.

Lawrence Stephen Lowry (1887–1976)

L.S. Lowry was born in Rusholme, the son of an estate agent. He studied at the Manchester School of Art (where he came under the tutelage of Adolphe

Valette) and later at the Salford Royal Technical College. Lowry was a great admirer of Valette, who demonstrated how the urban landscape could be used as a subject for art. Lowry called him 'a real teacher … a dedicated teacher' and said, 'I cannot over-estimate the effect on me of the coming into this drab city of Adolphe Valette, full of French impressionists, aware of everything that was going on in Paris.'

Having been brought up in leafy Victoria Park, it came as quite a shock to Lowry when he moved to Pendlebury and was surrounded by factories and mills. Initially he hated his new surroundings, but gradually came to see a kind of beauty in them. He worked as a rent collector and spent his days wandering the streets of a changing post-industrial city.

Lowry didn't find fame and (relative) fortune until he was in his 50s; his first London exhibition was held in 1939. Following the death of his mother, he led a very private, lonely life but in his later years he became something of a 'celebrity'. He was named Manchester's 'Man of the Year' in 1966, but turned down more national honours than anybody else, including an OBE, a CBE and a knighthood.

He died, aged 88, just months before a record-breaking exhibition of his work was staged at the Royal Academy in London. He left over 3,000 paintings and drawings; he had captured the industrial north like no other and had chronicled a vanishing world.

Lowry can be seen propping up the bar of 'Sam's Chop House' on King Street, one of his favourite watering-holes.

Adolphe Valette (1876–1942)

Valette was a French Impressionist painter, but his most famous works are urban scenes of a smoggy, but atmospheric industrial Manchester. These works are in stark contrast to his bright and colourful landscapes of rural France.

Born in St. Etienne, Pierre Adolphe Valette arrived in England in 1904 to continue his studies in London. A year later he arrived in Manchester where he found work designing greetings cards and calendars for a printing company. He attended evening classes at Manchester School of Art and in 1907 joined the staff as a teacher. It was there that he became tutor to the young L.S. Lowry.

Valette returned to France in 1928 and died in 1942.

Emmanuel Levy (1900–86)

Another of Valette's pupils, Emmanuel Levy was born in Manchester to Russian-Jewish émigrés and trained with Lowry at the Manchester School of Art. His work reflects both his northern and his Jewish heritage. He married a refugee from Berlin and helped her parents flee from Nazi Germany.

Arthur Delaney (1927–87)

Arthur McEvoy Delaney was born in Manchester, the son of a music hall artiste and (allegedly) the comedian Frank Randle. After leaving school at the age of 13 and spending thirty years as a textile designer, Arthur Delaney became famous for his paintings depicting Manchester and Salford.

John Cassidy (1860–1939)

A prolific sculptor, John Cassidy was born in County Meath, Ireland. He attended the Manchester School of Art before continuing his studies abroad. He then returned to and spent the rest of his life in Manchester, working from his studio in Plymouth Grove. Although his name is little known, his work is to be seen in various locations in the city (and in other cities around the country). His Manchester work includes a bronze bust of Charles Hallé in the foyer of the Bridgewater Hall, marble statues of John and Enriqueta Rylands in 'their' library and a bronze statue of Edward VII in Whitworth Park. Perhaps his most celebrated work is the bronze statue 'Adrift' (1907) which once adorned Piccadilly Gardens but now stands next to Central Library. Cassidy wrote that it represented 'humanity adrift on the sea of life'.

Musical Manchester

The Gentlemen's Concert Hall

In the 1750s, *Manchester Magazine* made mention of 'quarterly subscription concerts' which were probably held in the Exchange building. The Concert Rooms were built in 1775 for the Gentlemen's Concert Club and were situated at the corner of York Street and what is now Concert Lane. It was the home of classical music until the Gentlemen's Concert Hall was erected at the junction of Peter Street and Lower Mosley Street in 1830. The new Hall played host to numerous musical greats including Chopin, Liszt, Paganini and Mendelssohn. It was also where Charles Hallé began his Manchester career. Ladies were only allowed to attend concerts as guests of gentlemen who were members. Next door was another concert hall called the Casino, later the People's Concert Hall which offered a more varied programme. Both were sold to the Midland Railway Company in 1897 and the land became the site of the Midland Hotel.

The Hallé Orchestra

Among the many famous names at the Art Treasures Exhibition in 1857 was the German pianist and conductor, Karl (later anglicised to Charles) Hallé. Hallé had studied in Germany and then in Paris where he was living when the revolution of 1848 broke out forcing him to leave France; initially he went to London and then to Manchester. Hallé formed a sixty-member orchestra to perform at the Exhibition and the concerts were such a success that Hallé decided to form a permanent orchestra.

He asked two brothers, at the time working in London at Broadwood Pianomakers, to join him. The brothers were James and Henry Forsyth. Hallé employed them to look after the concert pianos and also to manage the business affairs of the orchestra. The Hallé Orchestra gave its first performance in 1858, thus becoming the first professional orchestra in the UK. It also lays claim to being the fourth oldest orchestra in the world. After Hallé's sudden death in 1895, James Forsyth, along with two other friends of Hallé, helped to secure the future of the orchestra by guaranteeing the next four concert seasons against loss.

The home of the Hallé Orchestra was the Free Trade Hall. At the onset of the Second World War the building was first requisitioned and then bombed during the Blitz. While the Hall was out of action, the orchestra played at various venues including the Albert Hall on Peter Street and the King's Hall at Belle Vue. In June 1996 the Hallé moved to the Bridgewater Hall.

> Charles Hallé (though not the accent) is remembered by having a 'mall' in the Arndale Centre named after him.

> **Barbirolli. Sir John (1899-1970)**
>
> Giovanni Battista Barbirolli was one of the Hallé's most famous conductors and the one who is credited with turning it into a world-class orchestra. He was born in London in 1899, the son of a Venetian violinist father and a French mother. Although slightly deaf in one ear, he played the cello and by the age of 10, was considered a prodigy.
>
> Whilst conducting the New York Philharmonic in 1943, he was offered the post of principal conductor of the Hallé Orchestra with an annual salary of £3,750. He accepted and remained with the Hallé for the rest of his life.

Manchester has long been at the forefront of popular music and its musicians include many famous names from the 50s, 60s and 70s, such as Freddie (Garrity) & the Dreamers, Herman's Hermits, Davy Jones (The Monkees), The Hollies, The Bee Gees, Elkie Brooks and 10cc.

The Ritz

When completed in 1928, this art deco building was a state-of-the-art dance hall (Grade II listed in 1994) with a revolving stage and a super-springy dance floor. It later became a live music venue playing host to many musical greats, including The Beatles, Frank Sinatra and later The Smiths.

> The first edition of *Top of the Pops* was broadcast, live, from Dickenson Road Studios (an old church hall) in Rusholme, Manchester on New Year's Day 1964 with 'miming' guests including the Hollies and the Rolling Stones. The show ended with the week's Number One - *I Wanna Hold Your Hand* by the Beatles. The show was commissioned for just six episodes, but in fact more than 2,000 have been made.

Anthony Wilson (1950–2007)

> Factory Records was an independent record label, founded by Tony Wilson, aka 'Mr. Manchester' and Alan Erasmus in 1978. It signed up groups such as Happy Mondays, Joy Division and many others. The establishment of this label is said to have marked the beginning of the 'Manchester Scene' in the 1980s.

Factory Records

It was in the 1980s that the city earned its sobriquet 'Madchester'; there was an explosion of music which centred on the Haçienda night-club which opened in 1982 and was part of the Factory Records empire. The Haçienda was set up as a platform for a new wave of post-punk bands which, being considered subversive, found it difficult to find a stage elsewhere. Joy Division appeared on the Manchester scene at the end of the 1970s, but following the suicide of its lead singer Ian Curtis in 1980, the remaining members formed New Order. The 'Madchester' scene included Happy Mondays, the Stone Roses and The Smiths, led by Morrissey and Johnny Marr.

Later Manchester bands included Simply Red, The Fall and Take That. Oasis is probably *the* Manchester band of the 1990s; their first concert was performed at the 'Boardwalk' in 1991.

Chapter 15

'Incomers'

As has been shown in previous chapters, Manchester is and always has been a city of immigrants; people have been arriving and settling here for at least the last 2,000 years. Romans, Saxons, Vikings and Normans may have been early incomers, but it didn't stop there. Flemish weavers came and with them the beginnings of the textile industry. As Manchester prospered and expanded, people from all corners of the globe flocked to the town, some in search of work, others fleeing from religious persecution and some simply to escape the threat of starvation. Here are just a few examples:

Jews

Jewish hawkers and pedlars had been frequent visitors to the town since the 1740s. However, in the 1780s, some 15 to 20 Jewish families arrived in Manchester, settling in the poorer areas of the old town around Withy Grove, Long Millgate and Shude Hill; the founders of Manchester Jewry are named as Jacob and Lemon Nathan, jewellers and slop-sellers (dealers in cheap, ready-made clothes) who lived at the house next to that which later became the Sun Inn. These early Jewish settlers initially rented small shops but as they prospered, they moved their businesses to the wealthier, more fashionable shopping streets, such as Deansgate and St. Ann's Square, providing goods and services to the ever-growing middle class. In 1829 the world's first ready-made tailoring shop was opened on Market Street by Benjamin Hyam, an immigrant who had arrived in Manchester only the previous year.

The first Jewish merchant to settle in Manchester was Nathan Mayer Rothschild who opened a warehouse on New Brown Street in 1799. He lived first on Downing Street in Ardwick and then in a grand house on Mosley Street before transferring his business to London in 1810. Jews were regarded with suspicion, at least initially. Many people considered them to be 'industrial spies', ready to steal the secrets of Manchester's booming textile industry.

> In 1785, a German by the name of Herr Baden was fined £500, then a colossal sum of money, for attempting to lure some cotton operatives back to Germany.

However, relations between Jews and Gentiles were mostly harmonious.

The Jewish community grew at a fairly slow pace over the next one hundred years as more families continued to arrive and make a positive contribution to the town. However, the Jewish population of Manchester was soon to double as a result of the Russian pogroms of the 1880s.

One person escaping Russia was Joseph Hyman; born in 1878, he finally came to Manchester. In 1912 he set sail to start a new life in America, leaving his wife and four children to join him later; he had a third-class berth on the 'unsinkable' RMS *Titanic*. He was one of the very few third-class male passengers to survive. The story goes that he, together with Bruce Ismay, chairman of the White Star Line, was put in charge of rowing one of the lifeboats. So it was that one of the richest and one of the poorest men on board the *Titanic* rowed the boat, carrying around forty people, to safety; they were rescued by the *Carpathia* and taken to New York.

There, Hyman stayed with his brother; his wife and children were too afraid to make the crossing to America and Joseph, understandably, was also reluctant to set foot on a boat again. Apparently, in 1913, one of his cousins plied him with drink and put him on a boat to England.

Following his return to Manchester, Hyman opened a delicatessen in Cheetham Hill; he had learned about the business while visiting various kosher delis in America. He called his shop 'J A Hyman Ltd'. However, as a survivor of the *Titanic*, Joseph became something of a local celebrity and his shop was always referred to as 'Titanics'. The name stuck and there were several shops in the chain. Titanics was the longest-running kosher shop in Manchester and in the fourth generation of the same family, until sadly, unable to withstand competition from supermarkets, the last shop closed in 2016.

> Joseph Hyman died in 1956, having been haunted by bad dreams of the disaster for the rest of his life.

Joseph Hyman

The Franks Dynasty

The Francks (anglicised to Franks) were a Jewish family who came to England from The Netherlands towards the end of the eighteenth century, settling first in Liverpool and then moving to Manchester where they were among the founders of the first Manchester Jewish community. Isaac Franks, the head of the family, was listed as a hawker of optical lenses. In 1819 Isaac's son Jacob opened an optician's on Oldham Road and in 1838 moved to new premises on Deansgate. After Jacob's death, two of his sons (Jacob had eleven sons, eight of whom also became opticians.), Abraham and Joseph, took over the running of the business which they named A & J Franks. They soon developed a reputation as makers of high-quality spectacles and scientific instruments – microscopes, telescopes, barometers, etc.

The firm moved into the fourth generation when Joseph's son Aubrey set up in business on King Street in the 1870s. It was here that in 1897 the first ever demonstration of Edison's cinematograph in the North of England was given.

In 1917 the business was taken over by Aubrey's son-in-law, Maurice Saffer, an entrepreneur with a great head for business. He kept the Frank family name and his was the first firm to bring wireless and television to Manchester. Under his management, the business expanded and at least five more shops were opened in the area. In 1927, Manchester's first television pictures were received at his shop on Market Street and three years later he started selling televisions at a cost of 25 guineas!

Chaim Weizmann (1874–1952)

Chaim Weizmann was born in 1874 in Belarus, then part of the Russian Empire, the third of fifteen children. He studied in Germany and Switzerland and gained a doctorate in organic chemistry. In 1904 he became a senior lecturer at Manchester University; four years later he was awarded British citizenship and anglicised his first name to Charles. He was to remain in Manchester for the next thirteen years. As a prominent Jew, his name appeared on Hitler's list of people who were to be arrested immediately after the Nazi occupation of Britain.

Weizmann was President of the British Zionist Federation and twice served as president of the World Zionist Organization. During his time in Manchester, he fought tirelessly for the establishment of a Jewish homeland in Palestine and is credited with having played a crucial role in the Balfour Declaration in which the government gave their backing to the proposal. He also met with the US President, Harry Truman, to gain American support in establishing the State of Israel.

Weizmann became the first President of Israel in 1949. He died three years later.

****

Many synagogues were built in and around Manchester. The first was a rented room at Ainsworth Court off Long Millgate, but as the Jewish population increased and became more prosperous, the synagogues became bigger and grander.

The Great Synagogue

Situated just outside the city on Cheetham Hill Road, this grand building was constructed between 1856 and 1858. It was in use until the 1960s when many of the Jewish families who lived in the area moved further afield. It was demolished in 1981.

The Great Synagogue

The oldest surviving synagogue in the area is that which today houses the Jewish Museum. It was built in 1874 for Sephardic Jews from Spain and Portugal.

The Irish

Manchester has not always welcomed its 'incomers' with open arms. The Irish immigrants of the nineteenth century must surely count as the least welcome group of people ever to come into the city. They were castigated on all sides and became scapegoats for all the ills of society. Even the liberal *Manchester Guardian* seemed unimpressed.

> **To Quote:**
>
> 'The extensive immigration of poor Irish has inflicted a deadly blow upon the health and comfort of the working class.'
>
> *Manchester Guardian*

> **To Quote:**
> 'They [the Irish] are the most serious evil with which our labouring classes have to contend.'
> *Manchester Guardian*

Even before the Potato Famine of the 1840s there were many thousands of Irish settlers in Manchester. Often coming from the most deprived conditions in Ireland, they were prepared to take the worst housing and the worst jobs; they were also prepared to work for less money which often led to tension with the 'native' working-class population.

Little Italy

In the second half of the nineteenth century there was an influx of Italian immigrants, many of them settling in the Ancoats area of Manchester, an area which soon came to be known as 'Little Italy'. About seventy of these Italian families set up businesses making and selling ice cream. These were small businesses, the ice cream often being made by hand, in the cellars of family homes.

At that time, a scoop of ice cream would come in a 'licking glass', also known as a 'penny lick'. The glass was returned to the vendor who then rinsed and reused it. The authorities deemed this to be a health hazard, spreading diseases such as typhoid and cholera and they threatened to ban the sale of ice cream. Luckily, Valvona and his edible ice cream cone arrived on the scene. Antonio Valvona of 96, Great Ancoats Street was first an ice cream maker then a biscuit maker. He is credited with being the 'inventor' of the ice cream cone (cornet). He was certainly the first to patent his invention as an 'Apparatus for Baking Biscuit Cups for Ice Cream' in 1902. On Blossom Street in Ancoats there was a warehouse used for storing fruit, vegetables and fish and attached to this was an ice-making factory. The Italians made great use of the surplus ice in making and selling their ice cream.

In the early years, the ice cream was carried by horse and cart, bicycle-cart or push-cart. After the Second World War motorized vehicles were widely introduced, enabling the vendors to travel much greater distances. The shouts of the vendors to attract their customers' attention were replaced by jolly musical chimes. Some ice-cream-making businesses which started in Ancoats at that time are still in business today such as Rea, Sivori, Granelli, Meschia, Levaggi and Bernado Scappaticci. ('Ben's Ices' is still going strong on Market Street.)

Granelli's ice cream cart on 'Sucker's Alley' in Shudehill - quite often there would be a line of ice cream vendors here.

'Little Italy' was known for ice cream, but also for its music and music makers, including the Gaviolis, makers, sellers and hirers of barrel organs. Italian musicians would wander the streets of Manchester, playing their music; some would have been accompanied by monkeys in red waistcoats and hats or, occasionally, by a dancing bear.

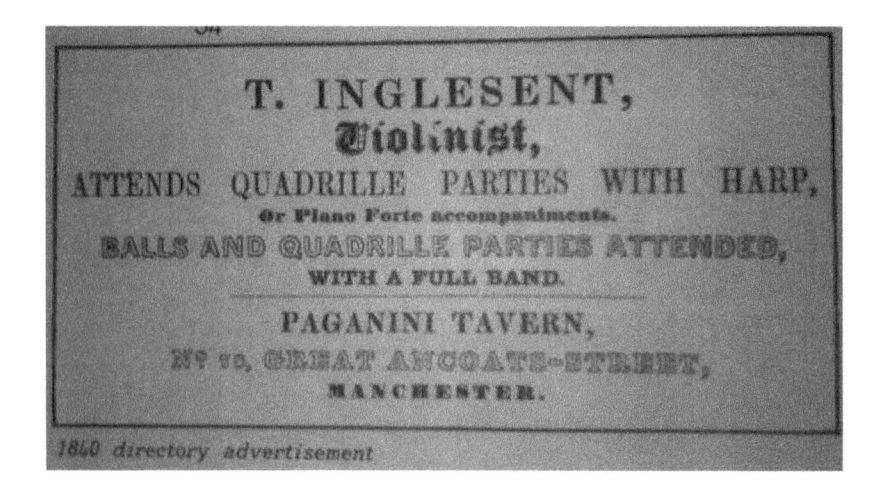

> T. INGLESENT,
> *Violinist,*
> ATTENDS QUADRILLE PARTIES WITH HARP,
> Or Piano Forte accompaniments.
> BALLS AND QUADRILLE PARTIES ATTENDED,
> WITH A FULL BAND.
> PAGANINI TAVERN,
> N° 70, GREAT ANCOATS-STREET,
> MANCHESTER.

1840 directory advertisement

When Italy allied itself with Germany in the Second World War there was a great deal of anti-Italian feeling and riots against Italian communities occurred in many towns and cities. Italian-born males between the ages of 17 and 60 were interned; they were seen as a threat to national security, even those who had fought for Britain in the First World War and those who had taken British citizenship. Bizarrely, many of those same internees had British-born sons who were serving in the British armed forces. Internees were transported to camps around the country and sometimes further afield. In July 1940, a boat heading for Canada and carrying German and Italian internees (many of them from Manchester) sank off the coast of Ireland with huge loss of life, including 470 Italians. Those left behind in 'Little Italy' were put under a strict curfew and were banned from holding public meetings.

Chinese &

The first Chinese immigrants arrived in Manchester in the early twentieth century and opened a couple of laundries and eateries. However, it was not until after the Second World War that the immigration boom occurred, turning the area into one of the largest Chinatowns in Europe. The frst restaurant opened here in 1948.

The Chinese Imperial Archway was built by engineers from China, cost £350,000 and was opened by Prince Philip in 1987.

Chapter 16

Disaster!

Earthquake

Just before 11 o'clock on the morning of 14 September 1777, an earthquake shook Manchester and the surrounding districts. The shock was felt over an area of 9,000 square miles and extended as far as Macclesfield, Rochdale and Preston.

The fourteenth of September was a Sunday and many people were in church. One observer, who was in St. John's Church, Deansgate at the time, wrote, 'It was at first heard like the rumbling of a coach at a distance, but in a moment, the noise exceeded the loudest thunder-clap I ever heard.' He went on to describe how the noise increased even further as the walls and the pews began to shake and the church bells began to ring, leading the congregation to believe that the church was about to collapse 'about their ears, and, impressed with this fear, every person, unmindful of any one else, endeavoured to make his escape'. People were knocked over and trampled upon in the rush to get out of the door. 'Every face gathered paleness, for I believe, it made the stoutest heart quake.'

In the records of 'Baptisms at the Collegiate Church in the City of Manchester' the entry for 14 September reads:

'No service in the afternoon occasioned by a violent Earthquake'

St. Ann's church, in the centre of the city, originally had a three-stage cupola with a vane at the top; after the earthquake, it was in danger of falling and had to be taken down.

In Seventeen Hundred and Seventy-seven,
The town was alarm'd by a token from Heaven;
One Sunday, when folk were assembled at prayer,
A sensation was felt on the earth, and in air,
Which appalled e'en the stoutest of hearts on that day,
And Courage itself would have fain run away:-

The Earth shook to its centre, for on it had trod –
And well might it shake then, - the Almighty God.
From the Churches all rush'd – risking life and their bones,
Breaking Sabbath-day's silence, by shrieking and groans;
Not only the wounded – but all look'd aghast –
As if, on conviction, the day was the last.
Church Devotion was over – yet sure on that day
Did many a prayer make to Heaven its way;
For nothing makes mortals to Heaven draw near,
So soon as when urged to't by grief or by fear.

(from the *Metrical Records of Manchester* by Joseph Aston, 1822)

Emma

The *Emma* was built by the New Quay Company which used boats to carry people and goods between Manchester and Liverpool. Located on the east bank of the River Irwell, the company had been established in 1822 but 29 February 1828 was the first time that a launch had been accompanied by such pomp and ceremony. Cannon were fired, a band played, the area was festooned with banners and streamers and a large crowd dressed in their 'Sunday best' had gathered to enjoy the festivities. The day was clear and breezy with occasional glimpses of the sun. To the sound of much clapping and cheering from the spectators, the two daughters of the company's manager smashed a bottle of wine on the ship's bow and the *Emma*, a fully-rigged river flat (flat-bottomed boat) with around 200 people on board set sail.

Unfortunately, it sailed only as far as the opposite bank where it crashed and capsized throwing many of the passengers overboard into the Irwell's icy (not to mention dirty and fairly polluted) water. Luckily, however, there was no shortage of heroes on that day. One, a dyer from Salford, jumped into the water immediately and rescued three people before he himself drowned while trying to rescue a fourth. Another was drowned when the man he was trying to save panicked and both were dragged under the water when they had almost reached the bank. Yet another hero, a fishmonger, had been watching events from his stall and saw the boat listing; he immediately removed his clothes and dived in. Having rescued many people from the water, he returned to the river bank only to find that his clothes had been stolen. Suffering from exhaustion and now exposure to the cold, he never recovered and died a few months later.

Around thirty-eight people died in the incident. One of the victims was 20-year-old Elizabeth Bradshaw, who was going to be married the following day. Those who were rescued were treated with all the remedies and medical procedures that were known of at the time including brandy, hot baths and 'constant friction'. Several people who were struggling to breathe had a hole cut in their windpipe into which a bellows was inserted; the bellows were then pumped in order to reinflate the lungs. It was also reported that as a last resort, the 'blood of a man, or of a dog, was transferred into the veins of a patient'.

The Great Flood(s)

Up until the late 1700s the River Irwell's water, described as 'translucent', was clean enough to drink and eels, fish and other wildlife were to be found in abundance. At one time, it was even possible to catch a salmon or two there. As one observer described it, 'The Irwell, gliding clear and pleasantly by, the pellucid waters inhabited by innumerable trout.' Gradually however, the river banks became lined with mills, dye-works, tenement blocks and other poor-quality housing; by 1850 the river was filthy, polluted and toxic with the waste from various local industries. Geoffrey Gimcrack described the river in 1849: 'The muddy Irwell oozed as black as Styx in all the sable majesty of filth.' Hugh Miller, a Scottish geologist, described how it looked in 1862 – 'less a river than a flood of liquid manure, in which all life dies, whether animal or vegetable'.

In November 1866, after three days of torrential rain, the Irwell burst its banks causing the worst flood in living memory. After the first day, the water level had risen fourteen feet above normal in places and everything came to a standstill; no street-lights could be lit and mills and factories had to be closed. All in all, £1 million of property was damaged, wooden bridges were lifted up and carried away, eleven hundred acres were flooded and hundreds of people were made homeless. If you walk through Peel Park in Salford today you may come across a granite flood obelisk on which is recorded the level the water reached on 16 November. Along with 700 other people in the vicinity, the park keeper had to be rescued from the upstairs window of his house. Some people, however, were able to enjoy the floods – 'The elders seek refuge in their upper storeys, while the youngsters make light of their troubles by floating upon the drawers in the lower rooms, guiding their raft with long brushes and brooms instead of oars.'

Wading through the flood

Peel Park obelisk

Amazingly, only one person seems to have perished (though whether by drowning or swallowing the poisonous water is unclear).

The terms 'climate change' and 'global warming' may not have been around in 1866 but the weather was even then causing some concern; one newspaper reporter wrote, 'This year would indeed seem one, in every sense, of exceptional phenomena.' 1866 came to be known as the 'Year of the Great Flood' in Manchester and Salford, but not for long! In 1872 there was another 'great flood' and this time it was the River Medlock that caused the most damage. This flood was described as 'the most disastrous flood which ever visited Manchester' and came after a month's rainfall in just two days. The flood was responsible for a huge amount of damage; bridges were swept away, businesses were destroyed in an instant and many homes were inundated with the filthy poisonous water. In some mills and factories situated by the river banks, the water level reached fifteen feet above normal. In parts of Ancoats the water rose as high as the bedrooms with many people having to be rescued by rafts.

The area around Philip's Park took the full force of the floodwater which ripped through a stone wall and into the Roman Catholic section of the adjoining cemetery, sweeping away headstones and carrying coffins with it. The coffins were soon smashed to pieces in the raging torrent of water and bodies in varying stages of decay were swept downstream. The exact number of bodies is uncertain, but more than fifty were later recovered and reinterred. A song 'The Great Flood' was written to commemorate the incident and included the following verses:

> Still on the mighty water came,
> Where lay the silent dead,
> And soon, alas! the coffins were
> Uplifted from their bed.
>
> Ghastly forms of old and young
> Lay open to our view;
> God grant that such appalling sights
> May ne'er be seen by you!

The Irk Valley Railway Disaster

On Saturday, 15 August 1953, at 7.40 am, an electric train and a steam train were involved in a head-on collision on the viaduct over the River Irk, close to Victoria Station. The electric train crashed through the parapet and plunged into the river below. Ten people, including the driver of the train, died and many others were seriously injured.

In 2010 one of the survivors of the tragedy finally met the person who had rescued him fifty-seven years earlier.

Woolworths

On the afternoon of Tuesday, 8 May 1979, around 500 people were in the six-storey Woolworths building at the corner of Piccadilly and Oldham Street. Shortly after lunchtime, a fire broke out in the furnishing department on the second floor. The fire brigade arrived within minutes of the first 999 call and spent 2½ hours bringing the fire under control. The fire had started when a faulty electrical cable ignited the cheap furniture filled with polyurethane foam, producing dense, toxic clouds of smoke.

Ten people died and 53 people were injured, including six firefighters. Most of the people who died were in the second-floor restaurant, trapped by the poisonous black smoke. There was no sprinkler system fitted and the upper storeys had bars on the windows; the fire crews had to wait for specialist cutting equipment to arrive before they could rescue the six people trapped behind them.

As a result of the fire, Assistant County Fire Officer Bob Graham campaigned tirelessly for almost ten years for a change in the law. Finally, in

1988, a law was passed obliging manufacturers to use only flame-resistant materials. This legislation has been responsible for saving many thousands of lives.

In 2012 a video of the Woolworths fire caused controversy when it was used as part of a Turner prize-winning art installation 'The Woolworths Choir of 1979'.

Chapter 17

Manchester Characters

Elias Hall

Elias Hall, who came to be known as the 'Manchester Prophet', was born in Manchester in 1502. By trade he was a draper; he was extremely successful and amassed a large fortune. In 1551 he claimed to have had a dream in which an angel spoke to him. The following year when he was seriously ill and confined to bed, he claimed to have again been visited by an angel who chastised him for his worldliness and told him he had been chosen to spread the word of God. He then (in his dream) went on a journey through heaven and hell which lasted a day and two nights. He recorded his experiences in verse in the imaginatively-titled *A Book of Visions*. He abandoned his trade in favour of becoming a full-time 'seer'. He seems to have had some success in this area too and he soon built up a large following. He dressed in a camel-hair robe (in imitation of the prophet Elijah), fasted and abstained from 'all things pleasante to the flesshe'. He left Manchester and headed for London where he hoped to gain an audience with Queen Elizabeth I, believing he had been sent as a messenger from God to 'the Quene and to all princes'. Elizabeth though had other ideas – Hall was interrogated, denounced, arrested and pilloried. He was then committed to Bridewell House of Correction (originally a palace built for Henry VIII) where he died in 1565.

The 'Wunderkind' of Manchester

When Manchester was still a small town there lived a poor, honest and industrious linen weaver named Philip Bennett. In 1676 the weaver's wife gave birth to a son whom they named Charles. By the time he was 3 years old, Charles Bennett had not only mastered the English language, he was also a fluent speaker of Greek, Latin and Hebrew; until his talents were recognized, his parents had assumed that their son was talking 'gibberish'. The boy claimed that these other languages had come to him 'by inspiration'. People came from far and wide to take a look at this infant prodigy and his fame spread throughout the kingdom; eventually even King Charles II had learned of the boy's great gifts. In 1679 Charles Bennett (with his parents) travelled to London for an audience with the king; the journey took many days as whenever the party stopped, the boy was greeted by large crowds of people wanting to hear him speak and he was often summoned to the houses of 'the great and the good' where, apparently, he was able to answer, in depth, any question relating to the Bible. Although some people believed he had been possessed by evil spirits who spoke for him, others believed that he was an 'extraordinary gift from God' who had been sent to call sinners to repentance and claimed that Charles preached only 'of piety and virtue and warned against wickedness'. There were several pamphlets written about this 'child genius' at the time and there seem to have been many witnesses to his remarkable talents. One such wrote 'The Miraculous Child or wonderful news from Manchester, a most true and certain account of how one Charles Bennett, a child but 3 years old …. the like thereof hath not been heard of in any age'.

In London the party stayed at the Bear Inn in Smithfield where hundreds of spectators came to see him and hear him speak. However, following the Royal visit, Charles Bennett seems to have disappeared and his fate remains a mystery.

A Lonely Heart

The first lonely hearts advert?

In 1727, a lady by the name of Helen Morrison placed a small advert in the *Manchester Weekly Journal*. In what was probably the first time a newspaper had been used for such a purpose, Miss Morrison expressed a desire to meet a 'pleasant gentleman with whom to spend time'.

The Mayor subsequently committed her to a lunatic asylum for four weeks!

The 'Manchester Mummy'

In the eighteenth century there was a wealthy spinster called Hannah Beswick who lived on a large estate, Birchin Bower, which lay just a few miles outside Manchester. During the Jacobite rebellion of 1745 when Bonnie Prince Charlie and his supporters were marching through Lancashire, Hannah became afraid of looters and so she buried all her valuables in various places around the estate. Even when the danger had passed, they remained buried and she took the secret of where they were hidden to her grave (eventually!).

At the end of the eighteenth century there was great hardship and deprivation among the handloom weavers of Manchester. One weaver who went by the name of 'Joe at Tamers' and lived on the Birchin Bower estate seemed not to be affected by the prevailing poverty. While others were on the brink of starvation, he and his large family were both well-fed and well-dressed. Although suspicions were aroused, it was only years later that he confessed to having found a buried tin which, when opened, was found to be full of gold bars. He took the gold to Oliphant's, an exclusive goldsmith's in St. Ann's Square, where he was given seventy shillings for each bar of gold.

Some years before her own death, Hannah's brother John had a rather disturbing experience; he had been pronounced dead and laid out in his coffin. The lid was just about to be fastened down when he suddenly sat up – very much alive and with a good few years in him yet! Perhaps unsurprisingly, this episode left Hannah with a morbid dread of being buried alive. She left a legacy to Dr. Charles White (one of the founders of Manchester Infirmary and also her own private doctor) on the condition that she was to be kept above ground and not buried for 100 years. She also stipulated that her body should be checked at regular intervals for signs of life. After her death the doctor kept his side of the bargain; he embalmed her in tar and wrapped her tightly in bandages, leaving just her face showing. Hannah had been considered eccentric, but Dr. White seems to have taken eccentricity to a whole new level; he later put the 'mummy' in a grandfather clock, the clock-face of which was replaced by the face of the mummified Hannah! The event caused a bit of a sensation and Hannah became something of a celebrity; visitors (of whom the writer Thomas de Quincey was one) were allowed to view the 'mummy' in the doctor's house on King Street. It seems that the good doctor had a collection of 'curiosities' which included the skeleton of the infamous highwayman Thomas Higgins. Hannah's body was subsequently placed in the entrance hall of the Natural History Museum on Peter Street, where she earned the nickname 'The Manchester Mummy'.

Soon after her death, stories of Hannah's ghost walking around the Birchin Bower estate were reported. Sightings of a woman, sometimes headless, sometimes in a black silk gown and a white lace cap, were seen heading to the barn which would glow with a strange ghostly light.

In 1868, one hundred and ten years after her death (and with little probability of springing back to life) Hannah Beswick was finally buried in Harpurhey Cemetery. One newspaper correspondent at the time commented, 'It may well be that her after-death wanderings have at last ceased.' But no! The ghost of Hannah Beswick has been sighted frequently. The estate was gradually broken up and built upon. In 1956 and in 1981, during a night shift in the Ferranti Works which now stood on the site, thirty factory workers claimed to have seen the apparition of a 'Grey Lady'.

The fear of being buried alive (taphephobia) was so widespread in the nineteenth century that many coffins were fitted with bells and whistles. In 1895 an English doctor, J.C. Ousley, claimed that around 2,700 people were buried 'prematurely' (i.e. alive) each year in Britain. The claim was disputed by the medical authorities who said that the true figure was only about 800 a year (only?) and accused Ousley of sensationalism.

Apparently, even today some people ask to be buried with their mobile phone. How annoying would that be – to wake up and find the only dead thing in the coffin was the battery?

'Spanking Roger'

The eponymous Roger in the title is Major Roger Aytoun, after whom the city centre street is named. He was born in Scotland in 1749 and was the Ninth Laird of Inchdairnie in Fife; he came to Manchester in the late 1760s with the regiment of the Marquis of Lothian's Dragoons. He soon became a well-known character around the town; he was 6 feet 4 inches tall (in his socks) and cut a dashing figure. He also had the reputation of being a drunkard, a gambler and a spendthrift. In 1769, at the age of 20, he married a wealthy widow 45 years his senior; she was Mrs. Barbara Minshull, aged 65. Her late husband was the apothecary Thomas Minshull, whose family also gave its name to a street in the centre of town. Roger Aytoun and Barbara Minshull had met at the Kersal Races in Salford. The story goes that a fellow officer bet a large sum of money that Aytoun wouldn't propose to her. In the eighteenth century it seems it was not uncommon for naked men to race across Kersal Moor in Salford in front of a female audience. Aytoun proceeded to win a 'foot race in a nude state' and succeeded in attracting the attention of the merry widow. Whether this unlikely-sounding tale is true or not, what's certain is that four weeks after their first meeting they were married. On their wedding day Aytoun was so drunk that he had to be held up by his friends during the marriage service. Their alliance, unsurprisingly, was not a happy one and within a few days Roger had abandoned his wife (though not her money).

Roger Aytoun went on to found (and fund) his own regiment – the '72 Regiment of foot' (or 'Manchester Volunteers'). He would scour the streets of Manchester to look for recruits; he would challenge likely candidates to a fight (hence his nickname) on the understanding that if they lost, they would have to enlist. His regiment formed part of the garrison involved in the Siege of Gibraltar, which had been invaded by the Spanish and the French. When the regiment returned to Manchester, Aytoun was hailed as a hero.

Mrs. Aytoun died in 1783 and by 1792 Roger Aytoun had squandered her vast fortune and, to pay off his debts, he had to sell all his land and property. He returned to Scotland where he died in 1810.

The story of 'Spanking Roger' is recounted in the *Metrical Records of Manchester* (1822) by Joseph Aston:

> And Manchester, nothing behind her compeers,
> Provided a reg'ment of brave Volunteers,
> For, anxious to form for their Country the vanguard,
> Men eagerly flock'd to the Manchester standard,
> Disregarding the bounty – though sometimes a keen dodger
> Would make a good bargain with fam'd 'Spanking Roger',
> A nick-name which AYTOUN, the Grenadiers' Captain,
> Had found MYNSHULL's widow was very much wrapt in.
> Though with age paralytic – and he a mere boy –
> She laid siege to his person and gained the toy;
> For nothing could take her colt's tooth from her head,
> Till she bribed him with riches to share in her bed.
> She gave him a fortune – he gave her his name –
> And the world had a laugh at the wanton old dame.

'Spanking' Roger Aytoun

Elizabeth Raffald

Elizabeth Whittaker was born in Yorkshire in 1733. Little is known of her early life, but her father was a teacher and she obviously received some schooling in the '3 Rs'. She went into service in her early teens, working her way up to the position of housekeeper for what she later described as 'great and worthy families'. In 1760 she became housekeeper to Sir Peter and Lady Elizabeth Warburton at Arley Hall – a grand stately pile in Cheshire. She remained there for several years on a salary of £16 a year. Following her marriage to John Raffald, the head gardener at Arley, they relocated to Manchester where John ran a market stall selling flowers and seeds.

The mid-eighteenth century saw the onset of the Industrial Revolution. Being a shrewd businesswoman, Elizabeth was quick to notice a gap in the market in the rapidly expanding town – high quality food for the newly-rich merchant class that was emerging at this time. She opened a confectionery shop in a busy shopping area next to the Market Place. In addition to selling 'possets, jellies and flummery', she also prepared meals in her shop and delivered them to the new 'elite'.

The ready-made meal was born!

> Flummery: – a sweet dish made with beaten eggs and sugar
> Posset: – hot milk curdled with ale or wine and mixed with spices – once considered a delicacy

She soon came to realise that many of her customers had little or no experience of 'fine dining' and this encouraged her to write *The Experienced English Housekeeper: for the use and ease of Ladies, Housekeepers, Cooks & Co*. Published in 1769 (100 years before Mrs. Beaton), it consisted of 'near 800 Original Receipts most of which never appeared in Print'. It was a huge success and she quickly became the 'celebrity chef' of her day. It soon came to the attention of a London publisher who paid her £1,400 (in cash) for the copyright. A century later, Queen Victoria had one – she used to copy recipes from it into her diary!

The publisher, a Mr. R. Baldwin, wanted her to change some 'northern' words as he thought that people in 'the South' wouldn't understand them. She refused. She said she had written it in plain English 'so as to be understood by the weakest capacity'.

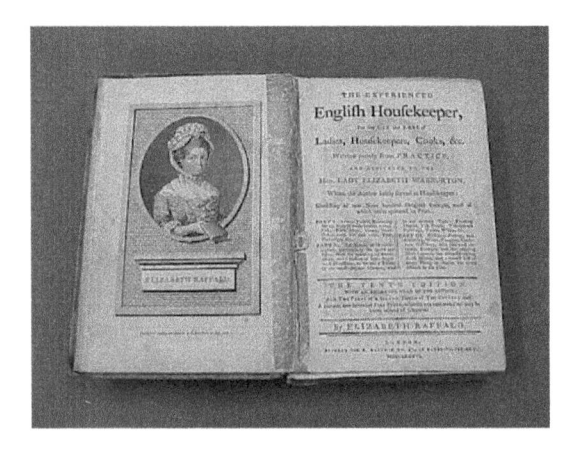

She dedicated the book to her former employer, Lady Warburton, and records show that she supplied Arley Hall with luxuries from her shop, for example, teas, oranges and sturgeon.

What a remarkable lady! Not only did she

- run a successful business,
- write a best-selling cookbook,
- run a cookery school,
- produce the first trade directory in Manchester,
- run an employment agency supplying domestic staff (The number of employers and employees was growing daily at this point in the town's history.),
- provide outside catering for Kersal Moor races,
- write a book on midwifery,

she also opened the first register office in Manchester that allowed servants to marry. This, in addition to giving birth to seven children (or perhaps it was sixteen – the exact number varies in different accounts of her life) – all girls! Sadly, only three of them outlived their mother.

Elizabeth Raffald is credited with the 'invention' of the modern-day wedding cake as she was the first cook to combine almond paste and royal icing on a 'bridal cake'. She also wrote a recipe for 'sweet patties', forerunner of the Eccles cake.

She later ran two pubs – The Bull's Head Inn in the Market Place (though this is disputed) and The King's Head in Salford.

At this point in history, in fact until 1882 when 'The Married Women's Property Act' was passed, married women had no legal rights and were not allowed to own property. Therefore, all her assets would have been in her husband's name. Unfortunately husband John was (allegedly) a notorious alcoholic and a bit of an all-round bounder; it seems he drank away much of the profits from Elizabeth's various businesses. Elizabeth died suddenly in 1781. She was commemorated with a new plaque in 2012, the original having been damaged in the IRA bombing of 1996. It is located on the Selfridges building, close to the original site of her shop.

> Some of her more unusual recipes give guidance on how:
> To make a dish of snow
> To make turtle and calf's foot pudding
> To spin a silver web for covering sweet-meats

'Old Billy'

The distinction of being the world's oldest-ever horse goes to 'Old Billy' who died in 1822, aged 62 years. The average lifespan of a horse is around 20-25 years. Billy, a brown horse with a white blaze, was born in Woolston, Lancashire in 1760 where he was 'put to plough' by Henry Harrison. When he was a few years old, Billy was bought by the Mersey and Irwell Navigation Company and worked for them towing barges and Mersey Flats along the waterways between Liverpool and Manchester. He carried on working for the same company until 1819 when, at the grand old age of 59, he was put to pasture and a life of ease on a farm near Warrington which belonged to one of the company directors.

Old Billy became something of a celebrity and, decorated in ribbons, he took part in a procession as part of the Manchester celebrations of King

George IV's Coronation. Old Billy was the subject of various lithographs and paintings, one of which was by the Manchester-born artist William Bradley who was commissioned by the owners of the Navigation Company. Old Billy was painted alongside Henry Harrison who, having been the one to train the horse, was able to verify its age.

Old Billy's head is, bizarrely, exhibited in two different museums – his skull is in Manchester Museum and his taxidermied head is at Bedford Museum, where it is described as one of its 'chief curiosities'.

Henry Harrison and 'Old Billy'

'The Ice Maiden'

The winter of 1813-14 was the coldest in living memory; snow lay thick on the ground and the rivers were frozen solid. Against this backdrop there was an incident which excited and intrigued the people of Manchester and beyond. For several weeks, newspapers across the country speculated on the likely cause of the mysterious disappearance of Lavinia Robinson.

Lavinia was one of many children born to William and Frances Robinson of Bridge Street, Manchester. They had previously lived in the Clockhouse area of Droylsden and Lavinia had been educated at Fairfield Moravian Boarding School. Her mother died when she was 12 and her father when she was 17. She was left as one of nine children, most of whom continued to live in the family home on Bridge Street; it was there that Lavinia opened a school which she ran successfully for the next four years. An attractive and intelligent young lady, she soon became engaged to Mr. Holroyd, a young surgeon who lived on the same street. Their wedding was due to take place on 12 January 1814. In 1811 John Holroyd was listed as being a 'midwife' at the Manchester Lying-in (Maternity) Hospital.

On the evening of the 16 December 1813, Lavinia was seen in the company of her fiancé; a bitter dispute followed during which the doctor made (unfounded) accusations against Lavinia for having encouraged the advances of another man and berated her for her 'want of chastity'. According to his testimony, despite her pleas of innocence, he had knocked her to the ground and left her near the New Bailey Prison on the banks of the River Irwell, where, by chance, a very temporary thaw had set in. When the police searched Lavinia's house they found a note in which she declared both her innocence and her unwillingness to live under the shadow of suspicion. 'With my dying breath, I attest myself innocent of the crime laid to my charge. Adieu! God bless you all! I cannot outlive his suspicion.' The note appeared to be in Lavinia's handwriting, but her family were not convinced of its authenticity. A reward of 100 guineas was offered and a description of the missing girl, given in all the newspapers, read: 'She was of a middle size, and good figure; of a fair complexion, with long light brown hair; she had on a fawn-coloured twilled stuff dress; a pink and yellow shot figured silk kerchief on her neck; a brown cloth mantle; a black beaver cottage bonnet; and her linen is marked L.R.'

Many people joined the search party, but it was almost two months later when the thick ice began to melt that her body was found. A Mr. Goodie, walking by his mill at Mode Wheel, which was located three miles downstream from the site of Lavinia's disappearance, saw a lady lying on a sandbank, enshrouded in ice with icicles hanging in her long light-brown hair. The freezing water had perfectly preserved her body.

Lavinia was described as having 'a high sense of religion, honour and character'. Was she the kind of person to take her own life? An inquisition was held at the Star Inn; a witness testified to having seen the couple arguing near the bridge over the river and had observed the man striking the woman. He described the pair in detail, including the clothes they had been wearing on the night in question. Despite a public outcry against John Holroyd, a jury concluded that there was no evidence to suggest how Lavinia came to be in the river. However, the great citizens of Manchester came up with a different verdict and hounded Mr. Holroyd, breaking his windows and throwing stones at him as he walked along the street.

> Poor LAVINIA! – But peace to thy ashes fair maid!
> The monster who dug thee thy grave has dear paid

> For his crime! – He wanders the earth like a Cain!
> A hell in his bosom! To fly from it, vain!

(from the *Metrical Records of Manchester* by Joseph Aston, 1822)

Now convinced of his fiancée's innocence, Holroyd left Manchester and turned up in Stafford where in 1814 he attempted to drown himself in the canal. The attempt failed and he chose a more reliable means of committing suicide: poison. The case of Lavinia Robinson had aroused much interest and thousands of people attended her funeral. The 'Manchester Ophelia' was buried in St. John's churchyard on Byrom Street. She was just 20 years old.

Sarah Taylor & Harriet Stoakes

In 1814 a middle-aged woman called Sarah Taylor applied for and received 'poor relief' from the churchwardens' office on Fountain Street. She told a remarkable story.

Sarah Roberts was the daughter of a bricklayer and from a young age she would assist her father at his work. She always dressed in boys' clothes (which seemed better suited to such labour) and with so much manual work she became a tall, strong and healthy young woman. When she was 14, she enlisted in the army, using her father's name, William Roberts. At that time, recruits were desperately needed and the process of enrolment was very cursory. (It must have been!) She remained in the army for twenty-one years, rising from private to corporal to sergeant. When her discharge was tendered, she elected to join another regiment which was then called up to serve in the West Indies. It was there that she contracted yellow fever; being so seriously ill and believing she was about to die, she confessed her long-held secret to a sergeant's wife. When she recovered, it was a secret no longer! She returned to living as a woman and married a private (presumably Mr. Taylor) from her regiment with whom she had three children. The Taylors were later captured and incarcerated in a French prison for two years, an experience she described as the worst of her life. Shortly after their release, her husband died and Sarah returned, albeit reluctantly, to her parents' house on Newton Lane (later renamed Oldham Road) and applied for an army pension. In the meantime, she was forced to claim poor relief. As far-fetched as this tale seems, it appears that the facts of the story were verified by some reputable citizens of the town.

****

Another tale in similar vein is that of Harriet Stoakes, who from an early age had worked as a bricklayer, adopted male dress and called herself Henry, the name she lived under for the rest of her life. 'Henry' married in 1816; it was a very short honeymoon as his 'wife' left the following day declaring that her husband was 'not a man'. Henry went on to form an 'alliance' with the landlady of a pub. For several years Henry acted as a special constable in Manchester and was involved in the Chartists' riots of the 1840s. Henry became a master builder but later in life lost the business. He was found dead in the River Irwell in 1859, still wearing a bowler hat! The corpse was taken to the coroner where it was identified as that of Henry Stoakes and the death was very nearly dismissed as just another 'simple suicide'. It was only when a colleague remembered the comments of 'Henry's wife' that the body was revealed to be that of a woman. Needless to say, the case caused quite a sensation amongst the friends and neighbours who had seemingly suspected nothing.

The 'Lion King'

John Gill, who became known as 'Manchester Jack' was born in Salford c. 1810 and is reputed to have been the world's first lion-tamer. He worked as the 'Lion King' for George Wombwell who owned the first travelling menagerie, which included two famous lions, Nero and Wallace. In 1810 these two animals had 'performed' in a barbaric bet which involved them being placed in a ring with six bulldogs. Nero, who went first, had merely played with or ignored the dogs but then Wallace entered the arena and proceeded to tear them to shreds. Some time later Wallace, together with a tigress, escaped from their cages and went on the rampage, killing four people.

In 1835 (ish) when he appeared on stage before an audience, Manchester Jack was sitting on Nero's back while holding the lion's mouth open. Fortunately Nero had always been a docile and good-tempered lion and by 1835 he was also an old lion. Manchester Jack performed in the UK and around Europe for many years. Rumours that the 'Lion King' had had his head bitten off during one of his acts were greatly exaggerated; he actually lived to a fair old age, leaving the world of lion-taming to take over the running of a pub in Taunton.

Madame Malibran

In 1836 a Music Festival was held in Manchester, the like of which had never been seen in the town before (or probably since). The festival hosted sacred and secular music which was performed at various venues, including the

Cathedral and the Theatre Royal. The festival was to end with a fancy-dress ball, the largest in Manchester's history and preparations for the occasion were made on a huge scale. Windows were taken out of the upper floors of the Assembly Rooms, the Portico and the theatre and the three buildings were linked with wooden bridges, built especially for the night of the ball – the window spaces now becoming the doorways. Next to the three buildings a supper-room was built on trestles and beams.

There were many famous names present at the Music Festival, but the star of the event was Madame Maria Malibran who was considered to be one of the greatest opera singers in the world. She had found fame at a young age, mainly owing to her tyrannical father who pushed her to sing in Paris, London and New York. It was while in America that Monsieur Malibran, a French merchant, supposedly fell in love with Maria Garcia Sitches (as she was then) and proposed to her. Maria was revolted by him; he was 50 and she was 17. Nevertheless, her father insisted on her marrying him, thinking that he would be gaining a very wealthy son-in-law. Just a few weeks after the wedding, however, Malibran was found to be bankrupt and heavily in debt. Maria's father fled, leaving his daughter to her fate.

Madame Malibran was a spirited lady and a fighter and she started up her own opera troupe. A year later she left her husband and returned to Paris where she went from strength to strength, travelling to perform in the great Opera Houses of Europe. Her husband made a brief reappearance in her life, presumably wanting a share of the 'spoils', but fortunately the Paris courts declared the marriage null and void.

It wasn't long before she married again, this time to a famous Belgian violinist, de Bériot. It was to be a short honeymoon as six months later Madame Malibran-de Bériot was dead. Rumours circulated about the events leading up to and after her death, but whatever the true circumstances were, 'Husband no. 2' did not come out of it well. Mme. Malibran certainly didn't have much luck with the men in her life! A story was spread that she had died as the result of a riding accident, but there was also an alternative version of events.

Madame Malibran performed at the Manchester Festival to resounding applause and great acclaim. She and her husband stayed at the Mosley Hotel on Piccadilly, where every morning the diva would breakfast on oysters and drink diluted porter (a dark beer). What her audiences didn't know was that her husband had several times forced her to go on stage despite her being unwell and in the first stages of pregnancy. Following one performance she became seriously ill and a few days later she died in her hotel room. She was 28 years old. Public feeling against her husband was strong in Manchester and within an hour of her death de Bériot had fled for Belgium, leaving his wife's body behind. A public funeral, attended by thousands, was held at Manchester Cathedral and she was buried in the adjoining cemetery. Her husband later asked for the coffin to be returned to him in Belgium.

Madame Malibran, one of the greatest operatic divas of the nineteenth century

Mark Addy

Over a period of nearly forty years, Mark Addy rescued more than fifty people from the River Irwell. He was born in 1838 in a house on the banks of the river. His father ran a boat-building and hire business and from an early age Mark had tagged along with him. He made his first rescue when he was just 13; despite being unable to swim himself, he waded into the water up to his neck and pulled his friend, who had accidentally fallen into the river, to safety. Said friend obviously didn't learn his lesson and it wasn't long before he had to be rescued by Addy for a second time.

After the first rescue, Mark Addy learned to swim at Greengate Baths in Salford where he soon became an expert swimmer. In later years he was also a prize-winning oarsman.

After his marriage Addy became the landlord of the Old Boathouse Inn in Ordsall, which again was located in close proximity to the river. In Addy's younger days the Irwell ran with dirty, but relatively unpolluted water. By 1869 when the Suez Canal was being built, the now toxic Irwell was referred to as the "Sewage Canal". Undeterred, Mark Addy made many daring rescues, often putting his own life at risk; those he saved included people who had ended up in the water accidentally, but also many attempted suicides. On one occasion Addy left his Christmas dinner and jumped into the icy water to rescue Ellen Doyle who was trying to drown herself. In 1878 he was awarded 200 guineas by the people of Salford for his 'heroic deeds'. Many more medals and awards followed, including the Albert Medal of the First Class (then the highest decoration for civilian gallantry, later replaced with the George Cross). This was 'graciously conferred' on him on behalf of Queen Victoria in recognition that he 'under circumstances of imminent peril, both from the violence of the river and the pestilential nature of its waters, saved no fewer than six-and-thirty lives'.

Addy made his final rescue on Whit Monday, 1889 when, at the age of 51, he again jumped into the river to save a little boy who had fallen into a stretch of water heavily polluted with sewage. He saved the boy's life and in doing so contracted tuberculosis from which he died a year later. Even knowing he was about to die, he is quoted as saying, 'The best work I ever did was saving that little lad.' On the day of his funeral crowds of people lined the streets as his coffin passed by.

Mark Addy wearing his medals

Puck, King of the Fairies

Many years ago, in a farmhouse on the main road leading out of Manchester, there lived a chap called Daniel Burton, nicknamed 'Owd Dannel'. His farm was the best farm around by a country mile. His animals were healthy and the corn in his fields grew tall and strong and golden.

His neighbours, who spent most of their time gallivanting around the town and left their cornfields to the weeds and the thistles, were jealous of Daniel. As Owd Dannel continued to flourish, his envious neighbours speculated about his success. Was he in league with the Devil? Was he just lucky? Some thought his good fortune was down to Puck, King of the Fairies, and they were right! Farm labourers, milk-maids, stable lads - all welcomed the Fairy King who made their lives so much easier. When the farm awoke to a new day, the animals had been fed, the cows milked, water had been fetched from the well, the yard had been swept and everything was neat and tidy.

Always the envy of his neighbours, Daniel's 'luck' continued for weeks, months, maybe even years. Daniel began to take Puck's hard work for granted; he became complacent and greedy. One morning, as Daniel was feasting on his eggs and bacon, one of the farmhands burst in. He greeted his master with the news that all the corn had been harvested during the night. Daniel rushed out; the previous evening he had looked upon fields of gold, now they were completely bare. Instead of being delighted that all the hard work had been done, Daniel hurried over to Puck and angrily shouted, 'Did you use my horses without giving them any rest?' As soon as he had said those words, he knew that he had made a terrible mistake. Puck's face turned as black as thunder as he yelled,

> Sheaf to field, and horse to stall,
> I, the Fairy King recall!
> Never more shall drudge of mine
> Stir a horse or sheaf of thine.

and with that, he was gone! The next morning, the same farmhand came in with the news that the corn was back in the fields. And indeed it was. Daniel was distraught; his farm was now no longer the best on the lane and his neighbours were secretly delighted. One evening as he was strolling home, a neighbour asked Daniel what was troubling him. Just as he was about to reply, Daniel saw Puck out of the corner of his eye; the Fairy King was hiding behind a hedge. Thinking he had hit upon a clever plan, Daniel began singing the praises of his erstwhile benefactor. But to no avail! Puck was never again seen on the farm.

Chapter 18

What's in a name?

CROSS STREET

Was originally named Pool Fold. The pool in question is most likely that in which the town's ducking stool was located, in the grounds of Radcliffe (also known as Pool Fold) Hall. A narrow passage which lies off Cross Street still bears the name 'Back Pool Fold'.

DEANSGATE

<u>Dean</u> – either referring to the long-lost River Dene or to the Viking (Dane) invasion of the ninth century.
<u>Gate</u> – the Norse word for street.

At over one mile long, Deansgate is the longest road in the city centre. It is also one of the oldest, dating back to Roman times. Like many areas of the city, Deansgate was once a place of massive contrasts. At one end it was famous (or infamous) for slums, squalor and shady characters.

'The very scum of the city, the very essence of hell is concentrated here.'
Alfred Alsop (1876)

At the other end could be found shops such as 'Kendal, Milne and Faulkner' and 'Finnigans' which catered for the wealthiest in the city.

Kendal, Milne & Faulkner in the nineteenth century

This street has several claims to fame: it was home to the eminent scientist John Dalton and in the 1820s it became the site of the Manchester Eye Institution (later Hospital); it was also the location of the first public telephone exchange in Manchester which opened here in 1879.

The first ever telephone line to be installed in the UK was in Manchester - between Thomas Hudson's furnishing business in Shudehill and his offices in Dantzic Street. This happened just twelve days after Alexander Graham Bell had demonstrated his new invention to Queen Victoria. The year was 1878.

At the end of the nineteenth century there were not many career opportunities for 'respectable middle-class ladies', but being a telephone operator was considered one of them. However, it seems one needed to be of a robust disposition to take on the job. An 1896 magazine suggested that 'if of a nervous temperament and at all subject to headache and neuralgia pains, it would be well to choose some other calling'.

&

Faulkner Street now lies at the heart of Chinatown. Erected in 1987, the Imperial Arch which spans the street was the first, and still remains one of the largest in Europe. The street is now lined with supermarkets, medicine shops and restaurants.

GREAT ANCOATS STREET

This area changed from being a rural idyll of fields and country houses, such as Ancoats Hall, to being one of the worst and most notorious slum areas in the country, filled with ramshackle houses and cellar dwellings.

In the 1700s Ancoats Lane was a cart track leading from the markets at Shudehill to Ashton Old Road, then known as the 'cattle drovers' highway'.

Towards the end of the eighteenth century the lane was renamed, becoming Great Ancoats Street, reflecting its growing importance to the economy of the town. It was soon lined with commercial properties – shops, factories and warehouses.

LEVER STREET

On a map of Manchester, dated 1650, there is a solitary dwelling surrounded by gardens, pastures and cornfields. Levers Hall was situated in modern-day Piccadilly and was for many years the town residence of the Lever family. In the mid-eighteenth century Sir Ashton Lever owned the land between what is now Piccadilly and Great Ancoats Street, land which he later sold to William Stevenson. (Soon after selling the land, Sir Ashton Lever allegedly committed suicide by poisoning himself at the Bull's Head Inn on the Market Place.) In 1773 Levers Hall was converted into a coaching inn called the White Bear. Its horse-drawn coaches were advertised as 'London Flying Machines' travelling from Manchester to London in just two days! (In 1754 it had taken 4½ days.) With the growing popularity of railways, the coaching inn went into a decline and was demolished in 1904.

Lever Street is notable for several reasons: it contains five original Georgian town houses built in 1787, it has some impressive old warehouses (such as Sevendale House), and it was also home to James Herriot, a deaf tailor who founded the Manchester and Salford Deaf and Dumb Benevolent Association.

MARKET STREET

In medieval times this thoroughfare led to the Market Place and was known as Market Stead Lane. It was here in 1650 that the first brick building in Manchester was erected.

> Before 1822, when it was first widened, Market Street was described as 'a winding tortuous thoroughfare' and was mostly lined with old timber and plaster houses. It was only fifteen feet wide and with the increase both in commerce and population, it was regarded as the most congested street in Europe.

An image of Market Street in 1822

Print: Courtesy of 'The Victorian Web'

Between 1821 and 1834 the road-widening of Market Street and surrounding streets (then still unfinished) cost a massive £233,000. The street soon became lined with shops, hotels and inns. In *Manchester as it is*, the author Benjamin Love describes the transformation of Market Street: 'From a dirty narrow lane it has been converted to one of the handsomest streets in England.'

Minshull Street

Thomas Minshull came from a very well-to-do family after whom Minshull Street (site of the impressive Crown Court) is named. Thomas worked as an apothecary (chemist) on this site on Hanging Ditch and was medical attendant to Humphrey Chetham and also a governor of Chetham's Hospital and Library.

Mosley Street was built over fields towards the end of the 1700s. It was named after the Mosley family who were Lords of the Manor of Manchester from 1596 to 1838. It soon became one of THE places to live and wealthy manufacturers began building their grand houses here. One such resident was Nathan Meyer Rothschild, the founder of the famous banking dynasty. John Dalton described it as 'The most elegant and refined street in town'.

However, in around 1830 these large houses began to be converted into textile warehouses and the 'gentry' moved out to the suburbs. It quickly became a busy, bustling commercial street.

Now a tram route linking Piccadilly and St. Peter's Square, Mosley Street has many listed buildings of architectural and historical interest: the Portico Library (the ground floor of which is now a pub) and Manchester Art Gallery (once the Royal Manchester Institute) are located here.

It is thought that this street was named after Adam Oldham (and not after the nearby road which leads to the town of Oldham). Before 1772, the year in which it was opened to the public, it was a private track described as 'an ill-kept muddy lane' and was bordered by fields and hedgerows. The land was owned by Adam Oldham, a wealthy felt-maker and hatter (and chum of John Wesley, founder of the Methodist movement); it was here that he built his own house – one of the first buildings on the street. It soon became a built-up area and was home to shops, businesses and residences for the wealthy. One such was the birthplace of Mrs. G. Linnaeus Banks, author of *The Manchester Man*.

This was one of the streets at the centre of the birthplace of the world's first industrial city and the modern world. Bordering Ancoats and the soon-to-be infamous Angel Meadow, it was an area of huge contrasts; a place of great wealth and even greater poverty.

Oldham Street became renowned for high-class stores and was one of *the* best places to shop. However, with the opening of the Arndale Centre, the street fell into a rapid decline which continued until the 1990s when 'The Northern Quarter' sprang into being. This street has many fantastic buildings which are falling into disrepair; hopefully the regeneration of the area will continue before other buildings meet the same fate as the wonderful art deco 'Dobbin's' building (fire and demolition).

Oxford Street runs from St. Peter's Square, becoming Oxford Road as it crosses the River Medlock (further along, it becomes Wilmslow Road). The street was once home to a myriad of cinemas and theatres including St. James' Theatre where Manchester's first film shows were held. The first purpose-built cinema in Manchester was also on Oxford Street: the Picture House was built in 1911 and is now, predictably, a pub.

The area now known as Piccadilly was once owned by the Mosley family. It had long had the nickname 'Daub Holes' referring to the large holes that were dug here to extract the daub for making wattle and daub houses. The Mosley family gave the land to the town for the building of a new infirmary, but made certain stipulations, one being that an ornamental pond was to be made out of part of 'Daub Holes' and another that the land must never be built upon and must always remain open to the public. Should these conditions be breeched, the land would revert back to the ownership of the Mosley family. The 'pond' supplied much of the town with drinking water for many years! In 1833 the pond was drained and filled in, later becoming part of Piccadilly Gardens. The Infirmary (extended to include a lunatic asylum) was on this site from 1755 to 1908 when it moved to its new home on Oxford Road.

The name Piccadilly was chosen in 1812. Before this, the road linking Market Street and what is now Piccadilly Station was called Lever's Row. The booming textile industry inspired the town to emulate London and that included pinching some of its names, hence Pall Mall, Oxford Street and Piccadilly.

The word 'Shambles' was originally used for a street of butchers' shops where animals were both slaughtered and sold. It is derived from the Old English word for a small wooden bench on which the meat would be displayed; a 'shambler' was the term for a butcher. It would not have been a pleasant place to be; the gutters would have been running with blood and guts – literally (hence the modern use of the word 'shambles' – meaning mess).

Shambles later came to mean a place of traders and market stalls. The Shambles in Manchester was just off the medieval Market Place – approximately where New Cathedral Street is now. It would have been home to fishmongers, oyster dealers, butchers, fruiterers, florists and poulterers as well as several taverns. Much of the Shambles area fell victim to Victorian redevelopment. What was left was flattened during the bombing of Manchester in the Second World War. Miraculously, the Old Wellington Inn survived both these events (and the 1996 IRA bomb).

The name Shudehill was first recorded way back in the sixteenth century. At that time and for the next 200 years it was a rural area and the site of large, grand houses. One such was Bradshaw Hall, a timber and stone house which stood on the site from 1512 to 1910. John Bradshaw was a magistrate and High Sheriff of Lancashire and he it was who gave the order to break up the Shudehill Fight of 1757.

What's in a name? 239

> In 1757 Shudehill Market was the scene of a riot owing to food shortages. In what came to be known as 'The Shudehill Fight', 4 people were killed and 15 wounded when soldiers opened fire on the protesters.

During the second half of the eighteenth century Shudehill became increasingly built-up with commercial properties.

It was home to one of Manchester's first cotton mills; owned by Richard Arkwright and opened in 1782, it was a large five-storey mill which became the first to use a steam engine as a source of power. The mill was destroyed by fire in 1854 but was rebuilt and survived until the Manchester Blitz in 1940. The site is now a car park.

In 1958 a building which had stood on Shudehill since 1306 and had once been home to 'Ye Olde Rovers Return Inn' was demolished. Another historic building bites the dust!

Shudehill is now mainly known as a transport hub, busy with a constant stream of trams and buses.

In the mid-1700s, Sir Ashton Lever sold his land to William Stevenson, after whom this square is named. He, in turn, sold off pieces of the land to various other landowners and entrepreneurs.

Stevenson Square became the place where people would meet to catch up with and discuss the latest news. It was also the scene of frequent speeches across a wide political spectrum; in 1911 Harry Pollitt, founder of the Communist Party of Great Britain spoke here, as did William Joyce in the 1930s. Better known as 'Lord Haw-Haw', Joyce held a rally here for the British Union of Fascists. Annie Kenney the suffragette spoke here in 1905 shortly after being released from prison, cheered on by around 2,000 people.

Stevenson Square was also the site of demonstrations and many an interesting debate! One such involved Dr. Grinrod, a champion of the Temperance Movement and Mr. Youil, a brewer – an event which attracted a crowd of over 3,000 people.

Tib Street was originally the footpath along the River Tib – a grand name for what was essentially a stream. The 'river', such as it was, was culverted in 1783. As the area became increasingly industrialised, the Tib turned into an underground sewer.

In earlier days, part of the street (nearest Piccadilly) was called Stable Street as it adjoined the stables of the Bridgewater Arms, a coaching inn.

For around 100 years Tib Street was known as 'cats and dogs street' or 'pets' paradise'; this was owing to the fact that there were so many pet shops here. The last one closed in 2002. Perhaps the most well-known was R. Groves & Son who were in business for over a century; their shop is now occupied by Abakhan Fabrics. The pet shops had animals on display in their windows and in cages outside on the street. Other pet shops on the street included R. Kremer (birds and birdcages), Walters and T.W. Watts.

The novelist Howard Spring wrote a children's story called *Tumbledown Dick: All People and no Plot*. It is the tale of a young boy who goes to stay with his uncle, owner of a pet shop on Tib Street, at Christmas time. The book gives a fascinating insight into 1920s Manchester.

After many years as a street to be avoided, Tib Street is now part of the thriving Northern Quarter, lined with shops, cafés and bars.

The name dates back to a time when this area was covered in pleasant country lanes. 'Withy' was the Old English word for 'willow' so Withy Grove suggests there were willow trees growing here. At one time willow was used in the construction of timber-framed buildings.

Withy Grove was the site of the Seven Stars Inn which claimed to be one of the oldest licensed houses in the country, having been there since the 1350s. Withengreave Hall, once home of the philanthropist William Hulme, was also situated here in a plot of 8½ acres. It was following the sale of the hall in 1763 that the nature of the area began to change. Thirty years later it was completely built up with houses and commercial properties. Engels described the maze of narrow winding streets around Withy Grove in *The Condition of the Working Class in England* (1845): 'the houses dirty, old, and tumble-down and the construction of the side streets utterly horrible'.

Withy Grove has played a significant role in the history and radical politics of Manchester; it has seen food riots, strikers demonstrating for better pay and working conditions, and clashes between Catholics and Protestants after the legend 'No Popery' had been daubed on the walls.

Later in the nineteenth Century it became the centre of Manchester's newspaper industry; what is now the Printworks was once part of the largest newspaper complex in the world, printing such diverse papers as the *Manchester Evening Chronicle*, the *Daily Mirror* and the *Sunday Times*.

****

Other streets in the city have come and gone. Some have unlikely-sounding names, such as Snow Hill and Cupid's Alley (now Atkinson Street). Others sound quaint, like Smithy Door, Toad Lane and Clock Alley. The latter was so named because the people who lived and worked there were mostly employed in making 'clock-lace'. The street was lost under the CWS buildings.

One name which cannot be left out is perhaps the most famous street in the country: Coronation Street. The original name for the series was *Florizel Street* and was only intended to run for thirteen episodes, the first of which was aired on 9 December 1960. Within six months, it was the country's most-watched television programme and is now the longest-running TV soap in the world.

Chapter 19

Shopping

Made in Manchester

With the rise of industrialisation, there was money to be made for those with the ability, ambition, hard work, luck and what most people did not have, the opportunity to set up in business. Of course some retail businesses were set up by wealthy entrepreneurs, but others grew from humble beginnings into companies still in business today and worth many millions of pounds.

In the eighteenth and nineteenth centuries the ever-widening gap between rich and poor was evident in every aspect of life, not least in shopping. For the first time in history, shopping became a leisure activity for those with plenty of time and money to spare, while for the majority of people it was merely another chore in a long, exhausting day. The shopping experiences for these two groups could hardly have been more polarized; while many struggled to buy necessities such as food and clothing, opulence and luxury were on offer in those shops which marketed themselves as catering for the 'elite', for example Kendal, Milne & Faulkner and Finnigan's.

Kendals

Johnny and Betty Watts opened a draper's 'bazaar' on Deansgate in c.1796. As the business expanded, Thomas Kendal, James Milne and Adam Faulkner joined the firm and in 1836 they bought the business from the Watts brothers. Thus was born the department store Kendal, Milne and Faulkner. The store was always at the forefront of new innovation and the business prospered; they had fifty horse-drawn vans to deliver their goods. When Adam Faulkner died in 1862 his name was dropped and the store became Kendal Milne & Co.

KENDAL, MILNE & FAULKNER

IMPORTERS OF
IRISH LINENS,
SHEETINGS, TABLE LINENS,
French Cambrics, &c.

SILK MERCERS,
HABERDASHERS, HOSIERS, GLOVERS,
Lacemen, Furriers,
CLOAK, MANTLE AND SHAWLMEN,
CARPET FACTORS,
Printed Furniture, Moreen, Damask, Family Linen and General Manchester Warehousemen.

KENDAL, MILNE AND FAULKNER,
THE BAZAAR,
95 to 99, Deansgate,
AND
3 to 7, Police Street,
MANCHESTER.

By the end of the nineteenth century the store employed 900 people. The business was conducted in two separate buildings facing each other across Deansgate; on one side of the road was the draper's department and on the other was the furniture department. At this time the firm not only sold their goods, they also made them. Behind the Kendal Milne furniture shop was a seven-storey factory employing cabinetmakers, etc. In 1920 an underground tunnel was built to connect the two retail buildings.

Kendal Milne was not a shop for the man in the street; it boasted of catering 'for the elite of town and country' and earned the label 'The Harrods of the North'. In 1919 it became just that when Harrods bought the shop for £650,000 and changed its name. After many complaints from staff and shoppers, it reverted back to Kendals. Adam Faulkner had long ago been consigned to history and he was now joined by James Milne.

> 'Hell hath no fury... ' and all that. In 1872 an assistant at Kendals received a sound thrashing from the young lady he had recently jilted!
>
> The headline read:
> **'Horsewhipped at Kendals'**

Recovering from a major fire and preparing for the inevitable outbreak of the Second World War, the two lower floors which had already been excavated were reinforced with walls of concrete and steel, providing sixteen air-raid shelters in the sub-basement, twenty-five feet below the ground. In the early years of the war the upper three floors were requisitioned by the government, the top floor being used as a NAAFI. After the war, the store continued to expand and by the 1950s it employed around 2,000 people.

The name Kendals remained and the inhabitants of Manchester continued to regard it as an upmarket store. It changed its name to House of Fraser in 2005 and even though it had been owned by them since 1959, many people felt that in losing its name, it also lost some of its character and uniqueness.

The building on the other side of the street (now occupied by Waterstones) and the subway were closed in 1981.

> The store lays claim, somewhat contentiously, to being the oldest department store in the world.

&

W. Mountcastle
Hatter to the Queen
21, (late 11) Market Street
Manchester

Mr. Mountcastle was a fashionable hatter of his day. In the 1820s, his became the first shop in Manchester to have (2) plate-glass windows, rather than small square pieces of glass. They cost a massive £30 and became a bit of a tourist attraction as people flocked to see them.

Jewsbury & Brown

Henry Jewsbury entered into a partnership with Whitlow in 1826. They founded a business selling perfumes, medications and a variety of non-alcoholic drinks, including ginger beer and lemonade.

> **To Quote:**
>
> **To thirsty souls the name be ever dear**
> **Of Jewsbury's 'Celebrated Ginger Beer';**
> **And let the meed of cool-tongu'd praise be paid**
> **To Whitelow's effervescing lemonade.**
>
> From *Gimcrackiana; or Fugitive Pieces on Manchester Men and Memories* by Geoffrey Gimcrack

The partnership was later dissolved and in 1845 Jewsbury formed another with his apprentice William Scott Brown; 'Jewsbury & Brown' was to become a famous name, not only in Manchester, but around the world. Their first shop was at 52 Market Street, but they later moved into newly-built premises at 113. The main factory and laboratories were located in Ardwick Green.

In 1964, the still locally-based company was taken over by the multinational corporation Schweppes.

Tom and Jerry shops

1821 saw the publication of the first edition of a monthly journal about the exploits of *'Jerry Hawthorn Esq. and his elegant friend Corinthian Tom'*. The stories were hugely popular and were soon transferred to the stage where the plays also proved to be a great success. The names *'Tom and Jerry'* became synonymous with any kind of raucous and riotous behaviour.

The Beerhouse Act, passed in 1830, permitted almost anyone (for a small fee!) to sell alcohol in their own home. Often this was illegally distilled liquor of dubious provenance. These houses became the refuge of drinkers and gamblers and were also used as pawn shops and often as the trading places of stolen goods. The term 'Tom and Jerry' or just 'Jerry' was applied to these 'low-drinking houses' of which there were many in Manchester and the surrounding areas. (The unlicensed equivalent of these 'Jerry shops' were known as 'Hush shops'.)

Mr. Hyde's shop on Market Stead Lane in 1823

Print: Courtesy of 'The Victorian Web'

The first mention of a shop in Manchester dates back to a document entitled 'Rental of the Manor of Manchester' of 1413. The shop was in the Market Place, where previously all goods had been sold from open stalls.

&

SMITHFIELD MARKET

Manchester was a market town. There were markets everywhere; a good few of them were in the Shudehill area where traders had been selling fish, fruit and vegetables for decades. Many of these markets came together in the first half of the nineteenth century; such were the beginnings of Smithfield Market which was officially named as such in 1822. Markets were held in the open streets until 1853 when four huge glass and cast-iron arcades were constructed over the various markets.

Smithfield Market was extended several times. The retail fish market was added in 1873 and various market buildings and offices were built; by the turn of the twentieth century it was reputed to be the largest market complex in Europe, covering around six acres.

Manchester's Smithfield Market in 1854

Trading would begin at 6am and any fruit and vegetables left over at the end of the day were sold cheaply to the residents of nearby Angel Meadow, one of the most deprived areas of the city. Smithfield Market would have been a bustling hive of activity from morning 'til night; the area surrounding the markets would have been alive with pubs, eateries, barrow boys, street musicians and entertainers – many people would visit for a good 'night out'.

> Shortly after the loss of twenty-seven lifeboat men, a fund was set up to help the bereaved families and £50,000 was raised. A Lancashire businessman came up with the idea of 'Manchester's Lifeboat Saturday', the first of which was held in 1891. Amongst other activities, the orphans of those lost at sea paraded through the markets. The event attracted 30,000 people and the city's annual contribution to the RNLI rose from £200 to £5,500.

Smithfield Market in the 1960s

Before finding fame and fortune in *The Sweeney* and *Inspector Morse,* John Thaw worked at the fruit market here.

When the market was demolished, the façade of the building with the fantastic stone carvings was retained and is now the frontage of a residential development.

manchester craft & design centre

Burgess lived in Monaco until his death

The building which now houses the Manchester Craft and Design Centre was once part of the retail fish market, built in 1873 adjacent to the wholesale fish market, both part of the huge Smithfield Market complex. Trade here continued for a hundred years until 1973 when the market moved to Openshaw.

This striking Victorian glass and steel building was renovated to become home to a craft centre in 1982, beginning the regeneration of what was to become the N4; the name 'Northern Quarter' was in fact coined in this very building. The history of the building is evident, many features having been retained, including some of the original fishmongers' booths.

Shopping 253

WILLIAM WHITAKER,
FISHMONGER,
DEALER IN LONDON NATIVE OYSTERS,
FISH MARKET, SMITHY DOOR,
MANCHESTER.

Tenders his grateful acknowledgements to the Public, for the liberal share of Patronage and Support he has received for the last Ten Years, and begs to assure his Friends that no exertion on his part shall be wanting to merit a continuance of their favours. He is regularly Supplied with LONDON OYSTERS, which he warrants of the Best Quality.
W. W. guarantees the Fish he sells, so that the Public may have confidence in all purchases made at his Establishment.

OYSTER ROOMS
Fitted up with every Convenience for the Accommodation of Large or Small Parties.
FAMILIES SUPPLIED WITH BARRELLED OYSTERS, WARRANTED OF THE BEST QUALITY.
LOBSTERS, CRABS, POTTED SHRIMPS, &c. FRESH EVERY DAY.
ALL ORDERS PUNCTUALLY AND CAREFULLY ATTENDED TO.
LICENSED TO DEAL IN GAME.

Advert from the 1850s

Oysters

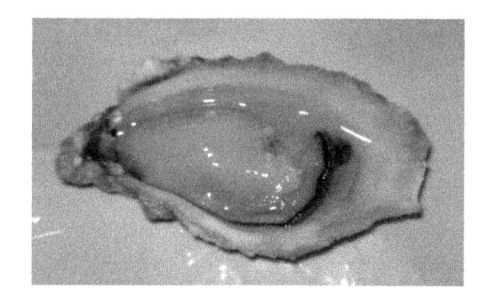

Now considered by some to be a (not so cheap) delicacy, pickled oysters were at one time (in the nineteenth century), part of the diet of the poor, especially in coastal areas; the first oysters arrived in Manchester by rail from London.

To Quote:

'He was a brave man that first ate an oyster.'

Jonathan Swift

(although oysters had been eaten for thousands of years)

To Quote:

'Poverty and oysters always seem to go together.'

Sam Weller in Charles Dickens' *The Pickwick Papers*

In 1862 Joseph Sykes opened a stall on Smithfield Market selling wet fish and Dutch shrimps. With the ever-growing network of railways and the use of zinc-lined boxes (precursor of the fridge) to store ice, seafood became more available and more affordable and the business prospered.

> Ice sellers sold ice to fishmongers, butchers and the wealthiest households. Blocks of ice were cut from frozen lakes in the winter, in countries as far afield as America, and shipped across the Atlantic. This photograph shows 'ice-harvesters' in New England. In the nineteenth century ice was America's second-biggest export; in 1890 three million tons of ice were cut in Maine alone with a workforce of 25,000 men and 1,000 horses.

The business continued to expand and by the 1930s Sykes had become one of the largest wholesalers on Smithfield Market. The firm moved to the new Market in Openshaw in 1973 and five generations later Sykes Seafood is still owned and run by the same family.

In 1844 a group of weavers set up the Rochdale Pioneers' Society. It was a co-operative, so was owned and run by its members between whom any profits were shared. It was one of many co-operatives being set up at this time, but this group is widely recognized as being the founder of the Co-operative Movement. In 1862 various co-operatives joined together to become the Co-operative Wholesale Society (CWS). The group's headquarters are and always have been in Manchester on a site of many buildings (most of them now listed) the latest being the striking and extremely eco-friendly head office, built in 2013, in the former slum area of Angel Meadow.

Manchester: Balloon Street and Garden Street.

An early CWS building

The company changed from wholesale to retail and became one of the most well-known brands.

An early Co-op supermarket

After a decline in fortunes towards the end of the twentieth century, the company underwent what was called 'the largest re-branding exercise in UK corporate history'. Their biggest-ever television advertising campaign was launched in 2009 featuring Bob Dylan's *Blowing in the Wind* – one of the rare occasions the artist has allowed his music to be used for commercial purposes.

Throughout its history, the CWS has incorporated and merged with other companies; one such merger in 2001 resulted in a change of name for the business, becoming the Co-operative Group (CWS) Limited. The Co-op Group is the largest mutual business in the world with 7,000,000 members and 100,000 employees working in its range of businesses – food, travel, banking and pharmacy to name but a few. It still retains its ethical stance on issues such as the environment and slave labour and operates a strict fair-trade policy.

Orme & Sons

The business was founded in 1845 when it began trading as 'Thomas and James Orme, billiards and bagatelle table manufacturers'; they later went on to become Orme & Sons. The company received the royal warrant and soon earned the reputation of being one of the best makers of billiard tables in the country. They also manufactured and sold all the accessories such as cues and balls, which at that time were made of ivory.

In 1887 they were commissioned to make a billiard table for Queen Victoria's Golden Jubilee Exhibition. The table was made from black walnut and carved with British birds and flowers, quotations from British poets and portraits of former kings and queens. The accompanying cupboard was carved with Victoria and Albert, royal palaces and scenes from Victoria's reign.

In 2010 the table was offered for sale at Harrods for £1,000,000! It is considered to be one of the most beautiful and THE most expensive billiard table ever made.

BEDDOE'S
General Mourning Warehouse,
71, DEANSGATE, MANCHESTER.

ESTABLISHED FOR THE EXCLUSIVE SALE OF
MOURNING GOODS,
Consisting of every Article for Deep or Slight Mourning, of the Newest and Most Fashionable Styles. A Large Assortment of
BONNETS, MILLINERY AND MANTLES,
Always on hand, and Families Supplied with every Article for Mourning on the Shortest Notice. Funerals Conducted and Supplied with Every Requisite.
John Beddoe, Proprietor, 71, Deansgate, Manchester.

Advert from c.1850

TIMPSON

William Timpson was born in Rothwell in 1859, the youngest of eight children. By the age of 8 he was already a budding entrepreneur, making and selling leather boot laces. When he was 11 he was sent to Manchester to work with his older brother, delivering shoes. However, following an argument, William returned to Rothwell to be trained in the art of shoemaking. When he was 16 he returned to Manchester and entered into a brief partnership with his brother-in-law, opening a shop in Butler Street in 1865. In 1869 he opened his own boot and shoe shop at 97, Oldham Street which he rented for £200 a year. This first shop was a great success and he went on to open more shops in the area. A new warehouse was built in Manchester in 1895 (apparently large enough to hold 40,000 pairs of shoes) and in 1897 a horse and cart were bought to make local deliveries. By the turn of the century there were fourteen Timpson shops in and around Manchester and by 1939 the company owned 189 shoe shops around the country.

Founder of the business, William Timpson

The Timpson family continued to play a leading role in the development of the business throughout the twentieth century, despite being taken over by other companies. However, in 1983 the chairman, John Timpson (great-grandson of William), paid £42 million to take back sole (ha ha) control of the family business. Four years later John Timpson sold all the shoe shops in order to concentrate on other aspects of the business. They now offer a range of services including processing photos and cutting keys. The only shoes to be seen are those waiting to be repaired.

The business is still based in Manchester. Nearly 150 years and five generations later, the business still remains in the same family and the name Timpson can be seen in roughly 800 branches around the country.

Pauldens

The Rylands building (now Debenhams) was built between 1929 and 1932 as a warehouse for the Rylands Textile Company founded by the Rylands family in 1819; it was one of the last great warehouses to be built in Manchester. The building was designed by Fairhurst in the art deco style and is clad in Portland stone; in 1994 it was given Grade II listed building status. In the 1940s a beacon was placed on the roof as a navigational aid for aircraft flying in and out of Ringway (now Manchester) Airport; it projected a revolving beam of light visible sixty miles away.

In 1865 Pauldens department store was established by William Paulden on Stretford Road. Mr. Paulden was quite the entrepreneur and it was one of the first shops to introduce electric lighting and lifts. Later, he attracted customers by having a moving picture show in the shop window. The shop even had its own band.

In 1928 Debenhams took over the business, but the shop continued to trade under the name Pauldens. It was one of the first shops in Manchester to use motorized vehicles; previously they had used horses and carts which were housed in stables at the back of the shop.

In 1957, the store underwent a complete renovation. On a Sunday evening and the day before the grand reopening, a fire broke out. Within a few hours the building was completely gutted.

This dramatic photograph was taken just as the old Pauldens building collapsed!

Following the fire, Pauldens continued trading in an army barracks annexe on Medlock Street. A year later they moved into the former Rylands warehouse on Market Street.

In the 1970s the name on the building was changed to Debenhams.

> A couple of years after the fire, the 103 bus to Wythenshaw drove into the crater, i.e. the basement of the old building. Lots of people were injured in the crash which happened on a foggy day. No Health & Safety in those days!

> At one time, tea was regarded as a luxury drink - the privilege of the wealthy. It was only at the beginning of the Victorian era that tea became more available and affordable for the masses.

Arthur Brooke was the founder of the Brooke Bond tea company. Bond was not a partner; Brooke just liked the sound of the name Brooke Bond, implying a bond of trust between himself and his customers. He opened his first shop in Manchester in 1869 in a prime location at 29, Market Street and sold only tea, coffee and sugar. He sold high-quality teas (unlike some tea dealers at the time) and his shop prospered. In the 1870s more shops were opened and the company's offices were established in London. The business also expanded into selling wholesale. It was a huge success and by the time he was thirty, Arthur Brooke was a very wealthy man!

The Brooke Bond shop at the corner of Piccadilly and Oldham Street

In the 1930s Brooke Bond launched PG Tips under the name Pre-Gestee implying that if drunk before eating, it would aid digestion. Tips, indicating that only the tips (i.e. the best bits) of the tea plant were used.

In 1952 tea rationing, which had been introduced in January 1940, had come to an end and the race to become market leader began. In 1954 Brooke Bond introduced collectable 'picture cards'. They proved a great success and by 1968 the annual production of the cards had reached 720,000,000. In all, 200 series of cards were issued covering a variety of topics from British birds to transport. There are still many collectors of these tea cards around the world; some of the early and rare sets of cards are much sought-after and can command prices of up to £1,000.

Brooke Bond was one of the first companies to successfully exploit television advertising and its first advert using chimpanzees was broadcast at Christmas in 1956. The trained chimps were taken from shows such as Billy Smart's Circus and the adverts became some of the most popular and successful in television history. Some adverts were parodies of James Bond – 'Agent Bond, Brooke Bond'. The advert in which the chimps are moving a piano ('Mr Shifter') was shown more times than any other advert on British television. Voice-overs were often provided by well-known stars, such as Peter Sellers and Bruce Forsyth. The chimps became so popular that they used to tour the country promoting Brooke Bond tea. The chimps proved to be a marketing triumph and soon twenty-five per cent of all British households were drinking Brooke Bond tea.

In the early 1960s, the company introduced tea bags into their range of products and they soon achieved second place in the British tea market, behind CWS. By 1967, however, Brooke Bond had become brand leader with its PG Tips range. In 1968 the company merged with Liebig Meat Company to become Brooke Bond Liebig. One hundred years after Arthur Brooke opened his first shop in Manchester, the business had become one of the largest food manufacturers and distribution companies in the UK with interests all around the world. The Brooke family connection to the company ended in the 1970s with chairman John Brooke. In 1984 the company was taken over by Unilever, but the Brooke Bond factory is still located in Manchester, at Trafford Park.

Cussons

Thomas Cussons opened a chemist's shop in Manchester in 1869. Thomas's son Alexander moved the business into manufacturing when he bought a bleaching factory in Salford in 1909. Several years later Marks and Spencer began selling products made by Cussons.

In 1918 the company began producing perfume. The business expanded rapidly and in 1920 they opened a soap factory, again in Salford. In 1934 the company launched one of their most famous products – Imperial Leather. In 1946 Alexander made Cussons, Sons & Co. a public company. Over the years Cussons acquired other firms including Bayley's of Bond Street, London. It continued to grow into a multi-million-pound international company.

In 1975 PZ acquired Cussons becoming PZCussons plc and business continued to prosper. During recent health scares, the company's profits soared as their anti-bacterial handwash, Carex, flew off the shelves! The company's head office is still based in Manchester.

Affleck and Brown

Once considered to be 'the Harrods of the North' Affleck & Brown was at one time perhaps Manchester's most famous department store, occupying the large elegant Smithfield building (formerly nine separate buildings) at the corner of Oldham Street and Church Street.

Founded by Robert Affleck and John Brown and opening its doors in the 1860s, it advertised itself as a 'Drapers and House Furnishers'. As can be seen from this later advert, the store was obviously at the forefront of technology – not only did it have a telegraph address, it also had twelve telephone lines.

The store was taken over by Debenhams in 1950 and in the 1960s it became home to British Home Stores. When BHS moved into the Arndale Centre, the building was left vacant.

In 1996 the Smithfield building became one of the first inner-city buildings in Manchester to be converted into flats. The multi-award-winning conversion by Urban Splash transformed the old shop space into eighty-one loft apartments built around two central atria while retaining many original features. There are also retail spaces on the ground floor.

Afflecks Palace opened in 1981 in a building opposite the old Affleck and Brown store and in what was to become the 'creative and Bohemian' Northern Quarter. It was an indoor market over four floors with an eclectic mix of dozens of off-beat and individual stalls and shops. It operated with a policy of low rents and weekly contracts; this opened the door to many people wanting to start a business with minimum funds. Frequent visitors included Happy Mondays and Inspiral Carpets. Despite two serious fires, the business flourished for twenty-five years; rumours that it was to be sold prompted an online petition which attracted thousands of supporters.

Afflecks Palace ceased trading on 31 March 2008 and reopened the following day under new management and a new name – Afflecks. This 'Manchester icon' and 'emporium of eclecticism' is still going strong.

H. Samuel

In 1821 Moses and Lewis Samuel began a clock-making and silversmith wholesale business in Liverpool. In 1862 Moses' daughter-in-law Harriet took over the business and moved it to Market Street, Manchester. The first retail shop opened in Preston in 1890 and in 1912 the company moved its headquarters to Birmingham.

This engraving for the bookseller Samuel Mallet Johnson dates from around 1830.

'Tommy Shops' (the Truck System)

The Truck System became widespread in the eighteenth and nineteenth centuries, especially in the industrialised cities of Britain, where it also became known as the Tommy System. In this system, the employees were paid not in money, but 'in kind', for example, in notes or tokens which could only be exchanged for goods in certain shops. These shops were usually owned by the employer and sold inferior goods at higher prices than similar shops, thereby returning all the profits to the owners' pockets. These came to be known as 'Tommy shops' and would 'sell' food, clothing, supplies and even furniture.

> The word 'truck' in this context comes from the French 'troquer', meaning to barter or exchange; it came into Middle English as 'truke'. The expression 'to have no truck with' meaning 'to have nothing to do with' has the same derivation.

&

> The descriptive phrase 'tommy rot' refers to the overpriced, poor quality goods sold in these shops.

In 1827 a (very brave) employee took his employer, a Manchester cotton manufacturer, to court. He gave evidence that he had only received two shillings (10p) in cash in nine months; the rest was paid in tokens which had to be exchanged at the shop owned by the employer's daughter!

An example of a token from 1812

It was only in 1887 that this practice was made illegal in Britain.

> **'Tick shops'** – where one could buy goods 'on tick', i.e. 'buy now, pay later'; many shops would have offered this service, especially in times of severe hardship.

Barton Arcade

Inspired by Crystal Palace in London and built in 1871 at a cost of £25,000, Barton Arcade is a beautiful Victorian structure made of cast iron and glass; it was one of the first buildings on the newly-widened Deansgate. The arcade, named after the Bartons, a wealthy Manchester family, is a four-storey building with three tiered galleries overlooking a central area; in 1972 it became a Grade II* listed building of special architectural interest. It underwent a complete restoration in the 1980s at a cost of more than £1 million. Sadly, this is the only survivor of three such arcades that were built in Manchester in the nineteenth century. Another was the curved Lancaster Arcade, erected c.1853 and one of the earliest shopping arcades in the city; it was left to fall into wrack and ruin and was eventually demolished in the 1970s.

Finnigan's

> The Finnigan family came over from Ireland in the early 1800s. Benjamin Finnigan first began trading on Market Street in 1875, later moving to premises on Deansgate. It was a pioneer department store in that it catered only for the needs of the 'elite'. In 1900 the company expanded when it opened another branch in New Bond Street, London. It also opened a store in Liverpool.
>
> Finnigan's established itself as makers of high-quality luggage and leather goods, but later widened the range of products on sale to include furniture and household goods, catering for the needs of Lancashire's wealthiest.

Even today, items labelled 'Finnigan's Ltd, Deansgate' are highly collectable and can be found in exclusive salerooms such as Bonhams and Christies. Finnigan's perfected the ancient method of stretching the wet leather over a welded steel rod frame to produce the best, most durable material – very time-consuming and hence very expensive. It harks back to an age when only the very rich would go travelling with trunks, dressing-cases and hat-boxes, etc. Luckily, they had plenty of servants to carry them all! Items by Finnigan's of Manchester and Bond Street, London are still considered to be amongst the best leather goods ever produced.

In its heyday Finnigan's played host to art exhibitions and other public events; Fred Perry, Wimbledon Champion for three years running (1934-36) gave a series of lectures on tennis and Valette held exhibitions of his paintings here.

LEWIS'S DEPARTMENT STORE

Following the success of his store in Liverpool, David Lewis opened a branch on Market Street, Manchester in 1880. Unlike 'Affleck and Brown' and 'Kendal Milne', this shop was not aimed at the wealthy elite. Instead, it set out to appeal to the 'upper-working and lower-middle classes' and was run on the principle of mass turnover and small profits.

It worked!

It was a huge success and soon hordes of people were travelling to Manchester solely to visit Lewis's. In the next few years the store was extended several times to accommodate new departments. One extension incorporated two back streets which were covered over to become Lewis's Arcade. It also extended into the Royal Buildings which stood on the site of the Royal Hotel (where the football league was founded in 1888).

Including workshops, in which almost 600 tailors and shoemakers worked to produce the goods on sale, it soon became an impressive building with seven floors and a huge clock-tower (now long gone) looking out over Piccadilly. At this time, Lewis's in Manchester was the largest department store outside London. It also claimed to be the home to Manchester's first escalator. When the lifts were installed, each lift had its own attendant who would take shoppers up or down to their requested floor; this continued well into the 1960s when self-service lifts were installed.

In its early days Lewis's offered numerous attractions to entice people into the store, many of which were to be found in the sub-basement; for example, a penny in-the-slot Edison phonograph and stereoscopic pictures, not to mention the largest soda fountain in the British Empire! Lewis's also held the first ever concerts in a department store; they lasted about half an hour and cost a penny; many later-to-be-famous artists first performed here. By the turn of the century people who could afford it were beginning to visit halls and theatres to watch moving pictures. Way out of the price range of most people (a shilling or twelve old pennies) Lewis's began showing the Lumière Brothers Cinematograph, also at the cost of one penny.

On one occasion the sub-basement was flooded to become a 'Little Venice' and customers were able to ride on gondolas along the two-feet deep 'Grand Canal' and under the 'Bridge of Sighs' to see the sights of Venice. Again, all for the cost of one penny.

On the top floor was a silver-service restaurant which had an orchestra playing in the afternoons, and they had a ballroom in which local bands would play; it would also be used for staff dances and exhibitions. On top of the building was a glass dome which formed the top of a central atrium which extended all the way down to the ground floor.

The ballroom on the 5th floor

In the 1950s there was a saying – 'You're standing there like one of Lewis's'. This referred not to lazy shop assistants but to the 'working girls' who frequented Lewis's Arcade at night, waiting for passing trade while sheltering from the wind and rain!

Lewis's at Christmas was a magical experience for any child with its amazing grottoes, toys galore (in the days when most children only received toys for Christmas and birthdays) and fantastic window displays on Market Street.

A Lewis's toy display

The central atrium became the scene of many Christmas grottoes.

Photographs: Roy Tootell

In the 70s, a time of heightened IRA activity, 'traffic light bomb alerts' were dotted around the store. Apparently the general public were not supposed to know about these, but of course they did. When the light turned red, it was time to drop your shopping and leave. In 1975 the IRA planted an incendiary device in the store which, when detonated, injured nineteen people.

When Lewis's closed in 2001, the building was taken over by Primark (the largest Primark in the world). It was a sad day for Manchester!

> **To Quote:**
>
> John Mahoney, better known as Martin Crane from *Frasier*, worked at Lewis's briefly before emigrating to America. He said, **'The worst job I ever had was probably selling clothes at Lewis's in Manchester.'**

Shopping 273

This photograph, taken in 1940, shows the Lewis's clock tower on the left and the Rylands building on the right.

A postcard showing Market Street with Lewis's on the right. The lady on the left is Maude Fealy (1883-1971) who was an American actress of stage and screen in the early twentieth century. Between 1900 and 1905 she made frequent tours of the UK with Sir Henry Irving's company. Presumably, it was during one of these tours that the actress visited Manchester.

FRED ALDOUS
ART, CRAFT & DESIGN MATERIALS

1886 was the year in which Queen Victoria celebrated her Golden Jubilee and Coca-Cola was invented; it was also the year in which Fred Aldous had a great idea. He had been working at a mill in which the cotton was moved around the factory in baskets. Aldous decided to set up a business importing cane to make baskets for the many mills and factories in the area. Initially he imported and sold just three products – cane, willow and yeast which he sold to cotton traders and brewers. He ran his business from a cart and it was not until 1902 that he had saved enough money to move into his first premises – a small, cramped shop in Elbow Street. This was also the year in which Fred Aldous's son, also called Fred, went to work for his father as an errand boy.

The decline of the cotton industry after the First World War could have heralded the end of the business had it not been for the inspiration of Fred (2). Craft products, which had previously been just a sideline, now became the main focus – a decision that secured the future of the company. Business boomed and several changes of premises followed. When Fred (1) died in 1936 he left the business to his five children. Fred (2) bought out his four sisters and three of his own sons joined the company. The business moved again, this time to Withy Grove. With over 100 employees, times were good – there was even a Fred Aldous Ltd company band. However, it was not to last. With the novelty of television, interest in handicrafts declined and the business began to flounder. With two of his sons having left and one having died, it was down to 77-year-old Fred to hold the fort. Enter another of his sons, Fred (3), under whose leadership the business got back on its feet. He took them into their last move – the present building on Lever Street. Fred (2) retired in 1970, sixty-eight years after joining the business as errand boy!

Over 125 years (and five generations) later, after the trials of war, flood and fire, the shop continues to go from strength to strength. The business is still in the same family and has grown from offering 3 to 25,000 crafty products selling to customers all over the world.

In 1884 Michael Marks arrived in Britain from the Russian Empire, a penniless Jewish refugee unable to speak a word of English. He initially traded from a handcart and then opened a stall on Kirkgate Market in Leeds. He called it 'The Penny Bazaar', using the slogan 'Don't ask the price. It's a penny'. This was not only a great marketing ploy, but also an excellent way of avoiding having to barter in his poor English. Marks was later joined by Tom Spencer.

Ten years after Michael Marks arrived in England, he and Spencer opened their first shop – at 20, Cheetham Hill Road in Manchester. Marks & Spencer opened their first warehouse in Manchester in 1901 and this was also the company's headquarters until the 1930s when it relocated to Baker Street in London. It was only after the First World War, long after the deaths of Michael Marks and Tom Spencer, that Michael's son Simon joined forces with Israel Moses Sieff and together they began building the shopping empire we know today. These two had grown up together, living in the same street. They both studied at Manchester Grammar School and Manchester University and later went on to marry each other's sister.

In 1928 the 'St. Michael' brand name was introduced by Simon Marks as a tribute to his father Michael and the name remained until 2000. They had a policy of selling only British-made goods and prided themselves on selling value-for-money quality items and outstanding customer service. A new slogan for the store was introduced – 'The customer is always and completely right.'

M&S later occupied a building at 46-50 Oldham Street. During the Second World War the basement was used as an air-raid shelter with room for 200 people. The staff of all the M&S branches raised £5,000 to buy a Spitfire. Perhaps unsurprisingly, it was named *The Marksman*.

Towards the end of the 1950s M&S saw the way the wind was blowing, i.e. the decline of Oldham Street, and in 1961 they moved to Cross Street.

In 1996, at about 11.15 am on 15 June, an IRA bomb exploded just outside M&S. The shop (and much of the area around it) was transformed from the busy Saturday-shopping hustle and bustle to a scene of utter devastation. There had been a warning and luckily the shop and the surrounding area had been evacuated of around 80,000 people, including many visiting Russian and German football fans. Following the bomb, this part of Manchester was given a much-needed facelift. While their store was being rebuilt, M&S moved into Lewis's department store.

Simon Marks and Israel Moses Sieff were friends and partners for sixty-three years, both becoming barons. Lord Marks died in 1964 and Lord Sieff in 1973.

In 1998, M&S became the first British retailer to make a pre-tax profit of £1billion. I wonder what Michael Marks, the penniless refugee, would have made of that!

> **&** The first M&S store in Asia was opened in the 1960s in Kabul, Afghanistan. It didn't last too long and was closed owing to 'political instability'.
>
> Nothing changes!

The history of M&S has not been without controversy. The company's links to Zionism go back a long way. When Israel Sieff became company director, he and Simon Marks were not only partners in business, but also in their Zionist activities. Marks and Sieff worked together with Chaim Weizmann, at the time a lecturer in Chemistry at Manchester University, towards the Balfour declaration of 1917, in which the idea of a homeland for the Jewish people in Palestine was put forward.

One of the fundamental objectives of M&S throughout the twentieth century, according to Lord Marcus Sieff in 1990, was 'to aid the economic development of Israel'. Since the death of Lord Sieff in 2001, M&S have tried to distance themselves from their controversial past:

'M&S is a secular organisation embracing all cultures, nationalities, races and religions. We do not support or align ourselves to any countries, nations, states, governments, political parties and religious bodies.' (2010)

Shudehill Booksellers

1930   **1958**

Forsyth

Originally, the shop founded in 1857 by brothers James and Henry Forsyth was on the corner of Deansgate and St. Ann's Street but in the 1880s the business moved to 126, Deansgate where it has remained ever since. Initially the shop specialised only in pianos, but gradually they extended their range of goods to include orchestral instruments, sheet music and books on music. Later, they went on to sell wirelesses and gramophones. They also established a music publishing business and had their own concert hall in which recitals were given, a practice that continued until the 1970s. Always keeping up with the latest technology they moved on from records to tapes to CDs to acoustic and electronic keyboards and guitars. James Forsyth's son Algernon, a director of the business, worked until three weeks before his death in 1961 -at the age of 98! After 150 years of business, the shop is still owned and managed by the fifth generation of the Forsyth family. It is the largest general music shop with the largest display of pianos in the UK. Since the sad demise of Edward's Shoe Shop, Forsyth is now also the oldest continuously open shop (keeping the same name) in the city.

This original sign for one of the oldest jewellers in Manchester dates back to the early 1900s.

Founder, John Nichols

The original recipe for Vimto was invented in 1908 by John Noel Nichols who owned a business in central Manchester selling herbs, spices and medicines. In the early part of the twentieth century the Temperance Movement was gaining momentum and Nichols saw an opening for a new non-alcoholic drink. It was marketed as a health-giving tonic, going under the name of Vim Tonic. In 1912 the name was shortened to Vimto.

Vimto is made from grapes, raspberries and blackcurrants and is flavoured with a secret mix of herbs and spices. That mix is a closely- guarded secret, known to only a few people.

280   2,000 Years of Manchester

A 1913 advert claimed that Vimto 'eliminates that out-of-sorts feeling' and 'builds up the system'.

Vimto started exporting as early as 1919, initially to outposts of the British Empire. It was especially popular in India and later in the Middle East.

A 'temperance' Vimto shop in 1921

Vimto adverts from the early days

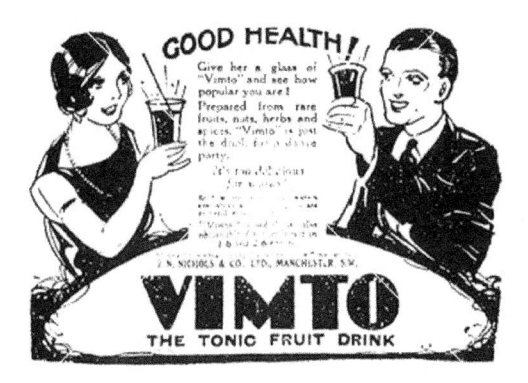

'Give her a glass of 'Vimto' and see how popular you are!'

Vimto is now sold in over sixty-five countries all over the world and the company remains in the fourth generation of the Nichols family.

> The Vimto Monument was carved out of an oak tree by Kerry Morrison. It stands on Granby Row - the site where Vimto was first made.

> 'Tizer' was also born in Manchester. It began life as 'Pickup's Appetizer' in 1924 when it was developed by Fred and Tom Pickup. It was later changed to Tizer with the slogan 'Tizer the Appetizer'. It was sold, first to Armour Trust, and then in 1972 to the Scottish company Barr plc for £2.5 million. The exact recipe remains a closely-guarded secret.

UCP shops

What a load of …

In 1906 there were 260 specialist tripe shops in the region. Today, there seems to be just one. (It's in Stalybridge, should you want to rush out and buy some. See below.)

UCP – United Cattle Products – was formed in 1920 when fifteen tripe companies joined forces to become one. They ran a chain of offal butchers in the north of England, many with cafés attached, selling tripe, cowheel, chitterlings, oxtail and other delicacies of the bovine variety.

> This picture shows a UCP premises at the corner of Market Street and Pall Mall. It opened in 1964 in a new building with a banqueting suite, a shop and a self-service café. In earlier days the UCP restaurants were grand affairs with tablecloths, waitresses clad in elegant black and white uniforms and long queues of people waiting for a table.

> **What is tripe?**
>
> (If you are of a squeamish disposition, look away now.)
> Tripe is the lining of animals' stomachs, usually the first and second stomachs of cattle. Once the stomach has been removed it is cleaned, it has the outer membranes removed and is then boiled. After cooking, the tripe is bleached in a very diluted peroxide solution, rinsed and trimmed. It is then ready to be sold.

MONOTONY
in meals can be avoided by
dainty meals contrived with
U.C.P. Tripe and Cowheels

> In some areas, black (unbleached) tripe was called 'slut' from the old Lancashire dialect word slutty, meaning dirty.

Tripe has had a long and varied history. In Greek and Roman times it was considered a delicacy and was eaten by the 'great and good'. At the other extreme, tripe was the staple diet of industrial Lancashire; it was cheap and quick and easy to cook – the fast food of its day!

> **To Quote:**
>
> 'Tripe ... is enjoyed by society's two extremes, the topmost and the lowermost strata, while the multitudinous middle classes of the world look upon it with genteel disdain and noses tilted.'
>
> *The Wise Encyclopaedia of Cookery*

UCP Ltd marketed its tripe as:
>Easy on the digestion
>Easy on the purse!

By the late 1960s as prosperity grew and tastes changed there was a fairly rapid decline in the sales of tripe and offal.

Photo: Courtesy of Ashton Market

> **To Quote:**
>
> 'The unlucky person finds bones in his tripe dinner.'
>
> Egyptian proverb meaning: You can't escape your fate.

Wiles

If you were a child growing up in Manchester in the first half of the twentieth Century, then Wiles Toy Shop was the place to be. The business was established by H. Wiles in a former chemist's shop (Standring's) and was considered by many to be the best toy shop in Manchester. It was situated on Lewis's Arcade which linked Market Street to Mosley Street – Lewis's on one side of the arcade and Wiles on the other.

Photo taken in 1927

The front of the shop can be seen in *Hell is a City*, a 1959 film based on a novel by Maurice Proctor and featuring his detective, Inspector Harry Martineau. The film starred John Crawford, Billie Whitelaw, Donald Pleasance, Warren Mitchell, and Stanley Baker as Martineau; it has since become something of a cult 'film noir'.

The world premiere of Hell is a City was held at Ardwick Apollo, then a cinema.

Goulburn's

Goulburn's Grocers and Poulterers was situated on the Market Place roughly where Harvey Nichols now stands. Underneath the building was (and presumably still is) a maze of tunnels leading in all directions. Amongst them was one tunnel which had long been used for archery, a skittle alley and a shooting gallery; the gallery stretched as far as the boundary of Manchester Cathedral. Goulburns later used these tunnels to store their cheese and eggs (once all the rats had been disposed of!).

During the Second World War, Goulburn's received a telegram from Winston Churchill requesting cheese. Obviously exempt from rationing, the cheese was immediately dispatched and the telegram was put on display in the shop window. Luckily for Churchill, this was before that section of the city was hit by German bombers which resulted in the destruction and later flattening of the area. (The only survivors of the bombing here were the Old Wellington Inn and Sinclair's Oyster Bar.)

Goulburn's went into liquidation in 1964 after 117 years of trading.

Silvana

> John Simon left Germany in 1933 and arrived in Manchester in 1937. He set up a clothing business in Phoenix Mills, Ancoats. In 1954, C&A (a clothing store on Oldham Street) rejected an order of his coats. Simon came up with the novel idea of selling directly from his mill. The business was known as **Silvana** and was in an old Victorian building of several storeys with rickety wooden lifts. On Saturdays he organized a free bus (coincidently the bus stop was outside C&A) to bring customers to his warehouse.

Arndale Centre

When the Arndale Centre was built in the 1970s, it was the largest shopping centre in Europe (and also the ugliest, according to many people). The land on which it is built was a maze of characterful cobbled streets, courts and narrow alleys lined with mostly commercial and industrial Victorian buildings plus a few much older buildings. It was only after the latter had been destroyed that people realised what had been lost and what had been gained –

> **To Quote:**
>
>   '**brutal obliteration'** Avery & Cruikshank (1975).
>
>   '**a distinctly lavatorial Arndale Centre'** Spring (1979)

Work on the Centre began in 1972 and when it was finished in 1979 the total cost was a whopping £100 million (the projected cost had been £11½ million). The centre had one million square feet of retail space.

In the 1990s the Arndale Centre became the target of terrorists. There was an arson attack in April 1991 and in December of the same year the IRA planted fire-bombs which caused considerable damage to four shops.

On 15 June 1996 an IRA bomb exploded on Corporation Street between the Arndale Centre and Marks & Spencer. Around 1,200 properties on 43 streets were damaged. Following the bomb, M&S had to be completely rebuilt and the Arndale Centre underwent major rebuilding and refurbishment. It is now the largest inner-city shopping centre in the UK and receives about 41,000,000 visitors a year.

Chapter 20

Iconic Buildings (past and present)

Despite falling victim to German and IRA bombs, ill-conceived town planning in the post-war era (what were they thinking?) and pure neglect, Manchester remains a city full of architectural gems. Many old buildings were obliterated during the Blitz, some were badly damaged and left to fall down, while others were damaged but were restored or in some cases rebuilt. In the 1960s many of Manchester's great civic buildings were soot-blackened, a legacy of the city's industrial past. A big clean-up to restore them to their former glory began as is shown in this striking before and after photo.

Spot the difference!

There are buildings of many different architectural styles and periods in the city from the medieval Chetham's buildings to the Tudor building which is home to the Old Wellington Inn, the Victorian Gothic Town Hall to the art deco Sunlight building. Many buildings have been described elsewhere in this book and it would be nigh on impossible to feature all the fantastic buildings in the city. Here are a chosen few:

The Royal Exchange

The first Exchange was built in 1729 by Sir Oswald Mosley and was situated in the Market Place. It was the town's first public building, the upper floor of which was used for exhibitions, travelling acting companies and even cockfights. The ground floor was at one time occupied by a meat market and became the haunt of 'idlers and petty criminals', earning it the nickname 'the Lazaretto' (a leper colony). It served until 1806 when it was replaced by a larger building which earned the 'Royal' prefix after a visit from Queen Victoria in 1851.

The second Exchange building, 1835

When the present (third) Royal Exchange was finished in 1874, the Great Hall boasted the largest trading floor in the world, a place where merchants and brokers met and deals worth millions of pounds were struck. At its peak, eighty per cent of the world's finished cotton was traded here. The building suffered extensive bomb damage during the Blitz of 1940 when it took a direct hit; sadly it lost some of its features when rebuilt and the Great Hall was halved in size. Trading ended in 1968 and the building was left empty and threatened with demolition. Worse still, there was talk of it becoming a station for the proposed Manchester Underground. Thankfully it was saved, becoming the home of a theatre company; it was officially opened in 1976 by Sir Laurence Olivier and remains the largest theatre-in-the-round in Britain. The theatre is a seven-sided glass and steel structure suspended from four huge pillars. The building was again damaged in 1996 when an IRA bomb exploded less than fifty metres away; it took two years and £32 million to carry out restoration work.

Sadly, the impressive portico of the Royal Exchange on Cross Street was removed during one of the building's extensions.

Free Trade Hall

This building (the third of three halls on the site) was erected in 1856 on land donated by Richard Cobden and known as St. Peter's Fields, site of the Peterloo Massacre. It was built to commemorate Manchester's fight against and the resulting repeal of the Corn Laws; it was a grand building in the Lombard-Venetian style and was large enough to hold 10,000 people. It was used for concerts, plays and public meetings. Many famous speakers graced its stage including Dickens, Disraeli and Churchill. Following the Christmas Blitz of 1940, only the outer walls of the building remained. It was rebuilt, and reopened by the Queen in 1951.

The Hall was home to the Hallé Orchestra from 1858 until the opening of the Bridgewater Hall in 1996 (bomb-damaged years apart) and also hosted rock and pop concerts (incl. Bob Dylan, David Bowie and Queen).

In 1976 the Sex Pistols played in the Lesser Free Trade Hall in what has been described as one of the most influential concerts of all time, marking the beginning of the 'Punk era'. Although thousands claim to have been at this 'historic' event, there were actually only about fifty people present.

Now a hotel, the façade and grand staircase of the Grade II* listed building were retained. The suites in the hotel are named after some of the Hall's most illustrious entertainers.

Town Hall

The Town Hall originally stood on King Street; it was opened in 1819 but soon became inadequate for the booming town that was 'Cottonopolis'. When the new (present) Town Hall opened, the old building became home to the Free Reference Library; it was demolished in 1911, but the portico was salvaged and now stands in Heaton Park.

The present Town Hall, a Grade I listed building, was completed in 1868 at a cost of over £1,000,000. Both the exterior and the interior were designed by Alfred Waterhouse whose designs were selected from well over a hundred entries. Luckily, it was before he entered his 'blood-red' terracotta period and was built of Collyhurst sandstone. The architect later earned the sobriquet 'Waterhouse Slaughterhouse'.

In the Great Hall are a series of twelve murals by Ford Madox Brown. Painted between 1876 and 1888, they depict the history of Manchester, dating back to the Roman occupation. Unfortunately, the Peterloo Massacre is not featured as it was felt that the image might offend Queen Victoria when she came to open the Town Hall which, in the event, she refused to do. The mosaic floors feature bees, a symbol of Manchester's industry.

Following the destruction to the city in the Second World War, the 'Manchester Town Plan' was drawn up in which the chief surveyor proposed knocking down the (undamaged) Town Hall and replacing it with a 'Modernist' building. Considering many of the post-war buildings in the region, one can only imagine what an eyesore that might have been!

> **Albert Memorial** &
>
> In 1867 the citizens of Manchester raised over £6,000 for the erection of a memorial to the late Prince Albert. It was Grade I listed in 1963.
>
> It was once included in a book entitled *The World's Most Ugly Objects*.

Corn Exchange

The original Corn and Produce Exchange was built in 1837 as a trading place for farmers and merchants. The building became too small to accommodate the thousands of people who came to do business here and so it was rebuilt in 1903. The building was badly damaged but not completely destroyed in the air-raids of 1940 and many of the original Edwardian features were saved. However, trading there declined and finally ceased altogether.

In the 1980s and 90s the building became home to an eclectic mix of shops and stalls – an 'Aladdin's Cave' and centre for 'alternative' shopping. This continued until the building again suffered bomb damage, this time in 1996. After extensive renovation and remodelling, it reopened as the Triangle shopping centre. The Triangle was aimed at the 'cash to splash' end of the market, but it gradually entered into a decline. Thankfully, the Triangle name was lost and once again it became The Corn Exchange.

This fantastic Grade II listed building has now undergone yet another change and become home to various eateries.

Midland Hotel

Central Station was owned and operated by the Midland Railway Company. When the decision was made to build a 'showcase' hotel, the ground directly opposite the station seemed the obvious location. At that time the site was home to Lower Mosley Street School, Mr. Cooper's house and garden and the Gentlemen's Concert Hall owned by Charles Heywood who agreed to the demolition of his Hall on condition that the new hotel would include a Concert Hall. It did! The Midland Hotel was the last word in luxury, with no expense spared. The site had cost £365,000 and the hotel, which took almost five years to build, a further £1,125,000.

In addition to the Concert Hall, the hotel also had a sub post office (complete with its own Midland Hotel franking), Turkish baths, ballroom, billiard room, gentlemen's reading room, a barber, a tailor and a chemist. For the ladies there was a hairdresser, a ladies' tea room and a Parisian milliner. There was also a roof garden in which Israel Sieff and Rebecca Marks (as in M&S) held their wedding reception in 1910. The architect, Charles Trubshaw, had evidently heard of the city's rainy reputation so gave the hotel a covered walkway which stretched across Windmill Street to link it to the railway station. (Windmill Street was the site of a mid-eighteenth century windmill; in 1766 it was offered for rent at £10 per annum, payable to Edward Byrom.) Consideration was also given to the hotel's murky surroundings; a revolutionary system of air-conditioning was installed to pump pure, clean air into the building. The hotel had 400 bedrooms, each with its own fireplace. Each room also had an electric clock with illuminated dial which could be operated from a switch by the bed – quite a novelty in 1903.

In later days, opulence gradually began to give way to commerce. The Concert Hall was no more and the huge space it occupied was converted into three floors of bedrooms. Ceilings were lowered, glass-covered areas were boarded over; the glory days were gone.

> **&**
>
> In 2004 a centenary dinner was held to commemorate the historic meeting at the Midland Hotel, one hundred years earlier, of Messrs Rolls and Royce. Owners of the illustrious cars came from all corners of the world to attend.

> In the 1930s a lady (obviously an extremely wealthy lady) lived in the Midland Hotel and declared that she never wanted to live anywhere else. So, following her eventual demise, the lady returned to the hotel as resident ghost and continued to inhabit her first-floor room. In life, she had always worn a grey taffeta dress which rustled as she walked. Although 'The Lady in Grey' was never seen by any of the guests, she was certainly heard as she rustled around in her taffeta, spreading an icy-cold chill about the room. After many complaints, the room ceased to be used for guests and became a store room. The lady was apparently not too happy at being left with only mops and brooms for company and she took to wandering the corridors instead!
>
> **Legend has it ...**

> **To Quote:**
>
> The Midland Hotel was once described as
>
> **'the ugliest building of any pretensions'.**

Britannia Hotel

The Grade II* listed building which is now home to the Britannia Hotel on Portland Street was once the S. and J. Watts Warehouse; it cost £100,000, took two years to build and opened in 1858. The warehouse was built on land which had been home to various buildings, one of which was a cottage occupied by Mrs. Bridget Monks. She had been a casualty of the Peterloo Massacre during which her arm was severed; however, she lived to tell the tale and survived for another thirty-two years.

This was the largest and most opulent warehouse in the city and epitomised the wealth and prestige of Manchester's textile industry. It was the also the first building in Britain to have a roof almost entirely of glass. Charles Dickens, on one of his many visits to the city, referred to it as 'the merchant palace of Europe'. Warehouses became showcases where goods were displayed and sold. It was designed in the Italian Palazzo style and each of its five floors has a different architectural style including Dutch, Elizabethan, Italian Renaissance and one based on the Versailles Galerie de Glaces.

Johnny and Betty Watts (who had six sons) opened a draper's 'bazaar' on Deansgate in c.1796. As the business expanded, Thomas Kendal, James Milne and Adam Faulkner joined the firm and in 1836 they bought the business from the Watts brothers. The brothers then founded S & J Watts and Sons which became the largest wholesale drapery in Manchester. James Watts, the youngest son, became one of the city's wealthiest cotton merchants, moving to Abney Hall in Cheadle where he played host to the rich and famous, including Prince Albert when he visited the city to open the Art Treasures Exhibition in 1857.

The building was badly damaged during the Blitz and remained derelict for many years. It was threatened with demolition in the 1970s but was luckily bought, restored and turned into a hotel at a cost of £5 million.

Manchester Museum

John Leigh Philips was a Manchester textile manufacturer and a keen collector. After his death a group of wealthy, like-minded enthusiasts bought his collection and in 1821 formed the Natural History Society; they founded the Natural History Museum in 1835 at the corner of Peter Street and Museum Street (street still there, museum long gone). It was yet another impressive building as is shown in the following sketch.

It closed in 1868 and its contents were acquired by Owens College; the collection formed the beginnings of Manchester Museum which opened to the public in 1890. The new museum, on Oxford Road, was designed by Alfred Waterhouse and later additions to the building were designed by his son and grandson. It is now home to millions of artefacts from all corners of the world.

London Road Fire Station

Manchester Fire Brigade was founded in 1615 in response to a fire which had destroyed part of the town. The Court Leet splashed out on 24 buckets, 6 ladders, 4 ropes and 4 hooks. Seventy-five years later, two manual pumps were bought at a cost of £40 and were stored in the churchyard. In 1839, Manchester's fire brigade was described as 'the most effective in Britain' and it is also credited with the invention or pioneering use of much labour- and life-saving equipment.

The 'new' fire station was built at a cost of £142,000 and opened in 1906, replacing the old fire station on Jackson's Row. It was not only home to the fire station, but also to a police station and an ambulance centre, plus living quarters for the firemen and their families. At that time fire engines were still horse-drawn but in 1911 the first motorised vehicles were introduced at the station. In 1942 the station was visited by King George VI and Queen Elizabeth in recognition of the fire crews' efforts during the bombings of the city in 1940/41. In the early 1950s it became the first station in the country with the equipment to record emergency calls.

The building became Grade II* listed in 1974 but from 1986 it stood empty and despite being bought by Britannia Hotels in the '90s, it remained derelict and was allowed to fall into disrepair. However, it was bought in 2015 and is set to become 'Manchester Firehouse' – a hotel, apartments and offices.

Victoria Baths

Victoria Baths in Chorlton-on-Medlock cost around £60,000 to build. When opened in 1906 it was described as 'the most splendid municipal bathing institution in the country' and 'a water palace of which every citizen of Manchester can be proud'. This was a time when Manchester was still an affluent city and no expense was spared on the building or its beautifully-tiled interior. There were three swimming pools: 1st class males, 2nd class males and a women's pool. The building also housed private baths, a laundry and a Turkish bath. During the winter, the main pool was boarded over and used as a dance floor. In 1952 the baths installed the first public jacuzzi in the country, then known as an Aeratone.

The baths were closed in 1993 and, like so many architectural gems in the city, the building was left to fall into disrepair. After winning the BBC's *Restoration* programme in 2003, the building received Lottery funding and the restoration began.

Ethel 'Sunny' Lowry was the first British woman to swim the English Channel. She was born in Longsight in 1911 and was a member of the Ladies Swimming Club at Victoria Baths. Her first two attempts to swim the Channel were unsuccessful, but it was third time lucky. On 28 August 1933, Lowry swam from France to England in 15 hours, 41 minutes. She caused quite a sensation in her choice of swimwear and was branded by some as a 'harlot' for her skimpy costume. She died in 2008, at the grand old age of 97, three years after receiving an MBE for services to swimming in the North-West.

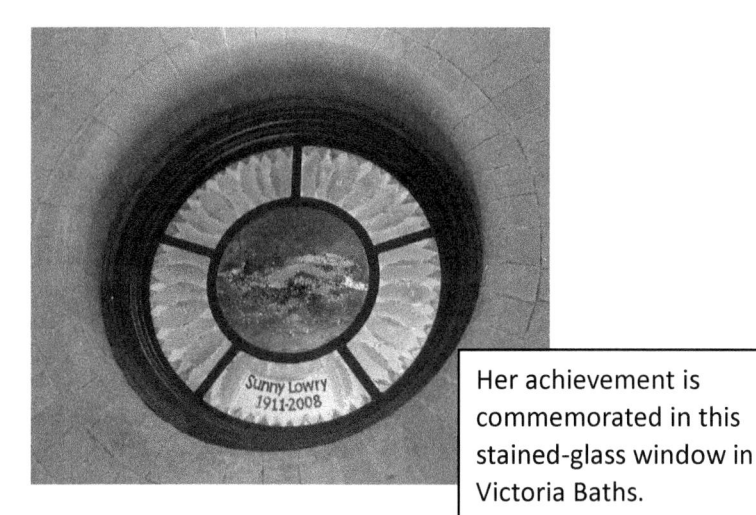

Her achievement is commemorated in this stained-glass window in Victoria Baths.

Edgar Wood

This fantastic Grade I listed building was the first purpose-built Christian Scientist Church in Britain and sits on Daisy Bank Road in Victoria Park, Rusholme. It was designed by Manchester architect Edgar Wood in the Arts & Crafts style and opened in 1906. It closed in 1971 and fell victim to vandals; it was later restored and is now home to the Universal Church of the Kingdom of God.

Edgar Wood set up in business in his home town of Middleton and later moved to Cross Street in the city centre.

Sunlight House

There are several outstanding examples of art deco buildings in the city, for example the old Midland Bank (now Hotel Gotham) and the Express Building on Great Ancoats Street. One building recently lost was the wonderful rocket-like Northcliffe House at the corner of Deansgate and Quay Street.

With fourteen storeys, the art deco Sunlight House was the tallest building in Manchester when it was completed in 1932. It was built by architect Joe Sunlight as the headquarters of his property business; inspired by a visit to Chicago, he also wanted to construct a thirty-five-storey building next door but this was vetoed by the council. He was an innovative designer and the building boasted high-speed lifts and a self-vacuuming system.

Sunlight's eccentricity started early; he was a Russian immigrant who needed an English name and so chose that of his favourite soap! Although one of the richest men in the city, he would man the lift during lunch hour himself so as not to have to pay anyone else to do the job. Yet he was also a massive gambler and was reputed to have spent around £1 million a year on horse racing. Perhaps more bizarrely, he wanted a mausoleum built on top of the building after his death in which he would be laid to rest. This never happened. When he died, he was the biggest taxpayer in Manchester.

The building still retains its original basement swimming pool which was opened in 1933 by Hollywood legends Carole Lombard and Douglas Fairbanks Jnr.

CIS Building

When the Co-operative Insurance Society Building opened in 1962, it was the tallest building in the UK (a record it held for only one year) and the third tallest in Europe. At 387 feet tall and with twenty-five storeys, it remained the tallest building in Manchester until Beetham Tower was completed in 2006.

Before it was built, the architects and engineers went on a 'fact-finding trip' to America and Canada; the main inspiration for the design came from the Inland Steel Building in Chicago. A later fact-finding trip to Sweden inspired the interior art work. The building was given Grade II listing in 1995.

Iconic Buildings (past and present) 299

Death-defying construction work on the CIS building in the early 1960s. Were they paid danger money?

Chapter 21

Sport

Football

Football has not always been such a popular pastime in Manchester. In 1608 the Court Leet ordered 'that no manner of persons hereafter shall play or use the footeball in any street within the said toun of Manchester'. However, times change and on 17 April 1888, the Football League was founded in Manchester, in the Royal Hotel (which stood at the corner of Market Street and Mosley Street) making it the first national football league in the world.

> The Royal Hotel was originally a mansion with large gardens. It was converted to 'The Royal Hotel and New Bridgewater Arms' in 1827 and was one of the town's main coaching inns; the gardens were turned over to stables and coach sheds. The coaches were usually red and black and the coachman and guard wore elaborate uniforms. Ever on the lookout for lurking highwaymen, the guard would always have his horn and a pair of pistols handy.
>
> The hotel was later demolished to make way for an extension to Lewis's department store.

Manchester City

The club was founded in 1880 by two wardens from St. Mark's Church in Gorton and was originally called 'West Gorton St. Mark's'; their first playing field was a piece of waste ground near the church. At that time unemployment in the area was high and the club was started as one of a number of activities aimed at providing an alternative to the increasing levels of gang violence and alcoholism. During its first season the team won only one match (against a team from Stalybridge). The club's links with the church were soon severed and the club changed its name to Gorton Association FC. It then moved to a site in Ardwick and again changed its name, this time to Ardwick Association FC. The first match in the new ground on Hyde Road was something of an anti-climax – the opposing team, Salford, failed to turn up! In 1887 one of the players was awarded five shillings (25p) a week, thereby promoting the club from amateur to professional status. In 1881 the first Manchester derby was played and the teams met again in 1889 when they played a benefit match following an explosion at a coal mine on Hyde Road in which twenty-three miners were killed. In 1894 in a bid to draw support from the whole city, the club officially became Manchester City Football Club. In 1904 the team won its first major trophy: the FA Cup.

> In 1902, defender Di Jones cut his knee during a match; the wound became infected and within a week he had died.

&

Allegations of corruption, financial irregularities and match-fixing are nothing new. As far back as the early twentieth century, the world of football was mired in scandal involving one of City's most famous and talented players, Billy Meredith, aka the 'Welsh Wizard' who was considered by many to be the greatest footballer of his generation. He, along with others, was forced out of the club, following which he joined Manchester United. However, he returned to City in 1916. In 1923 Manchester City moved to Maine Road which had a capacity of over 80,000.

In 1949 City signed up the former German prisoner of war, Bernhard (Bert) Trautmann amidst much controversy. Trautmann had been a Nazi paratrooper and fervently anti-British. However, his opinion of the English shifted dramatically after being captured and interned here and after the war he declined to be repatriated. Despite mass demonstrations against his appointment, his skills on the pitch soon earned him popularity; he was regarded as one of the greatest goalkeepers of his time and was elevated to hero status by many fans. In 1956 Trautmann was injured during the FA Cup Final; he soldiered on to the end, not realising that he had a broken neck! In the same year he was named FWA Footballer of the Year. He stayed with City for twenty-five years.

Both City and United have their origins in East Manchester, but both spent the greater portion of the twentieth century on the other side of the city. However, in 2003 City moved back east to its new home in the former Commonwealth Games stadium.

Mad about football! A Manchester shop window c.1900

Manchester United

The 'Newton Heath Lancashire & Yorkshire Railway Football Club' was founded in 1878; the team earned an early nickname of the 'Heathens'. The club soon lost its links with the railway and LYR disappeared from its title. By 1902 the club was in severe financial difficulties and was served with a 'winding-up' order. It was saved from bankruptcy by John Henry Davies, a wealthy Manchester brewer who became club president and changed the name of the club to Manchester United. (Manchester Central and Manchester Celtic were also considered as possible names.) He also changed the team colours to red and white. In 1910 Manchester United moved to a new stadium at Old Trafford, again with the help of Davies who invested a whopping £60,000 in the project. In 1915 three members of the team were found guilty of match-fixing and were banned for life.

In 1931, several years after the death of Davies, the club was again on the verge of bankruptcy and was rescued by another Manchester businessman, James Gibson. He invested £30,000 with the proviso that he become chairman of the club. After Old Trafford was heavily bombed in the Second World War, the club had to share the stadium at Maine Road with Manchester City.

Sir Matt Busby

Born in 1909 Matt Busby, whose name is forever linked with Manchester United, actually played for rivals Manchester City from 1929 to 1936 when he joined Liverpool FC. His footballing career was interrupted by the outbreak of war; when he came out of the army he was signed up as manager of Manchester United, a post he held until 1969. In 1958 when the team was taking off from Munich airport, the plane crashed, killing twenty-three people including eight players (known as 'Busby Babes') the team trainer, secretary, coach and eight journalists. Although suffering multiple injuries in the crash and spending two months in hospital, Busby returned to football and built up another winning team. The name 'Busby Babes' was no longer deemed appropriate and so the nickname 'Red Devils' was coined. Under Busby's leadership the team won every major football trophy and in 1968 it became the first English club to win the European Cup. Busby was knighted for his services to sport and received a papal knighthood from the Pope for his services to charity. He died in 1994.

In the 98/99 season, under manager Alex Ferguson, Manchester United was the first English team to win the 'Treble'.

When a talent scout first spotted the young Belfast lad George Best, he told Matt Busby, 'Boss, I think I've found you a genius.' He wasn't wrong! Once dubbed 'the greatest-ever player' by Pele (himself regarded by many as the greatest footballer of all time), Best joined Manchester United in 1963. He became the world's first footballing superstar, but his celebrity lifestyle and troubled personal life inevitably turned him into an erratic and temperamental player. He later asked that he be remembered for back-page headlines and not those on the front page.

****

In 1967 Best and his pal Mike Summerbee, a Manchester City player, opened a 'fashion boutique' on Bridge Street. The shop 'George Best Rogue' is featured in the opening sequence of *The Lovers* starring Richard Beckinsale and Paula Wilcox.

In 1901 the Football League put a £4 a week cap on wages. Today a top footballer can earn an incredible £300,000 a week: more than an average worker would earn in ten years! Both Manchester United and Manchester City are consistently in the 'Top 5 Richest Clubs in the World' list; in January 2017 United was named the world's richest club with an annual revenue of £355.3m.

Cricket

Old Trafford Cricket Ground, formerly meadows on the de Trafford estate, has been home to Lancashire County Cricket Club since 1864 and is one of the most prestigious grounds in the country. It is England's second oldest Test ground and in 1884 was the venue for the first Ashes test held in England; the first day was lost to rain and the ground has maintained its reputation for bad weather ever since. During the Second World War the ground was used as a transit camp for troops, but was bombed in the Manchester Blitz. Ironically, it was German PoWs who restored the ground after the war.

Commonwealth Games

After two unsuccessful bids to bring the Olympic Games to Manchester, the city was awarded the Commonwealth Games in 2002, the year in which Queen Elizabeth II celebrated her Golden Jubilee. At the time, with 281 events across 17 sports, it was the largest multi-sport event ever staged in the UK and it was also the largest ever Commonwealth Games. The Games cost £300 million and were considered a huge success. It left Manchester with the lasting legacy of continuing regeneration and some world-class sporting facilities, including the stadium which is now home to Manchester City, the Velopark and the Aquatics Centre.

Bibliography

Books

Banks, Mrs. G. Linnaeus *The Manchester Man*
Bradshaw, L.D. *Origins of Street Names in the City Centre of Manchester* (Neil Richardson 1985)
Brooks, Ann & Haworth, Bryan *This Good Old Town* (Carnegie Publishing 1997)
Buckley, Angela *The Real Sherlock Holmes* (Pen & Sword 2014)
Engels, Friedrich *The Condition of the Working Class in England* (Penguin Classics 1987)
English Heritage *Ancoats Cradle of Industrialisation*
Fielding, Steve *Hanged at Manchester* (The History Press 2008)
Glinert, Ed *Manchester Compendium* (Penguin Group 2008)
(Selected and Edited by) **Cliff Hayes** *Stories and Tales of Manchester* (Printwise Publications 1991)
Kidd, Alan *Manchester*
Kirby, Dean *Angel Meadow*
O'Neill, Joseph *Crime City* (Milo Books 2008)
Wyke, Terry & Rudyard, Nigel *Manchester Theatres* (Manchester Free Press 1994)

E-books

Aston, Joseph *Metrical Records of Manchester* (1822)
Axon, William *Annals of Manchester* (1886)
Everett, J. *Panorama of Manchester and Railway Companion* (1834)
Love, Benjamin *Manchester as it is* (1839)
Procter, Richard Wright *Memorials of Bygone Manchester & Memorials of Manchester Streets* (1880)
Roby, John *The Traditions of Lancashire* (1872)
Swindells, Thomas *Manchester Streets and Manchester Men* (1906)
The Court Leet Records of the Manor of Manchester

Websites
archive.org
bbc.co.uk
cheethams.org.uk
friends-of-angel-meadow.org
manchestereveningnews.co.uk
mancuniensis.info
msg.org
theguardian .com
workhouses.org.uk

Photographs
Huge thanks to Chetham's Library and to Greater Manchester Police Museum
Many photos in the book have come from the Manchester Local Images Collection – Many thanks to them

Places
Central Library
Chetham's Library
Greater Manchester Police Museum
John Rylands Library
Manchester City Art Gallery
Manchester Cathedral
Manchester Jewish Museum
Manchester Museum
Museum of Science and Industry
People's History Museum
Portico Library
U.C.K.G. Church
Working Class Movement Library

Index

Acres Fair 9
Addy, Mark 227–28
Ainsworth, William Harrison 142, 179–80
Alcock and Brown 124–26
Aldport 4
Alsop, Alfred 24, 230
Altars, Roman 1, 49
Angel Meadow 15–17, 27, 89–90, 99, 101, 110–11, 236, 250, 255
Angel Stone 51
Anti-Corn Law League 32–33, 108, 184
Art Treasures Exhibition 172, 192–93, 196, 294
Assize Courts 79
Atkinson and Barker's Royal Infant Preservative 20, 22
Aytoun, 'Spanking Roger' 217–18
'Baby' 127
Bancroft, Joseph 94
Banks, Mrs. G. Linnaeus 145, 184, 236, 305
Barbirolli, John 197
Barlow, Saint Ambrose 58–60
Beck, Isabella 102
Belle Vue Zoological Gardens 7, 77, 163–69, 196
Bennett, Charles 214–15
Beswick, Hannah 215–16
Blackfriars Bridge 152
Blanketeers 28, 38
Blitz 48, 57, 79, 106, 155, 196, 239, 288–90, 294, 304
Bradford, John 60–61
Bradley, Mary 108–09
Braid, James 119–20
Bridgewater Canal 1, 129
Brighouse, Harold 156, 187–88
Britannia Hotel 294–96
British Union of Fascists 7, 240
Brontë, Charlotte 181–84
Brookes, Joshua 56–57, 185
Brooks, William Henry 89
Brotherton, Joseph 65
Bull-baiting 69, 160

Burgess, Anthony 191
Burnett, Frances Hodgson 186–87
Busby, Matt 303
Byrom, John 144, 174–75
Caminada, Jerome 83, 87
   Manchester 'Cab Murder' 84
   Fancy Dress Ball 85–86
Cassidy, John
   'Adrift' 195
Cenotaph 48
Central Station 24, 133, 292
Chartists 35, 225
Chetham, Humphrey 105, 235
Chetham's Library 19, 56, 105, 164, 235
Chetham's School 4, 55, 105
Chinatown 206, 232
Chinese Imperial Archway 206
Chinese Settlers 206
Cholera 16, 99–101, 204
Chopin, Frederic 96, 196
Churches:
   Bible Christian Church 64–66
   Cathedral 4–5, 51–54, 57, 84, 104–05, 126, 134, 142, 145, 151, 158, 171, 173, 226–27, 286
   Christian Scientist Church 297
   Cross Street Chapel 44, 57, 106, 179–80
   St. Ann's Church 9, 58, 69, 158, 207
   St. Mary's Church (The 'Hidden Gem') 151–52
CIS Building 298–99
City Art Gallery 193
Civil War 43–44, 105, 186
Clogs 87–90
Cobden, Richard 32–33, 108, 290
Cockfights 158–60, 289
Communist Manifesto 19, 106
Corn Exchange 292
'Cottonopolis' 10–11, 291
Court Leet
Cowherd, William 64–66
Crabtree, William 115
Cricket 171, 304

308 2,000 Years of Manchester

Dalton, John 106–07, 115–117, 172, 231, 235
Dancer, John Benjamin 117
Danes 4–5, 123
Dawson, Jemmy 45–46
Deaf and Dumb Institute 108–09, 234
Dee, Dr. John 54–56
Delaney, Arthur 195
Dickens, Charles 37, 108–09, 113, 180–82, 192, 253, 290, 294
Dixon, Elijah 38–39
Doherty, John 33–34
Ducking stool 73–75, 94, 230
Earthquake 207
Emma 208
Engels, Friedrich 16–19, 26, 32, 78, 104, 106, 242
Exchange Station 133–34
Factory Acts 35, 159, 162
Floods 210
Football 90, 171, 188, 270, 276, 300–03
Franks, Isaac 201
Free Trade Hall 7, 30, 33, 40, 82, 96, 182, 196, 290–91
Garrett, Rev. George William 121–22
Garrottings 83
Gaskell, Elizabeth 57, 107, 180–83
Gentlemen's Concert Hall 195, 292
Giddy-Gaddy 68–69
Godfrey's Cordial 20
Golding, Louis 189–190
Grand Centrifugal Railway 119
Graphene 128
Great Synagogue 202–03
Groves and Whitnall 150, 240
G.U.T.E. 41–42
Hallé, Charles 181, 192, 195
Hallé Orchestra 196–97
Hall, Elias 214
Hall of Science 35, 51, 112–13
Hanging Ditch 5, 10, 235
Heywood, Abel 25, 37–38
Horniman, Annie 156, 187
Horridge, Bob 87
Hospitals:
   Garden Street 94
   Lock Hospital 97–98
   Lunatic Hospital 94–96
   Manchester Infirmary 61, 97–98, 149, 176, 216

Huskisson, William 130–32
Hyman, Joseph 200–01
'Ice Maiden' 222–24
IRA Bomb 53, 145, 221, 238, 272, 276, 287–89
Irish Settlers 15–16, 20, 77–78, 89, 99, 133, 203–04
Irk Valley Railway Disaster 211–12
Italian Ice Cream 204–05
Italian Settlers 204–06
Jacobite Rebellions 44–47, 57, 215
Jewish Settlers 66, 189, 195, 199–203, 275–77
Jewsbury, Geraldine 182
Jodrell Bank 127–28
Jones, Ernest 35, 39
Jordan, Joseph 97–98
Knott Mill 49, 161
Lee, Ann 61–64
Levy, Emmanuel 195
Libraries:
   Central 113, 195
   Chetham's 19, 56, 105, 164, 235
   Free Public Library 112–13
   John Rylands 113–14, 116, 189
   Portico 107, 177, 226, 236
Lind, Jenny 96
'Lion King' 225
Lit. & Phil. Society 33, 106–07, 116, 118, 177
'Little Ireland' 15–17, 99
'Little Italy' 204–06
Liverpool and Manchester Railway 130, 132, 221
London Road Fire Station 295
Lords of the Manor of Manchester 4–6, 105, 174, 235
Lovell, Bernard 127–28
Lowry, L.S. 58, 193–95
Lowry, 'Sunny' 296–97
Madame Malibran 225–27
Manchester City 149, 300–04
Manchester Evening News 140–41
Manchester Grammar School 56, 58, 60, 103, 115, 121, 146, 178, 180, 187, 189, 275
Manchester Guardian 32, 86, 90, 123, 139–41, 161, 187, 189, 203–04
Manchester 'Martyrs' 77–78
Manchester Mummy 215–16
Manchester Museum 2, 50, 163, 222, 294–95
Manchester Rebels 45, 180
Manchester Ship Canal 13, 129–30, 171–72

Manchester Underground 79, 134, 245, 289
Manchester United 301–03
Manchester University 40, 106–08, 114, 118, 121, 123–24, 126–28, 191, 202, 275, 277
Manchester Zoological Gardens 169
Marsden, William 36
Marx, Karl 19, 106
'Masque of Anarchy' 31
May Day 161–63
Midland Hotel 137, 156, 196, 292–93
Mithras 51
'Molly Houses' 163
Morrison, Helen 215
Mosley, Family 4, 6, 8, 58, 235, 237
Mosley, Oswald Emeld 6-8, 94, 289
Nadin, Joseph 31
New Bridge Street Workhouse 25–26
New Cross 91, 99
Newspapers 38, 81, 139–40, 222–23
Newton, Daniel 95
Night Asylum 23–24
'Old Billy' 221–22
Owen, Robert 33-34, 112
Owens, John 107
Pankhurst, Adela 39–41
Pankhurst, Christabel 39–41
Pankhurst, Emmeline 39–40
Pankhurst, Sylvia 39–41
Peterloo Massacre 29–32, 39, 64, 138–40, 185, 290–91, 294
Piccadilly Gardens 94, 195, 237
Pierrepoint, Alfred 80–82
Poets' Corner 145, 184
Pomona Gardens 151, 169–71
Prisons:
   Dungeon 70
   New Bailey 29, 38, 75–77, 79, 142, 223
   New Fleet 70
   Strangeways 70, 79–82
Procter, Maurice 191–92
Pubs:
   Circus Tavern 147
   Crown and Kettle 91
   Iron Dish and Cob of Coal 91
   John Shaw's Punch House 146–47
   Lass O' Gowrie 149
   Old Wellington Inn 144–45, 174, 238, 286, 288
   Oxnoble 98, 147
   Peveril of the Peak 148
   Seven Stars 142–43, 241
   Sun Inn 6, 145–46, 178, 184, 199
   Tommy Ducks 148–49
   Ye Olde Rovers Return 143, 239
Puck, King of the Fairies 229
Punishments:
   Pillory 71–73, 75
   Scold's Bridle 71–72
   Stocks 25, 69, 72
   Whipping Post 72
'Purring' 87–88
Quincey, Thomas de 107, 177, 216
Raffald, Elizabeth 219, 221
Ragged Schools 110–11
Resurgam 121–22
Right of Soke 5
Rivers:
   Irk 4, 5, 10, 11, 104, 168, 211
   Irwell 1, 4–6, 53, 69, 70, 75, 76, 150-52, 171, 208, 209, 221, 223, 225, 227, 228
   Medlock 1, 4, 16, 49, 149, 211, 237
Roe, A.V. 124
Ritz 197
Robinson, Lavinia 222, 224
Roget, Peter Mark 107, 176
Roget's Thesaurus 107, 176, 177
Rolls-Royce 14, 125, 137
Romans 1, 2, 4, 49, 161, 199
Roscoe, Henry Enfield 123
Royal Botanical Gardens 171–72
Royal Exchange 289–90
Royal Jubilee Exhibition 172
Rush-carting 161
Rutherford, Ernest 106, 123
Salford Bridge 43, 53, 70
S. & J. Watts Warehouse 294
Sator Square 50–51
Saxons 4, 199
Scott, C.P. 140
Scuttlers 88–90
Shakers 61–64
Shelley, Percy Bysshe 31, 66
Shopping:
   Affleck & Brown 265–66, 269
   Arndale Centre 134, 145, 196, 236, 265, 287
   Barton Arcade 268
   Brooke Bond 14, 262–64
   Co-op 39, 110, 112, 255–57, 298
   Cussons 264

Finnigan's 230, 243, 268–69
Forsyth 196, 278
Fred Aldous 274
Goulburn's 286
H. Samuel 266
Jewsbury & Brown 246–47
J. Sykes & Sons 254–55
Kendal, Milne & Faulkner 230–31, 243
Lewis's 270–73, 276, 285, 300
Manchester Craft & Design Centre 252
Marks & Spencer 264, 275–76, 287, 292
Mountcastle, W. 246
Orme & Sons 257
Pauldens 260–61
Silvana 287
Smithfield Market 215, 249–52, 254, 255, 265
Timpson 259–60
Tizer 282
Tom & Jerry Shops 248
Tommy Shops 267
U.C.P. 282, 284
Vimto 279–81
Wiles 285
Siege of Manchester 4, 43
Smith, Dodie 190–91
Smith, Robert Angus 123
Spring, Howard 188–89, 241
Stoakes, Harriet 224–25
Stopes, Marie 124
Streets:
    Cross Street 44, 57, 73, 74, 106, 117, 141, 179, 180, 230, 276, 290, 298
    Deansgate 4, 5,10,16, 24, 43, 98, 113, 118, 121, 136, 157, 175, 186, 199, 201, 207, 230, 243, 245, 268, 269, 278, 294, 298
    Faulkner Street 230-32, 243, 245, 294
    Great Ancoats Street 39, 140, 204, 233, 298
    Lever Street 234, 274
    Market Street 33, 73, 92, 117, 135, 148, 160, 199, 202, 204, 234, 235, 237, 246, 247, 261, 262, 266, 269, 271, 273, 282, 285, 300
    Minshull Street 235
    Mosley Street 6, 107, 183, 195, 199, 235, 236, 285, 292, 300
    Oldhan Street 37, 91, 184, 212, 236, 259, 263, 265, 276, 287
    Oxford Street 155, 157, 237
    Piccadilly 6, 8, 53, 66, 74, 94, 137, 183, 193, 195, 212, 226, 233, 236, 237, 240, 263, 270

Shambles 144, 146, 174, 238
Shudehill 9, 11, 94, 143, 205, 232, 233, 238, 239, 249, 277
Stevenson Square 240
Tib Street 11, 12, 160, 240–41
Withy Grove 29, 34, 142, 199, 241–42, 274
Suicide 82, 91–2, 96–7, 127, 176, 198, 224–25, 228, 234
Sunlight House 298
Swain, Charles 178
Sydall, Thomas (Father) 44
Sydall, Thomas (Son) 44
Tarquin's Castle, The Legend of 2–4
Taylor, Sarah 224
Textiles 1, 10, 12, 39
Theatres:
    Gaiety 156, 187
    Hippodrome 155–56
    Opera House 156, 226
    Palace Theatre 155
    Queen's Theatre 155
    Theatre(s) Royal 102, 151, 153, 226
Tinker's (Vauxhall) Gardens 168
Top of the Pops 197
Town Hall 38, 66, 79, 86, 99, 113, 115–16, 133, 288, 291
Trafford Park 13–14, 137, 264
Transport 73, 129, 131, 133, 135, 137, 239, 263
Turing, Alan 106, 126–27
Valette, Adolphe 194–95, 269
Vegetarianism 64–66
Victoria Baths 296–97
Victoria Square 27
Wakes Week 157, 159
Walker's Croft 99–100
Wardley Hall 59
Weizmann, Chaim 202, 277
White, Dr. Charles 94, 97, 216
Whit Walks 157–58
Whitworth, Joseph 12, 108, 120–21
Wilson, Anthony 58, 198
Wood, Edgar 297–98
Wood Street Mission 24
Woolworths (Fire) 212–13
World War One 14, 48
Wray, Cecil Daniel 57
Wroe, James 30, 140
'Ye Hearts of Oak of Manchester' 46